GRAVEN IMAGES

GRAVEN IMAGES

New England Stonecarving and its Symbols,

1650-1815

By ALLAN I. LUDWIG

WESLEYAN UNIVERSITY PRESS, MIDDLETOWN, CONNECTICUT

Grateful acknowledgment is made to the following for permission to reprint passages from works under their control:

To the Bollingen Foundation for permission to quote from Volume X of *Jewish Symbols in the Greco-Roman Period*, by Erwin R. Goodenough, copyright © 1964 by Bollingen Foundation.

To Frederick Burgess, Esq., for permission to quote from his *English Churchyard Memorials*, copyright © 1963 by Frederick Burgess.

To Doubleday & Company, Inc., for permission to quote from *The American Puritans: Their Prose and Poetry*, edited by Perry Miller, copyright © 1956 by Perry Miller.

To E. P. Dutton & Co., Inc., for permission to quote from *Mysticism*, by Evelyn Underhill.

To Princeton University Press for permission to quote from "Theology in America: A Historical Survey," by Sydney E. Ahlstrom, in Volume 1 of *Religion in American Life: A Historical Survey*, edited by James Ward Smith and A. Leland Jamison, copyright © 1961 by Princeton University Press; from *Abbot Suger*, by Erwin Panofsky, copyright © 1946 by Princeton University Press; and from *The Poetical Works of Edward Taylor*, edited by Thomas H. Johnson, copyright © 1943 by Princeton University Press.

To Random House, Inc., for permission to quote from *Basic Writings of St. Thomas Aquinas*, edited by Anton C. Pegis, copyright © 1945 by Random House, Inc.

To Yale University Press for permission to quote from *Images or Shadows of Divine Things*, by Jonathan Edwards, edited by Perry Miller, copyright © 1948 by Yale University Press; from *A Treatise Concerning Religious Affections*, by Jonathan Edwards, edited by John E. Smith, copyright © 1959 by Yale University Press; from *The Gentle Puritan: A Life of Ezra Stiles, 1727–1795*, by Edmund S. Morgan, copyright © 1962 by Yale University; from *Christographia*, by Edward Taylor, edited by Norman S. Grabo, copyright © 1962 by Yale University; and from *The Poems of Edward Taylor*, edited by Donald Stanford, copyright © 1960 by Yale University Press.

Library of Congress Catalog Card Number: 66–14665
Manufactured in the United States of America
First edition

To My Parents
and to the memory of Erwin R. Goodenough

"Idols are always the other fellow's symbols."
—Erwin R. Goodenough

Contents

Plates

PLATE 151. A. Detail of the Joseph Tapping stone, 1678, King's Chapel, Boston, Massachusetts. B. Engraving from Francis Quarles' *Hieroglyphiques of the Life of Man*, London, 1638. C. Detail of the John Watson stone, 1753, Plymouth, Massachusetts. D. Detail of the frontispiece of Isaac Watts' *Horae Lyricae*, London, 1727. Engraving cut in 1722.

152. A. Detail of the Samuel Hall stone, 1795, Meriden, Connecticut. B. Detail of a woodcut in Timothy Stone's *A Sermon Preached Before His Excellency Samuel Huntington Esquire*, Hartford, Connecticut, 1792.

153. A. Detail of the Pember children stone, 1773, Franklin, Connecticut. B. Detail of broadside published March 5, 1770. Courtesy of Dr. Robert Farris Thompson. C. Detail from a New England Primer published in Haverhill, Massachusetts, in 1811. D. Detail of the Sarah Swan stone, 1767, Bristol, Rhode Island.

154. A. Detail of a New England Primer. B. Detail of the Thomas Brenton stone, 1772, Newport Rhode Island. C. Detail of an 18th century English broadside. Courtesy of Dr. Robert Farris Thompson. D. Detail of the Polly Harris stone, 1787, Charlestown, Massachusetts.

155. A. Detail of a European Provincial wood carving. Probably 17th century. B. Detail of the Nicholas Larrance stone, 1710, Charlestown, Massachusetts.

156. Broadside cut for Rebekah Sewall, 1710. Courtesy of the Boston Public Library.

157. A. Detail from Isaac Watts' *Horae Lyricae*. B. Detail of the Sarah Hunt stone, 1799, Rumford, Rhode Island.

158. The 'E. L.' stone, Ipswich, Massachusetts, 1647.

159. A. The Samuel Danforth stone, 1653, Roxbury, Massachusetts. B. The Sarah [Hammond?] stone, 1674, Watertown, Massachusetts.

160. The Faithful Rowse stone, 1664, Charlestown, Massachusetts.

161. A. The Mehetabel Gearfeild stone, 1675, Watertown, Massachusetts. B. The Nathanael Hammond stone, 1677, Watertown, Massachusetts.

162. A. The Isaac Morgin stone, 1696, Enfield, Connecticut. B. The Henry Burt stone, 1735, Northampton, Massachusetts.

163. A. Detail of the Ann Erinton stone, dated 1653 but probably cut in 1674, Cambridge, Massachusetts. B. Detail of the Mary Allin stone, 1678, Malden, Massachusetts. C. Detail of the Dorcas Brakenbury stone, 1682, Charlestown, Massachusetts.

164. A. Detail of the Thomas Call stone, 1676, Malden, Massachusetts. B. Detail of the Thomas Kendel stone, ca. 1678, Wakefield, Massachusetts.

165. A. Detail of the John Watson stone, 1678, Cambridge, Massachusetts. B. Detail of the Joanna Ingles stone, 1678, Copp's Hill, Boston, Massachusetts. C. Detail of the Joseph Farnum stone, 1678, Copp's Hill, Boston, Massachusetts.

166. A. Detail of the John Cleverly stone, 1703, Quincy, Massachusetts. B. Detail of the Edward Thompson stone, 1705, Chelmsford, Massachusetts. C. Detail of the Ichabod Wiswall stone, 1700, Duxbury, Massachusetts.

All photographs not otherwise credited above were taken by the author.

Maps

Acknowledgments

I am grateful to those writers and publishers who have allowed me to reprint passages from copyrighted works under their control, as specified elsewhere in this volume. Here, I should like especially to thank Frederick Burgess, Esq., not only for permission to quote him but also for the use of illustrations from his *English Churchyard Memorials*. I am grateful, too, to Dr. Robert Farris Thompson, Jr. for allowing me to reproduce several broadsides from his collection, and to the American Antiquarian Society for permitting me to reproduce photographs from the Forbes collection. I am indebted also to the Boston Public Library for the use of a broadside; to the Yale University Library for photographs of several engravings; and finally, to the trustees of the British Museum for allowing me to reproduce certain Romano-British monuments in their collections. The manuscript of the present work was completed at Yale University, where it was awarded the John Addison Porter Prize in 1964.

Foreword

THE final work on New England stonecarving has yet to be written. The emergence of religious symbols in a culture heretofore thought to have been "iconophobic" suggests the possibility that we may not have been thinking the right things about Puritan image making for some time. It seems to me that these problems transcend any "hermetic" study of the monuments from a strictly art historical point of view and I have therefore modified the normative method of art historical studies by bringing in the data of the symbols.

Indeed, the relationship between Puritan art, theology, and ritual has rarely been studied in depth because such investigations often founder upon the rocks of what is derisively called "interdisciplinary studies." Few historians of art are equipped to deal with the problems of Puritan religion while conversely few documentary historians ever pay enough attention to visual art. Hence we always seem to study a culture by only looking at parts of it. Such are the drawbacks of specialization.

Recently, however, there has been a movement afoot both to bring together under the rubric of historical studies the diverse creations of religious man, and to weigh their influence in the light of all the evidence including the art. I have been most impressed by the monumental study of Erwin R. Goodenough called *Jewish Symbols in the Greco-Roman Period* which seems to me to be a pioneer attempt to gauge the religious lives of the multitudes by judiciously evaluating not only the scanty literary data of the intellectual elite, but by looking into the hearts of the people through the visual symbols which they created. As any student of the Hellenistic world knows, Goodenough reached some astonishing and invaluable conclusions and established a new method of looking at religious symbolism. I have been encouraged to follow this difficult path because the finding of religious symbols among the supposedly iconophobic Puritans parallels in many ways the finding of symbols among the supposedly iconoclastic Jews and I know of no better way of presenting this evidence to the community of scholars and readers concerned with the roots of American civilization.

The first chapter is an attempt to see the visual symbols in a broad historical context and may be skipped by those whose interest is strictly art historical, while the later chapters may be read only briefly by those whose real interest is Puritan religion and intellectual history and who find the tracing out of styles a tedious burden. Needless to say I hope that this book will be read in its entirety by those interested in Puritanism as a whole.

Knowing full well that as a scholar I am trespassing upon the preserves of many disciplines ranging from the history of religion to folk lore and anthropology, I am fully prepared to bear the burden of criticism for my academic temerity.

From the point of view of art history the study offers many unprecedented opportunities only faintly realized in this investigation. Eventually it will be possible to plot the diffusion of local and imported styles with an exactitude hitherto impossible in more conventional works of figural art which have moved from place to place and whose dating is still a matter of conjecture. The bright stone images provide a perfect microcosm for the study of the spread of artistic styles in pre-industrial societies. The dating of the monuments is almost always to be relied upon and once a stone was placed it no longer travelled, making its co-ordinates in time and space an historical constant and a methodological delight. The cycles of invention and borrowing, the time lapse between inland and coastal workshops appropriating new themes and designs can be studied without fear that our conclusions will be marred by "reconstructions" and imaginative conjectures. Of equal significance is the fact that until the present day the losses from the original body of work have been historically negligible, although the problem is now getting far more serious and vandalism is a constant threat.

Some years ago I was tempted to incorporate into the plates far more comparative material from the history of religious symbolism than is here included. Upon further thought it seemed to me that it would be more useful to publish materials which had never before been printed than to clutter up the illustrations with monuments which are widely known.

The term "ornamental style" is derived from continental usage and characterizes rural New England stonecarving which was relatively free from the influences of European art until late in the 18th century. The term is traditionally used to signify a condition present in all early art which conceives of form in linear rather than in fully modelled terms where all lines dissolve in sensuously shifting planes and undulating volumes. It is a type of seeing which substitutes surface articulation and the pleasing simplicity of large geometric shapes for a more mimetic handling of the problem of representing nature. It is a technique which abstracts essential pictographic elements from the seen world and transforms them into artistic conventions, rather than a method of representation which attempts to evoke the optical world as it appears to the eye. See plates 204–225.

The term "provincial baroque" will stand for those highly naturalistic, active, illusionistic Italianate and Flemish forms of sculpture and graphic art which were often diluted by local craftsmen when they appeared in England after *ca.* 1640 and which formed the urban background of both English stonecarving and popular art. See plates 126–140. Having crossed the Atlantic in the form of woodcuts and engravings these already popularized European forms were further diluted and reduced to cold formulas of frontality and stiffness by local New England carvers. See plates 150–157.

No study can move forward in this field without taking into account the invaluable contributions of both H. M. Forbes and Dr. E. Caulfield. My debt to both writers is enormous but particularly to Mrs. Forbes whose vision, patience, and foresight resulted in the first serious publication in this field in 1927.

The Bollingen Foundation provided the funds for the always expensive field investigations and photography between 1961 and 1964. None of this work could have been undertaken without their generous support and there is a real sense in which this is their project as well as mine. I am also indebted to Mr. Charles Seymour, under whose guidance I wrote a dissertation on this subject, for his constant encouragement and perceptive comments. Were it not for the vision of the senior members of the art history department at Yale University my interests in this subject could have easily been thwarted. Among those whose interest encouraged me in this work were Professors George Kubler, Vincent Scully, George Hamilton, and Sumner Crosby.

It should be more than apparent that my debt to Erwin R. Goodenough, my friend and mentor, cannot be adequately described. His works have provided me with a shining example of that rare combination of scholarship and insight which few attain but which I can attempt to shadow. Those conversant with his studies will know that I have relied heavily upon his method. Edmund S. Morgan taught me most of what I know about Puritanism and in addition always took the time to read over my innumerable attempts to say something sensible about the always elusive "Puritan Mind." I shall always remember the encouragement of Norman Holmes Pearson and his prediction that the Samuel Green stone would one day be famous (plate 218) long before it was published in various journals both here and in Europe. My good friends Susan and Melvin Woody and Saul Rogolsky are still largely unaware of the degree to which I relied upon their opinions when I was still wondering if I ought to study this material in depth. Many of the ideas which I have tried to work out in detail and which relate the symbols to Puritan religion were products of our many fruitful discussions.

I am also indebted to Rulon Wells whose continuing interest in my work has shaped many of my ideas.

David Hall was kind enough to read the first draft and his recommendations for cutting have been ruthlessly applied. His own studies of Puritanism substantiate many of my own findings and it was encouraging to hear that despite two independent points of view we seemed to agree in so many areas.

My warm thanks are extended to Frank Sommer, Charles Montgomery, and E. P. Richardson of the Winterthur Museum, for their lively interest in this project. Their purchase for Winterthur of some one thousand catalogued photographs allowed me to make an extended trip to England to search for prototypes. I am additionally grateful to Yale University for providing me with two consecutive summer research grants in 1959 and 1960 before the funds from the Bollingen Foundation became available, and to my parents who were on hand between 1956 and 1958 when no public funds were forthcoming.

The American Philosophical Society has happily granted support from the Johnson Fund for the printing of many of the negatives used here; their aid came at a most advantageous time. The Colonial Arts Foundation provided the funds for the drawing up of the maps and in addition they have taken on the burden of providing the funds for much of the film and processing and for the organization of the files so that this material may be used by other scholars.

While I was abroad, the National Buildings Record, the Society for Antiquaries in London, and the British Museum allowed me to use their resources with complete freedom. The American Antiquarian Society in Worcester, Massachusetts, has been most co-operative in allowing me access to the Forbes Collection. The staff of the rare book room at the Yale University Library has been more than patient with me and has guided me deftly in my researches there. I cannot but thank them for the six years of constant support. Mrs. Marilyn Schmitt has kindly consented to read this manuscript and to her I must extend my thanks.

I would also like to thank Mr. Tom V. Schmitt for preparing the several drawings of gravestones which have been included. Moreover I should like to extend my thanks to Mrs. Jeanne Hockley for typing the final draft of the manuscript and to the Dickinson College community which has made my year here a pleasant one.

Last but not least I must mention my patient wife Janine, who not only is busy rearing a noisy family of three but who has tirelessly filed, indexed, printed, corrected, and noted down seemingly endless bits of information for the past eight years without appearing to be a bit flustered by it all.

GRAVEN IMAGES

Introduction

I. THE PURITAN BACKGROUND

THE image of Puritanism has been badly distorted by history. Contemporary American society neither understands the values of a people devoted to God nor does it seem to want to; but, if we are going to understand the meaning of Puritan art, we must have some clear-cut notion about Puritan belief. If we are going to try to understand why Puritans cut graven images for their tombs but would not allow the same imagery into their meetinghouses, we will have to know something more about Puritanism than the story of the lamentable witch hunts of 1692. If we are going to comprehend why an iconophobic culture enthusiastically embraced the imagery of icons in stone we will have to understand what the Puritans thought of symbols and idolatry.

Over thirty years ago it was fashionable to come to the study of New England armed with the then traditional theory that Puritans came to America for every reason save a religious one.[1] Puritan motives became so confused that even today they are painted as either the precursors of democracy or its suppressors.[2] The Puritans are still thought by many to have had little figural art and no religious art. Both notions are fictitious.

Behind these changing historical fashions concerning Puritanism there is a chronic modern inability to grasp the essential nature of Reformed New England Protestantism.[3] This is fundamentally an inability to see the New England adventure as one of the last great efflorescenses of the English Renaissance and Reformation.[4]

The Puritans believed that a man could live in the world and yet not be of it. They considered it wrong-headed to abandon irresponsibly the affairs of the world for the sanctuary and security of a protected cloister.[5] They believed that if Christianity had any meaning at all it was for all men and not a special few hothouse personalities who found shelter from a dissembling world behind the high walls of a monastery. Surely this does not make them hypocrites.[6] God might grant grace to whom He pleased, but the Puritans believed that they could boldly hew their way forth in an evil world and transform it into a New Zion. This was the meaning of their historic "Errand into the Wilderness."[7] I have seen no evidence that leads to any other conclusions.[8]

More recent historical studies by Morison, Murdock, Miller, and Morgan have shown that the religiosity of the New Englander was not simply a cloak for economic, social, or political reform or repression but the root from which these forms of Puritan culture sprang.[9] Although the Puritans were not above advancing their own interests masked by the current theological jargon of the day, we must not go so far that we transform Puritan religiosity into Puritan hypocrisy because we have found the Puritans to have had human failings. No people are without their foibles and few societies have ever lived up to the ideals of their leaders.

Throughout this essay the term "Puritanism" will stand for something larger than Congregationalism; it will stand for those forces within the Church of England which strove for an even more purified form of belief and worship and either separated from it directly or simply crossed an ocean to put its own beliefs into practice. We might even go so far as to say that the Visionary Quakers formed the radical left wing of the English Reformation while the Church of England took a position at the far right. The Puritans who will concern us are neither radicals of the left nor the conservatives of the right but rather the vast multitudes who trod a middle path in New England between the two extremes. There is ample historical justification for such a broadened use of the term.[10]

These were the people who re-created the beginnings of a new religious art in New England just as surely as they had destroyed the vestiges of the old before leaving their mother country to cross the sea. Religious art is born only when there is a burning need for imagery. It is a need so ingrained that even when the mind dreads imagery for fear of idolatry, religious art endures. The New England Puritans found their need for imagery so great that not even their storied fear of idolatry could come between them and the thousands of stone images they carved and rooted in the hilly New England landscape for a period of some 165 years. In this hurried act of creation the Puritans drew their vision of the spiritual world with an intensity of expression, an honesty of means, a dignity, and a capacity for stylistic innovation hitherto unexpected.

Puritan funerary art shows a deep strain of passion and a naïve delight in mystical symbolism. Between 1668 and 1815 this art slowly deepened in meaning and ripened into forms and symbols which in any other culture would be immediately interpreted as the visual manifestations of a deeply mystical religion.

This study moves away from the Puritan's strictly intellectual pursuits, legalisms, and interminable internecine religious strife in order to focus attention upon a vision of a life to come which was frozen for posterity on the carved stones of New England. I should be the last to attempt to demonstrate that this shift in historical emphasis overshadows other facets of Puritan life. The Puritan mind was so spacious that it could have many mansions of the spirit.[11]

Nor have I invented the notion of Puritan "passion" and "subjectivity" to form a romantic backdrop for their art. Ahlstrom has written,

> Without ever forgetting their responsibilities for the clear "opening" of God's word, or the need to convince the human intellect, and prevent, rather than encourage a simple emotional "decision for Christ," they [the Puritans] sought to make a place in the economy of Salvation for *subjectivity*, for the acts of human consciousness.[12]

Puritan literature dazzles the modern reader with momentary displays of a passionate longing for God. One need only glance at diaries of men like Thomas Shepard,[13] or read the love-drenched poetry of Edward Taylor[14] to realize that many were intoxicated with the love of God. Miller noted this Augustinian strain of piety in their literature years ago and devoted a chapter to it.[15]

The stone icons are but another indication of a Puritanism about which we have until now been told little. The reliefs which animate the surface of stone after stone flicker into immediate life with the coming of the sun and reveal a Puritan vision of eschatology untainted by dogma. Taken with both the devotional poetry and diaries, the stone imagery of New England reveals a psychology much more rich and complex than had formerly been imagined and in many ways in sharp contrast to what has been taught about the Puritan heritage.

The visual and the documentary evidence, however, often point in different directions. For example, the literature of Puritanism has been interpreted as indicating a decline in piety throughout the latter part of the 17th and the entire 18th century; while the visual evidence, especially the symbols found in rural New England, attests to a flowering of religious sentiment until at least the beginning of the 19th century. The logic of the imagery will be followed closely because it seems to speak in the language of the multitudes. The logic of the imagery does not signify (1) what the intellectual elite supposed to be the belief of the people nor (2) what the ministerial profession took to be the people's thought. The art might aptly be described by the French term *art populaire*.[16]

The relationship between religion, symbol, and image is not easily drawn out. Stonecarvers did not consciously attempt to mirror theological dogma and the intellectuals never programmed any complicated cycles for them. Indeed, stonecarvers were almost always mute concerning their craft and the ministers had equally little to say about the imagery.[17] In addition, Puritan writings about religion are almost always cast into theological abstractions while the imagery speaks in the language of sensuous form. Yet both attempted to symbolize the joys of life to come and in attempting to express by symbols the unity and beauty of the "invisible world" both have much in common.

II. THE LANGUAGE OF RELIGIOUS SYMBOLISM

THE language of symbolism is common to both words and pictures but the study of religious symbolism is in itself something rather new.[18] There is as yet no established methodology for the historian to follow, although Goodenough has taken the first practical steps in that direction. Perhaps the lag in symbolic studies is due to the fact that it is always taught as a minor adjunct to other studies and never in and of itself. Perhaps it is due to the fact that the dust from the pioneers' plows has not yet settled and the great universities have not as yet institutionalized symbolism as a separate discipline. Perhaps it is because America is not an hospitable ground for the rapid growth of such studies. Indeed, European scholarship has been far ahead of Anglo-American efforts; it seems that the empiricism of the former and the pragmatism of the latter are not the most favorable of soils for the growth of such studies. The Europeans have made a notable effort to study these problems over the last hundred years and it is to their work we must turn in order to sketch out some of the backgrounds of symbolic studies which are all too unfamiliar in America.

One of the dominating figures on the recent European landscape was C. G. Jung whose work with symbols is as profound as it is difficult and obscure. While I profess no particular competence in the field of Jungian psychology, Jung's work is particularly useful in setting the stage for an analysis of the views of other thinkers. According to Jung symbols are manifestations of the archetype. Every symbol is archetypal, but an archetype is not always identical with a symbol. Symbols merely fill out the archetype and make it "visible."[19] Hence the Jungian archetype is encountered only indirectly through a symbol, or archetypal image. For the purpose of historical analysis it is more important to note what Jung said about the symbols themselves than to attempt to trace out their relationship to his notion of the archetype. Jung saw a clear-cut distinction between allegories, symbols, and signs.[20] The true symbol stands for the unknown. The allegory, on the other hand, is a symbol once removed so to speak. It stands for the unknown by virtue of having been transformed into the known. When the force of the sky becomes personified by the anthropomorphic figure of Zeus, an allegory has been created according to Jung. Throughout the history of western art, anthropomorphic figures with appropriate attributes have stood for the elements of nature, the vices and virtues, the liberal arts, and often whatever else the imagination of man could invent. According to Jung, a sign is different from a symbol because the former stands for a known quality; hence according to this view it is impossible to create a truly living symbol from wholly known associations.[21] Jung was making reference to the unknown or transcendental element which dominates all studies of symbolism.

In general, Jung defined three classes of symbolism: the true symbol standing for the unknown, the allegory standing for the unknown by virtue of the known, and the sign standing for the known. A great deal of confusion has arisen over these categories not because they are Jungian, but because the three are more easily distinguished in theory than in practice. All tend to blend at times when we leave the realm of categories and actually begin to look at objects. Purity, however, is an attribute of the gods, and the historian should not feel infuriated if the symbols with which he works will not fit into any of these pigeon holes.

Signs, then, define known things. An illustration of an apple in a botany book would be an example of a sign, but an apple in the hand of Eve in a Scriptural illustration would be a symbol—the entire picture an allegory. At just what point the apple changes from sign to symbol is difficult to determine because symbolic content depends upon usage. In a culture alien to our own, a person might simply see only a nude figure holding an apple, just as we might be unable to "read" their symbols. According to Jung this illustrates how a symbol can degenerate into a mere sign.[22] The problem of knowing whether or not we are dealing with degenerate symbols or signs, or living symbols thus revolves around that elusive word "usage." Perhaps more than any internal analysis of form or meaning, only usage determines where on the spectrum between sign and symbol an art object will fall. Jung believed, and many historians have come to agree, that only usage determines the ground on which the object must be interpreted. The calf of gold was an idol to the Jews but the same object transmogrified into a simple child's trinket might have been looked upon with equanimity by the great Moses himself.

Another aspect of symbols, according to Jung, is their ability to transcend consciousness. It is still a matter of conjecture whether or not such symbols are real or imagined, but they do have a reality as far as human consciousness is concerned and it is human consciousness that the historian of symbols seeks to describe, not ultimate reality. For the study of religious symbols this is a notion of paramount importance. Unless symbols attempt to express something beyond the capacity of discursive language there would really be very little need for them. Tomb art has persisted from prehistoric times until the present and almost twenty thousand years of human labor cannot be reasoned away as products of conspicuous consumption, as Erwin Panofsky has recently shown in his new publication on tomb sculpture.[23] If the Puritans could have said all they wanted to about the brutal reality of death they would not have created religious themes but would have developed secular signs to distinguish their tombs, such as armorial shields. They chose, however, to abandon the armorial shields in favor of the religious symbols, and this in itself is a significant fact.

The work of Jung on the nature of symbols not only comprises the ideas we have just discussed but far more complex ones as well. According to Jung by virtue of the symbol the known and the unknown are brought together in a new dialectic. Symbols are bipolar. Symbols bring together pairs of opposites. The Greek root of the word "symbol" means "woven together" according to Jung,[24] while in German *Sinnbild* means a combination of "sense meaning" and "image" or the raw material of the primordial womb of the collective unconscious which takes on meaning in its union with the first component and acts as an integrating factor in consciousness. The transcendent function of the symbol is seen in its ability to fuse opposites such as symbols of both life and death. Although the New Englander did not know anything about the arcane vocabulary of Jungian thought he did think in profoundly Jungian terms. The Gershem Holmes stone (plate 1A), shows a death's head spewing forth a profile soul effigy. Plates 4A and 4B show effigies suspended between images of life and death. Part soul effigy, part death's heads, they are among the most significant fusions of symbolic opposites in all New England.

Although we have not discussed Jung's concept of the symbol as a transfer of energy, nor his notion of individual and collective symbols, we have seen how useful many of his ideas can be when dealing with actual historical problems of making sense of the imagery which the New Englander created to symbolize his trembling expectations in the face of unknown death.

Long before Jung entered the picture, the study of symbolism in Europe was begun in earnest by F. Creuzer and Goblet d'Alviella,[25] who marred further and more prudent investigations into the field by their obvious enthusiasms. Accordingly, a reaction set in which strictly denied the symbolic function of religious art and classed all monuments as merely decorative. So deeply has this skeptical point of view been imbued in the minds of contemporary scholars that I have heard the New England symbols called "decorative and without meaning," by those who ought at least to have investigated the material more closely before making such definitive pronouncements. Had they cared to apprise themselves of the fact that the Puritans give us not only the picture but often the explanatory verbal key cut into the same stone, they could hardly then have held the tree of life to be decorative and without meaning.[26]

Upon rereading Creuzer and d'Alviella we find that some of their conclusions about symbols, if not the methods they used to develop them, are coming back into fashion. Creuzer was on the right track when he claimed that the symbol can make the divine visible with an irresistible power that draws the beholder to itself with the form of absolute necessity.[27] Oskar Doering said much the same thing in his *Christliche Symbole*,[28] by calling symbols metaphors of the eternal in the form of the transient fused into a new unity of meaning. J. J. Bachofen in his "Versuch über die Gräbersymbolik der Alten"[29] agreed when he said that symbols awaken intimations which speech can only explain. According to Bachofen symbols combine the most disparate elements into unitary impressions, see plates 4A and 4B.

Many philosophers since at least the time of Hegel have tried to probe the nature of the religious symbol. According to Hegel signs and symbols should be distinguished from one another because the symbol is bound up in with the notion of intuition and the mere sign is not.[30] H. Hoffding in his work on the philosophy of religion claimed that religious symbols were drawn out from intuition and used for more universal expressions which because of their inherent ideality could not be more directly expressed.[31]

Ernst Cassirer devoted many volumes to the study of symbols and symbol making and had an influential effect upon a small group of American philosophers who have carried on his work.[32] Cassirer believed that prior to the time of Kant philosophers had contented themselves with the object described both as known and given. In spite of the fact that knowledge itself impresses certain laws upon given data, philosophers continued to treat the problem of epistemology with a lack of real concern. After Kant, epistemological problems became of more primary concern until they now threaten to gobble up philosophy itself. According to Cassirer, Kant wanted to begin with the laws of cognition instead of rambling on about metaphysics because only the laws of cognition are accessible and certain in the primary sense. Once these fundamental forms of judgment were defined objectively metaphysics becomes possible in a philosophical sense. Kant meant to examine the "lenses" of reason by which we focus upon what we come to know so that men would once and for all be able to distinguish between the object in itself and the means by which it became known. Philosophers are still attempting to draw out the implications of Kant's revolutionary ideas. Cassirer saw both the importance of such studies and their futility. He hoped to extend the Kantian framework between objects and the schema by which they become known to a more general critique of culture.[33] He hoped to work his own Copernican revolution, and for historical studies perhaps he did. He believed that we ought to take as our starting point not the general concept of the world, but rather the general concept of culture, for the forms of culture cannot be separated from the fundamental forms of human activity. In Cassirer's terms, "being" can be apprehended only in action. Only in so far as there is aesthetic imagination is there a sphere of aesthetic objects and so too with other forms of man's activities. Mythological thinking, the most fundamental level of the religious consciousness, transforms reality into simple material existence. At higher levels of contemplation religious consciousness possesses its object only in so far as it relates itself to that object in a special way, hence it too becomes an activity which takes place within the confines of what Cassirer called the "culture forms."[34]

For those who are in one way or another involved with historical studies there can be no question that these culture forms exist, but just what these forms are and how they are to be elicited from the "facts" of history, indeed, if there are any "bare facts," is a matter of historical judgment. According to Cassirer, cognitive thought and the forms of culture exist side by side in consciousness. The third element which binds them is the universality of the human spirit and of human experience. It is unfortunate for those of us who struggle with symbols that death took him from us before he completed his major work on symbols. Susanne Langer took up the task and has devoted her professional career to these problems. In an early work, *Philosophy in a New Key*,[35] she made a clear-cut Cassirer-like distinction between denotative and connotative thinking which has now achieved a status far beyond the discipline of philosophy. Langer clearly saw that thinking in its broadest sense could never be limited to "linear" logical cognitions, which are so much the fashion these days, without running the danger of losing the very richness of man's psychological and imaginative life. In the course of her investigations she proposed that language be thought of as functioning on two distinct levels, namely denotative and connotative. The difference between the two is the difference between verbal and averbal, but not necessarily antiverbal, thought. For Langer the process of symbolization is to "project" feelings to external objects and thus objectify and "conceive" of those feelings. Symbols thus become objectified projections of feeling cast into form. Hence no symbol is merely "decorative" or lacking in meaning, but all are projections of feelings, all different, all significant.

William Marshall Urban, another thinker influenced by Cassirer, attempted a general theory of symbolism in his important but often overlooked book *Language and Reality*.[36] According to Urban no hard and fast line could be drawn between sign and symbol in ordinary discourse because all depended upon usage, a point which Jung never tired of making. Urban believed that signs could upon occasion become symbols and conversely symbols, signs. According to Urban, and this is where his basic position differs from that of Jung, the symbol was a special kind of sign.[37] Urban then divided signs up into three categories, designatory, expressive, and significant and defined the symbol as wholly bound up with the intuitive which could not attain adequate expression in any other way. Urban then divided symbols into three classes, the extrinsic or arbitrary, the intrinsic or descriptive, and the insight symbols.[38] Needless to say it is this latter category which will concern us. Urban borrowed the idea of "insight symbols" from H. F. Dunbar whose book *Symbolism in Medieval Thought*[39] dealt directly with the problem. Dunbar believed that certain types of symbols do not simply describe or make more concrete objects otherwise known (descriptive symbols), but provide a gateway to something belonging to the world of "spirit,"[40] apprehended through the sensuous symbol. Drawing upon Jung, Urban saw the symbol composed of two elements, the real and the fictional. If it were real it would not be a symbol and if it were fictional it would simply be empty imagining without the element of necessity which is a matter of primary importance in isolating the essence of symbolic processes. According to Urban the symbol blended the known and the sensuous with the quality of the discursively unknown and the "invisible." This is the paradox of symbolism. In addition, Urban believed that symbols had raw, naked power, especially religious symbols. Like Jung, Bachofen, and Creuzer, Urban spoke often of the immanential law of symbolism which extended itself outward in both directions. From what I can gather from the thought of Urban this immanential law was quite similar to the *Mysterium Tremendum* of Rudolph Otto.[41] According to Otto the *Mysterium Tremendum* is the infinitely holy working into intuition. According to Urban the religious symbol is not the idea of God, for example, but the inner essence of the idea.[42] This is the kernel around which the religious symbol crystallizes. Essence and existence melt together in the very quality of the deity.[43] The idea that an immanential law extends in both directions, toward the known and the unknown, is the key phrase for anyone hoping to study the nature of religious symbols carefully. Accordingly, in practical affairs religious symbols couched in immediacy allowed the believer to entertain the idea that not only is communication between symbol and symbolized open ended, but that the noumenal sense of divinity could directly saturate the symbols themselves with a thick layer of "spirit." According to Urban, the true religious symbol is so composed that if it is not saturated with divinity, if divinity is not immanent within the symbol, if essence and existence are not one, then the symbol is corrupt. The symbol has degenerated into a mere sign by usage.

Thus far three important notions concerning the nature of symbols have become apparent. First, symbols seem to mediate between the known and the unknown in experience, between ideality and the world of sense and form, if you will. Second, religious symbols have within themselves something both immanential and immediate which distinguishes them from the products of discursive mediate thought. Third, this immanential power permeates the symbol, saturating it with spiritual significance.

Perhaps the best expression of these ideas was developed by Rudolph Otto in his *The Idea of the Holy*. According to Otto, the Holy is a category of religious interpretation which cannot be derived from any other; it is neither aesthetic, ethical, nor rational.[44] It remains *a priori*. To express this evanescent sense which was beyond the Good of Kant, Otto chose the term "numen" from which the now far more famous term "numinous" derived. The numinous is a symbolic manifestation felt outside the self but in such a refracted manner that it becomes manifested as the *Mysterium Tremendum*.[45] Included in the feeling of the *Tremendum* are the elements of majesty, of the overpowering, of energy, and of urgency. The *Mysterium* is composed of those nonrational elements which are already inherent in religion being most often characterized by the mystics as the "wholly other." According to Otto in the experience of art the numinous finds form by creating a "magical" sense of reality independent of rational reflection while the "magical" itself is nothing more than a suppressed, a dimmed form of the numinous. He argues that only in the truly great work of art is the magical element transcended and the numinous confronted.[46] Hence in certain classes of art an image or icon can easily slip over into an idol by virtue of being so closely connected in imagination with elements of both magical and numinal concern. A religious symbol can descend into an idol when usage demands that the degree of numinal saturation reaches the point of no return and the mind no longer distinguishes between the symbol and the symbolized. In some cultures the boiling point is reached rather easily. Among the post-Hellenistic Jews no significant imagery at all was ever allowed for fear of idolatry but in the Catholic world the multitudes still pray to their legions of carved, molded and painted saints.

One of the most influential writers upon whom Otto relied for his ideas concerning religious art was Oswald Siren.[47] Siren, in writing about the great Buddha in the Lung-men Caves, said that anyone who approached the figure had to realize that it had religious significance without any knowledge of the particular motifs. It mattered very little what one knew about Buddhism to feel that the image was permeated or drenched with "spiritual will." The religious significance of such a figure was immanent, it created a presence, or an "atmosphere" of spiritual significance rather than formulated an idea, or a system of motifs which could be exhausted by iconographic investigation. The idea of "presence" is a familiar one to all art historians, because all great art whether it is religious or not has "presence." Presence in the sense of "spiritual will" is probably only confronted in the religious work of art. Of more significance than the notion of presence which we have come to expect from all good art, or "spiritual will" which we have come to expect from all good religious art, is the sense in which Siren said, and Otto agreed, that every motif need not be worked out systematically for the religious work of art to work its "magic."

On many New England gravestones there is such a profusion of arcane secondary themes that it would be foolish to imagine that the layman, or perhaps even the stonecarver himself, could read them all like a didactic text. It seems to me that in all symbolism the value of many secondary motifs was not so much didactic, although to be sure it could be that too, as it was "atmospheric." The secondary symbols were meant to fill out the "presence" of symbolism rather than to define any specific dogma. In many cases when art was still far more popular than aristocratic, when every theme did not have to be "rationalized" by humanist or medieval scholars, many secondary symbols were probably meant to be indeterminate rather than explicit and clear. It would be foolish to assume that because the rural New England stonecarver created literally thousands of variant forms of foliage for the border panels, that thousands of verbal shades of meaning were involved. It is far more likely that the variants were meant to make stylistic rather than iconographic sense. Conversely, it would be foolish not to look for meaning when the age-old symbol of the tree of life is involved. Needless to say the scholar must be guided in these matters by his sense of judgment and proportion. Another difficult factor is that what were once symbols of normative value in Europe came to be transformed by the rural New England stonecarvers into patterns of new meaning. Hence an old symbol had been corrupted so to speak. It is then the job of the historian to study each theme to decide if the symbol has remained a symbol or become merely a hollow, meaningless sign. For example, the European cherubim were transformed into soul effigies by the stonecarvers of New England

and it is often difficult to tell created angels from glorified souls. Although in extreme cases the stonecarvers made specific references in one direction or another, in the vast majority of cases they have left this subtle classification to our imaginations. A transformation in symbolic value took place on the long ocean voyage over the Atlantic. The more difficult question is whether or not the change so corrupted the symbol that no new meanings were possible. I do not think so. For example, the swastika was an ancient symbol long before the Nazis took it over and gave new meanings to it. Few Jews who experienced the dark night of barbarism which descended over Europe would agree that symbols could not exchange their meanings and still retain symbolic significance. They still shudder when confronted with the dreaded swastika.

Paul Tillich saw five characteristics in religious symbols: their figurative quality, their perceptibility, their power, their acceptability, and their unconditioned transcendence.[48] According to Tillich it is the power of the symbol standing for something higher than itself which distinguishes it from the mere sign. This is the quality which elevates the symbol to a level lost in ordinary usage. Added to this dimension of power, which so many other thinkers have seen in symbols, Tillich also stressed the compulsive power of the symbol. Tillich believed that all religious art was originally charged with magical power and when it became totally lost the genuine symbolic character of the art was forfeited. Accordingly, the social acceptability of the symbol conveys the notion that symbols can degenerate into mere signs depending on usage, a notion that every writer on symbols seems to have noted. For example, it is well known that the antique symbol of the shell originally represented the vulva but as centuries progressed the sexual meaning was played down and abstracted from its original connotations until the present day when the bare outlines of this ancient symbol are to be seen ornamenting many Neo-Georgian doorways. The owner of such a doorway might be astonished to know that those crossing his threshold are in point of fact re-entering a symbolic womb. A symbol had passed through a long period of transition,[49] where meanings were constantly changed and diluted until finally the symbol was transformed into mere sign. Such an analysis bears out what Tillich had been saying about symbols. In order to be symbolic a form must be socially rooted and socially supported. Tillich's fifth category of symbolism is that of unconditioned transcendence. This is where Tillich leaves the company of other authors and arrives at conclusions difficult for all but the specialist to follow. Tillich seems to think of the soul as religious and expressing itself through symbols. Accordingly, the real function of the religious symbols is to break through and transcend themselves and their immediacy and meet the "wholly other" at the point of transcendence. I must confess that I do not understand how a symbol can "transcend" the melting together of symbol and symbolized in immediacy and transcend itself, because then it would seem to me that we are no longer talking about symbols at all but something else again.

Thus far we have been engaged in a rather theoretical discussion of religious symbolism which seems to have only tangential bearing on the problems facing the historian of art. It was left to Erwin R. Goodenough to attempt to bring together the fruits of theory and history and forge them into a new method of historical analysis. Goodenough believed first of all that symbols speak in the language of paradox,[50] secondly that the rich diversity of Hellenistic symbols can be reduced to the single theme of supplications for immortality, and thirdly that no single theme or explanation can convey the rich atmosphere of the multitudes of symbols used to convey this single meaning. Thus Goodenough found that no explanation exhausted the limitless possibilities of the symbols. After eleven volumes of analysis Goodenough could still say,

> What, basically, is the character of the Judaism thus suggested to us? To try to put it into a few words would do violence to my own impressions, and to the synagogue itself. A great difficulty inheres in verbalizing an expression of religion which its exponents have left to us only in symbols. Words are exclusive and specific, symbols inclusive and suggestive. We are dealing with a period in religion which antedated the curse which the synods and scholastics laid upon Western civilization, the curse (in many ways, of course, a blessing) of supposing that conceptions must be expressed in words of clearly specific meaning. We dispute, excommunicate, and torture to death for the sake of words. The Catholic church rightly saw that the destruction of its icons would cut at the roots of its very life. The verbalism of Protestantism and rabbinic Jews has been their own greatest obstacle. Words are also symbols, I know, but the word "vine" can never be a symbol as the vine itself, in nature or in representation, can be. Always what contemporary thinkers have come to distinguish as the denotative meaning of verbal expression intrudes into the pure metaphysical connotation of the symbols themselves. Actually the symbol has little importance except as it takes us behind all formal thinking into a reality which perhaps we create but which simultaneously creates new forms in us. . . . Our creative metaphors create new dimensions in ourselves, whether they be metaphors of mathematics or scripture. We can no more paraphrase in

words the metaphors of painting or music than of physics. But all our deepest expression is metaphorical.[51]

A paradox in itself, Goodenough could say that after more than thirty years of study and eleven monumental volumes his words had not been enough to express the enormity of the symbols.

It is this very sense of paradox that is so difficult for the historian to live with, and yet a necessary condition for the understanding of all religious experience. Goodenough at one point explained why the most moving of all symbols of the Western world, a symbol which threaded its way through Egyptian religion, Orphism, Mithraism, and finally into Christianity, was a dead god symbolizing new life. It is by virtue of paradox that such symbols possess our minds and the New Englander was not unaware of such notions. The Puritan poet Edward Taylor knew about the language of paradox when he wrote,

> The Painter lies who pensills death's Face grim
> With White — bare butter Teeth, bare staring bones,
> With Empty Eyeholes, Ghostly Lookes which fling
> Such Dread to see as raiseth Deadly groans,
> For thou [Christ] has farely Washt Death's grim grim face
> And made his Chilly finger-ends drop grace.[52]

The New England stonecarver spoke in the same language of paradox when he carved a soul effigy in profile being ejected from the mouth of death in plate 1B. He traced in the language of paradox the transformation of death into new life when over a period of years he transformed his imagery, his eschatology, if you will, into symbols of angelic life from symbols of death in plates 2 and 3. He spoke in the language of paradox when he showed a living root and flowers bursting from a skull and a cinerary urn in plate 8. Nothing could be more clear and yet nothing has been more misunderstood. Before we can interpret these symbols we must know how to "read" the language of paradox. Apparently our understanding is no longer dialectical enough to encompass both life and death in one symbol, but this does not mean that the Puritans interpreted these figures in the same manner. No grouping of New England symbols has aroused more controversy than these symbols of transformation which purport to change grim death into sweet grace before our eyes. Apparently our modern conceptions of the soul are not complex enough to sense that the soul can abide in heaven only by first becoming lost in death. In the same sense our modern conceptions of symbols are not complex enough to see the peace of the soul in the suffering Christ on the cross. Modern civilizations cannot face Christian symbols directly so they have distorted the paradox of the Passion, eliminating all the suffering and replacing it with a sweet coat of sentimentality. Just as the ancients slowly worked the symbol of the vulva into the abstraction of the shell (foam-borne Aphrodite), so too the anguish of the Passion was dimmed after the Renaissance until our time when the images of Christ sold in gift shops throughout the nation are nothing more than vacuous faces exuding only sweetness and light. We are not going to understand the message of the New England symbols if we persist in reading them as our fancy dictates rather than as the Puritans themselves would have read them. The terror of death was the price of victory in Christ. The difficult journey from death to new life in Abraham's bosom revealed the true glory of the Resurrection in the terrors of death.

Religious art has been an adjunct for the expression of religious beliefs since before the dawn of recorded history. Nothing testifies more to the need for symbols than the supposed iconophobia of the Hellenistic Jews, the early Christians, and the American Puritans. All three, to judge from their literature, were aware of the dangers of idolatry and all three have subsequently been found to have had a wealth of religious art no matter what the intellectual elite of the time might have thought about imagery. It is now clear that the American Puritans had art in spite of the fact that their ancestors in England had obviously delighted in wrecking a great deal of religious sculpture before they sailed away and began to develop a religious art of their own.

After 1668[53] no Puritan family was ready to commit its loved ones to the cold earth without an appropriate cluster of symbols hovering protectively over the grave. It seems that only in art could the aspirations of men pierce the veils of discursive language and give the "invisible world" meaningful expression, and so it was to art they turned when confronted with the awful immensity of death and the long voyage of the soul.

Through analysis it is becoming more and more apparent that symbolism brings together what reason cannot logically comprehend. It is also becoming clear that only at the symbolic level of the gravestones did the Puritans dare to hope to find a path between time and eternity. As we shall see when we deal with the orthodox Puritan views of man's knowledge of God, the New Englander was also confronted on an intellectual level with reasoning out this complicated relationship. God, in being both transcendent and immanent, limited what men could know of the working of eternity. The visual symbols, on the other hand, opened up brightly lighted boulevards of the spirit where Puritan discursive reasoning revealed only dark labyrinths of thought about that which cannot be conceived. The Puritans believed that words were in the final analysis a very limited means of apprehending the Godhead. Edward Taylor wrote,

> Words are befould, Thoughts filthy fumes that smoake,
> From Smutty Huts, like Will-a-Wisps that rise
> From Quaugmires, run ore bogs where frogs do Croake,
> Lead all astray led by them by the eyes.
> My muddy Words do dark thy Deity,
> And cloude thy Sun-Shine, and its Shining Sky.[54]

Words were merely the building blocks out of which a cathedral of piety could be built upon the foundation of Scripture, but the bond of love which joined the two was not of human origin. God was the true architect of redemption. The making of a saint was a passive process; reason had to be irradiated by the light of the Holy Ghost. Verbal discourse was a valued instrument which could prepare a "vertical" route toward heaven, but the would-be saint still had to be carried into a state of grace. For the Puritans, reason prepared the way (indeed, if it could even do that without the taint of Arminianism) but the growing illumination of the spirit through Scripture mediated by reason was not the product of reason but of revelation as the Puritans understood the term.[55]

In these matters the Puritans differed from the Quakers. The Quakers wanted to open up the symbolic possibilities of a more heartfelt and immediate communion between man and God while the Puritans were always wary of such blatant displays of emotionalism which ensued whenever the symbols for God and God Himself became confused in the minds of the theologically unsophisticated.[56] For the Quakers, revelation did not come through the dusty pages of Scripture but immediately through the heart pierced with love and bathed in the bright light of the Holy Spirit. The Puritans had presentiments of what harm these babbling prophets could cause, each with his own special vision; each running about New England sowing the seeds of social confusion. The Quakers were brutally and summarily suppressed in the manner of the 17th century. Again, from the point of view of symbol making, the Quaker invasion of New England is particularly interesting. The Quakers presented normative Puritanism with a more immediate way of reaching out towards the invisible world and the

Puritans rejected the notion in no uncertain terms. The latter preferred to retain their own more academic version of the drama of redemption and they thus set the stage for the rise of visual symbolism.

Puritan sacramental symbolism was another area where there might have been greater possibilities for symbolic communication between the world of the flesh and the spirit but again the Puritans hedged and conceived of the sacraments as somewhere between the outright principle of transubstantiation of the Catholics and the symbolic barrenness of Zwingli's principle of the sacraments which merely "sealed" church membership. In these matters the Puritans once again rejected an immediate confrontation between man and spirit, between symbol and symbolized.

Every culture uses symbols in a variety of ways. The Puritans not only conceived of their God in terms of symbols; they also thought symbolically in language, the sacraments and many of the disputes which animated their lives in the 17th and in the 18th centuries. Symbolically, Arminianism, Antinomianism, and Revivalism may all be seen as bold approaches at injecting more blood, so to speak, into the watery veins of a Puritanism which was in fact risking decline into a new kind of scholasticism.

The emerging formula concerning the use of symbols seems to be this: the more the forces of the institutionalized church channelled symbolic activities into controllable areas of community expression the more the multitudes strove to find a form of numinal expression outside the context of institutionalized religion, but still related to it. After the first thirty years they found the gravestone and persisted in carving them well into the early 19th century in rural isolated pockets where the old ideas and ways endured the longest.

I

Puritan Religion

I. THE FUNCTION OF SYMBOLISM IN NORMATIVE PURITAN THEOLOGY

Samuel Willard, Vice President of Harvard College and a prominent Boston minister until his death, had a great deal to say about how language should function in investigating man's knowledge of God. Willard attempted to strip words of their ability to transcend the finite order of things without actually going so far towards agnosticism that religious symbols became mere signs without correspondence to religious truth. Language directed at investigations of the "invisible world" was then the historical correlative of what the multitudes expected of their bright stone icons. Puritan language made God's transcendence majestic in its aloofness while their visual symbols made His mercy immanent in its immediacy.

Orthodox Puritans were always ready to admit that their thoughts about God did not embrace a knowledge of His essence. Such a conception naturally limited the ability of verbal symbols to penetrate the Godhead in any significant way. To think out this complicated notion was the object of Willard who wrote the most systematic account of orthodox Puritanism prior to the work of Jonathan Edwards, who was not actually an orthodox Puritan at all.[57] The principle of verbal symbolism which Willard followed was first penned by Duns Scotus.[58] The object of Willard's sermons was to allow a knowledge of God only where God had taken attributes freely upon Himself which would correspond to attributes familiar to man. To know that God was good was possible because God took the attribute of goodness upon Himself so that men might know Him.

God's "incommunicable glory" was transcendent and had little if anything to do with the attributes God took freely upon Himself according to Willard. The problem was twofold: to avoid making God too transcendent for fear of agnosticism and too immanent for fear of blasphemy. The job of blending immanence and transcendence was not so much a matter of technical or philosophical concern but of religious conviction. Hence for Willard, the measures were already blended by force of social convention and needed reasonable confirmation. This may have been poor philosophy but it does establish clearly that the ground of most philosophical theology, no matter how artfully worked out, reduces itself in the final analysis to a belief in the efficacy of one set of symbolic conventions in preference to another. For example, the Quakers were more mystical in their social conventions, religious practices, and subjective feelings toward this issue and naturally their philosophical theology mirrors that symbolic concern.[59]

The problem was one of forging a Puritan view of how verbal symbols describe God, just as it was the stonecarvers' problem to depict the Resurrection and the soul in heaven without stepping outside Christian doctrine on the one hand or the very real fears of taboo and idolatry on the other.[60]

An overemphasis on God's transcendence would mean that nothing could be known of God by definition and thus the overt flashes of His being revealed in Scripture would be suspect and thus civilized religion would become impossible. If, on the other hand, man could come to know God by the exercise of reason alone then this would mean that there was no difference between reason and revelation, between Greek speculation and Christian mystery, between Creator and created.[61] In a single leap of the imagination man could theoretically elevate himself to the level of eternity without the intervention of grace which would then make the Passion a meaningless event rather than the core of Christianity itself. Thus the blend of transcendence and immanence had far more significance than simply a systematic one in Willard's eyes.

The job Willard faced was to make his verbal symbols tread a middle ground between agnosticism and anthropomorphism. Willard could not afford either to melt together the temporal and the eternal orders or to define terms *aequivoce* so that nothing could be known of the eternal.[62] In working out this complicated symbolic middle ground the Middle Ages produced St. Thomas Aquinas whose thought on the subject attracted the largest audience, although it would be naïve to believe that the late Middle Ages spoke only in his words.[63] The New England Puritans rejected out of hand the Thomistic view of verbal symbols, which involved the concepts of both proportion and proportionality, and attempted to follow Duns Scotus for reasons which are not at all clear even today. Perhaps it was because Aquinas had the official stamp of "Rome" upon him. Perhaps it was because the Puritans believed that theology was for all and the simplicity of the Scotistic system had far more to offer than the dark passages of Thomas. Although there is no easy way to state the Thomistic position, in its most simplified form it does assert that in order to make symbols for God valid in language, words must function neither *aequivoce* nor *univoce*, but by proportion or proportionality.[64] To deny this theory would, according to the Thomists, plunge the science of theology in the abyss of pure speculation. Willard attacked this position with little substantiating evidence, but despite Willard's antipathy the Thomistic system did allow theology to navigate the tricky waters between agnosticism and anthropomorphism.[65]

The Thomists claimed that one could not predicate terms *univoce* without running the risk of anthropomorphism. To call God good *univoce* would mean that God was good in the same way that a man may be said to be good only to a greater degree. According to the Thomists this is excessive anthropomorphism in which the transcendence of God has no meaning whatsoever. To call God good *aequivoce* would mean that God was good in some way which had no meaningful relationship to the way in which we ordinarily use the term good. According to the Thomists unintelligibility would naturally follow and from unintelligibility, agnosticism. Since neither excessive anthropomorphism nor agnosticism was a satisfactory alternative Thomas invented the idea of proportion and proportionality which Willard believed was far too complex and rather meaningless. Both Willard and Scotus believed that there was little sense in calling God good unless you meant that He was good in the same sense that a man could be said to be good only to a greater degree. Although God's goodness was perfect and man's far from it, the difference was in degree not in kind. The Scotistic system needed no complex middle ground of "proportion," only purification, as attributes moved from man towards God. The accretions of the finite order of things merely had to be stripped away to make a term such as "good" function both for man and God, remembering all the while that God merely took these predicates upon Himself in order to be known.

The thoughtful Willard knew that he could not enter these troubled waters without a guiding principle of symbolism. Having chosen to follow Scotus Willard believed that *univoce* predication would not allow the enthusiastic to assert that all the winds of heaven were gathered up in the sail of Scotistic reason. In this sense Willard's thoughts about symbols were indeed modern.

In sermon thirteen of his *A Compleat Body of Divinity*,[66] Willard wrote, ". . . God as he is in himself, is not to be comprehended by the creature."[67] This is the first indication that Willard was less than optimistic about what reason could know of God in spite of the fact that in sermon twelve he wrote that God was "Spirit, Infinite, Eternal, Unchangeable, Wisdom, Power, Holiness, Justice, Goodness and Truth."[68] The extended argument for man's inability to comprehend the Godhead is given by Willard as follows:

> The vast distance that the Creature stands from God! Shall the upstarts of time, equal themselves in Understanding with Eternity itself? Shall they that are of Yesterday, and know nothing, compare with him that is from Everlasting? Shall our purblind eyes challenge as much as he, who is light itself? . . . *He is without causes.* Humane knowledge comes to discern into things, by reaching the Causes of them. . . . He that apprehends the first being, is able to say what he is, to trace his original, to give a true and proper definition of him, to find out and discover the Nature of his essential and constituting principles; but this no Creature can do.[69]

Further along in sermon thirteen Willard claimed that, "All reason is too finite to comprehend the infinite; too shallow to contain the deep, the bottomless; too narrow to grasp the boundless; too little comprehensive to include this incomprehensible object."[70]

The dialectical unity of Puritanism is revealed in sermons twelve and thirteen. In sermon twelve Willard defined a number of attributes belonging to God as if there were going to be little subsequent danger of probing these relationships to their depths aided by the instrument of reason. In sermon thirteen he turned from the bright light of Greek rationalism to the legalisms of normative Judaism which cast God into an almost wholly transcendent role.

Similar tensions became apparent in the Greco-Roman world when Christian apologists had to compete with the riper rationalistic systems invented by the Greeks and proceeded to cast into a philosophical frame of reference what was originally a mystery religion.[71] But as we have already seen, there are some meanings in religion which thrive on paradox rather than logical clarity. For the truly pious rather than the merely puzzled, philosophical theology in and of itself was never enough. It was a beginning but never an end.

Indeed, philosophical theology was a rather late development in the history of religion and endemic only to the western world or those influenced by it. Ritual, symbolic art, music, dance, poetry, and literature and myth have far older pedigrees and there is sufficient reason to believe that if civilization ever loses these Orphic gifts society will be deeply impoverished. Apparently even the Puritans realized their loss very early and attempted to build up a vocabulary of symbolism of their own however crude it might now seem to modern sensibilities.

Willard relived the classical Christian dilemma when in sermon twelve he was buoyed up by his rationalistic optimism and in sermon thirteen depressed by his Hebraic pessimism. Just as the poet Edward Taylor came to realize that even if reason is the mere croaking of a toad in matters spiritual, man has no finer voice,[72] so too Willard attempted to forge a symbolic meeting ground in language between Athens and Jerusalem.

The moments in religious consciousness which dwell between transcendence and immanence, between agnosticism and anthropomorphism, between time and eternity had to be melted together in a synthetic unity. Willard chose to follow Scotus in this matter in order to eliminate the possibility of immediate revelation so that none could dare to think that the mind could distinguish its way into the Godhead. In laying to rest these fundamental issues Willard skipped over one of the most profound questions of Christianity. If Creator and created are distinct, and Willard made such a claim at every opportunity, then God is transcendent of the created order. But if God is transcendent of the created order He cannot be infinite because the predicate "infinite" includes His creation. If, on the other hand, God is Creator, He is immanent in creation by virtue of His infinity. But God cannot be immanent in creation because He is supposed to be distinct from the creature by virtue of His transcendence. The symbolic blend of transcendence and immanence cannot be reduced to the cold logic of a philosophical system without tampering with the basic symbols of paradox themselves. One wonders what Willard would have had to say about these issues. Perhaps he was wise to remain silent.

Willard was attempting to make another symbolic blend. The key passage which Willard believed was the scriptural justification for the introduction of Scotus reads,

> THIS Incomprehensible Being hath made such discoveries of himself in his
> Back-Parts, as present him a suitable Object for Faith to rest upon. There are
> some precious rays of the Divinity, that irradiate us by way of reflection; by
> which we may so far acquaint ourselves with God, as may make us happy. God
> is called a *Sun* . . . Now if we fix our eyes directly on the body of the Sun, it will
> wholly dazzle us; but if we look on the reflected light or beams of it, we are
> safe, and it is confortable; and so it is here. The Divine perfections are irra-
> diated upon our Understanding through a dark glass; they are held forth
> Aenigmatically; which displays of himself to his Creatures, God is pleased to
> call *his back parts*, which he promised he would eminently make known to
> Moses, . . . Now they are so called.
>
>   *BECAUSE they fall short of the plenary discovery of his Native Excellency,
> in the immediate unreflected manifestations of it.*[73]

Willard took this passage to mean a scriptural endorsement of the
Scotistic position. According to Willard *univoce* predication revealed
only God's communicable glory, or His "irradiations." Nothing more
nor less could be allowed because if the great Moses could not look
directly into the face of Jehovah without perishing, how could the
struggling Puritan? All knowledge of divinity was filtered through the
screens of *univoce* predication and reason itself only opened up the
attributes which God had freely taken upon Himself to reveal. Willard
wrote,

> *WHAT is the Discovery, which the first Being makes of himself, in his Back-
> parts?*
> . . . It is that whereby he reveals his communicable glory unto us, according
> to our manner and measure of receiving it. It is his speaking to us about himself
> in our own language and according to our capacity of receiving and apprehend-
> ing any thing of him.
>
>   . . . .
>
> Because Heaven's mode and way is not known unto us, therefore he speaks
> to us in the language and manner of Earth; (*Joh.* 3.12.) and that is in the way
> of created human Reason. . . . We know nothing of God but by putting some
> logical Notion upon Him. All things are conveyed to us in a Logical way, and
> bear some stamp of reason upon them, or else we should know nothing of
> them. Hence God, to fit his discovery of himself to our manner of entertaining
> it, takes the Rational and the Logical Arguments upon himself, admits of a
> Distinction or Description, utters Sentences or Actions about himself, speaks
> of himself as if he were an Effect, and had Causes; a Subject, and had Adjuncts:
> and by such a way we come to see something concerning him, who is in himself
> invisible: and this tells us how useful and necessary reason is to Faith; it being
> an instrument which is used to convey the discoveries of God unto it; and

therefore Faith does not relinquish or cast off reason; for there is nothing in Religion contrary to it, tho' there are many things that do transcend, and must captivate it.[74]

Reason was apparently not the mode of God, nor could reason plumb the depths of the spiritual world. Reason was merely the way in which God allowed Himself to be comprehended by the creature. Reason did not abandon faith. Faith merely transcended reason in a higher synthesis of consciousness. According to Willard, however, there was nothing to be revealed without reason, but reason had to be transcended in faith. This is where orthodox Puritanism parts ways with both Quakerism and with the neo-orthodoxy of the New Light followers of Jonathan Edwards. According to Willard and orthodoxy, faith and love grow in the soil of reason, but the bloom of grace could only come through a process called "preparation" which embodied and transcended reason without abandoning it. It was this very paradox of orthodox preparation which Edwards found too contradictory and attacked as being far too Arminian.

The allegiance of Willard to Scotus is further revealed in another passage from sermon fourteen. The limitation on Scotistic principles was spelled out with unmistakable clarity.

> WE cannot know more of God, and live. It is impossible that the created faculty should receive more into it . . . If *Moses* had seen God's face, it must have been with the eye of his Understanding; but that being finite and God infinite, it must have been extended beyond its capacity and so have been broken and destroyed. . .[75]

Sermon fifteen picked up the threads of the argument and attempted to weave a delicate garment which would blend together both the distinction between God's communicable and His incommunicable glory. Willard wrote,

> THOSE Back Parts of God, in which he discovers himself to us, are his Sufficiency, and his Efficiency.
> GOD'S Sufficiency (or his Alsufficiency) is his Divine Fulness, by virtue whereof he hath enough in himself, to answer all his own ends.
>
> . . . .
>
> A man is then said to be self-sufficient, when he hath not only enough for himself personally, but for all them too that have their dependence upon him; when he is able to live upon his own, without being beholding to others, and maintain his post, and do all that belongs to him, and his estate will bear it out without impairing the principal. Hence we make our guesses at God's Alsuffi-

ciency, by conceiving him to be such a Being, but after a more transcendent manner.

THE chief perfections of the Creature are, in the *most perfect* manner and measure, in God. If we speak of Justice, Wisdom, Power, Goodness, etc. there seems to be some Analogy between God and Man in respect unto these. Hence we give them the same name, and have Analogous formal conceptions of them in our minds. . . . . But we must remember, there is but *little* of this in the Creature; but they are *infinite* in God. They have them separably, he inseparably; he therefore hath them in a more sublime and superminent manner, than either is or can be in a Creature. Hence we would add the Epithet of Transcendency to them, when we ascribe them to him, ...[76]

Thus the ways in which the Puritans came to know God gave them a satisfactory conception of Him but did not exhaust His content.[77]

At this juncture it looked as if Willard had rested his forceful case. It looked as if he had successfully defended the faith against the intrusion of immediate revelation on the one hand and Arminianism on the other; the former because symbolic language was technically limited to *univoce* predication and the latter because meaningless *aequivoce* predication was summarily avoided as well. It looked as if Willard had blended just the right amount of immanence to make the children of Greek rationalism enthusiastic and just enough transcendence to make the heirs of the Hebrews true to their heritage.

Although a vertical analytical path between finite and infinite had been plotted with the aid of discursive language, although words formed a billowing canopy between meaning and the meaningless, the symbolic passivity of the process was consonant with the spiritual determinism of Calvinism. The Puritan soul was conceived as a spiritually insensate vessel awaiting the divine fluid of grace.

Willard was, however, going to have some trouble with the philosophical implications of his symbolic position before sermon fifteen came to a close. He wrote,

GOD is pleased to reveal his Essence to his people by diverse Attributes, which he assumed to himself.

. . . .

THE Attributes of God are his Essence which is in itself a Pure Act, diversely apprehended by us . . . Now because this act cannot be known to us altogether, at one sight of our Understanding; but we must needs have a diversified representation of it, it being too big for our single comprehension; Hereupon God hath taken Attributes to himself, which are so many several expressions of the same Essence and Act: and these are more properly said to be assumed by him, than to be so many several Perfections of him.

. . . .

NOW the reason, why this pure act must be diversely apprehended by us, is, because tho God be to be seen by an eye of Faith, yet he must be seen by an eye of Reason too: for tho Faith sees above Reason, yet it sees nothing, but in a way of Reason, which discerns all things by Arguments. . . .

. . . .

When we say, *God is Great, Wise*, etc., our reason looks upon God as the subject, and his greatness as one Adjunct, etc., and so we joyn these two together: and our manner of conception and expression, makes a distinction between his Being, and his Holiness, Wisdom, etc. Yea, it conceives a difference between the Attributes themselves: it distinguisheth between his Wisdom, and his Holiness, between his Justice and his Mercy. So that the Essence comes into our Understanding, under a various representation; through which, as through so many several glasses, we have so many discoveries made to us, of his glorious Essence, . . .[78]

According to Willard, we are to believe that God's essence transcends subject-predicate definitions. The latter merely allow men to distinguish between attributes which God takes freely upon Himself. Prior to this time Willard wrote,

there is no Essence or Nature (which) can be attributed to God. *He is without causes.*[79]

In contrast to this assertion Willard subsequently defined God's essence as "Pure Act" and later seemed to be saying that the attributes of "Pure Act" define God's essence. Willard wrote,

THAT these Attributes are in God, but one most *pure and simple act.* They are therefore called Attributes, because they may more properly be said to be ascribed to him, than to be really in him.[80]

We are suddenly supposed to believe that God is a "Pure Act" in spite of the fact that only a moment ago Willard was claiming that there was no Essence or Nature to be attributed to God and that He was beyond attributes and causes. It is in these places that it is hard to follow Willard. He made it even more difficult when he not only claimed that "these Attributes are in God" as a pure and simple act but that the attributes are more properly said to be ascribed to God than really in Him. Prior to this time Willard was saying that the divine attributes were merely being assumed by God in order to make Himself known in terms of the creature. Now Willard appears to be saying that these attributes are somehow truly in God ("that these Attributes are in God, but as one most pure and simple act"), but in reality ascribed to God at the same time ("they may more properly be said to be ascribed to Him, than to be really in him"). If these attributes are in God He cannot be conceived in terms of a pure and simple act because multiplicity and unity cannot inhere in the same substance at the same time. Willard seemed to be saying just this when he wrote,

> THE Attributes as they are in God, are not *distinct from the Essence*, nor *one from another*.[81]

Willard now seems to be saying that not only are the attributes in God but that they are not distinct from one another. One fails to see how attributes such as God's immensity and eternity can be "in" God and undistinguished from one another and still remain attributes. Further, I do not see how the attributes, even if they were somehow distinguished from one another in God, could be in His "Essence" without having multiplicity and unity inhering in the same substance at the same time.

Willard has gotten himself into serious difficulties because he wanted to follow Scotus only in so far as God's communicable glories were concerned. He wanted to follow Scotus only in so far as both God and man shared certain attributes. When Willard had to turn to a definition of God's incommunicable glories, or those attributes He did not share with the creature, Willard abandoned *univoce* predication and with it Scotus. With the abandoning of Scotus, Willard took up *aequivoce* predication where there are no qualities in the divine attributes which can be traced in the creature. If Willard abandoned Scotus without picking up the system of predication of the Thomists he is left with *aequivoce* predication which according to the best philosophical minds ends in unintelligibility. Willard never told us how he planned to avoid unintelligibility but he did claim that,

> OF his Attributes, some are said to be *Incommunicable;* others to be *Communicable*. The former are the Divine properties, which so belong to God, as there is no shadow of them in the Creature, and it is blasphemy to ascribe them unto it: such as Immensity, Eternity, Immutability.[82]

The most important question we can address to Willard's text is why was Scotus abandoned at this critical juncture when he had served so well? Surely these are not particularly intricate philosophical problems if met with consistency. It seems that when all has been said and done the problem lies in the nature of Puritanism itself which was always more concerned with symbolic truth than with ontological definitions. Willard wanted his terms to dance to his tune and his tune was orthodoxy. Willard wanted his terms to be true to the symbolic tenets of Puritanism and when they could no longer be managed after having been set into motion he merely attempted to change the tune. Willard knew full well that he could not apply Scotistic principles to God's incommunicable glory (factors such as immensity, immutability, and eternity), without giving to the creature that which almost certainly belonged to the Creator and running the risk of excessive anthropomorphism by blurring the sharp doctrinal edge between man and God. Willard thus abandoned the principles of Scotus in order to save what he believed to be a higher truth of Christianity. It seems that Willard ran directly into the problem of the paradoxical nature of religious symbols which cannot be neatly fitted into logical schemes. Religious symbols attempt to bring together the opposites of discursive logic in a new dialectical unity and Willard would rather keep to the truth of the symbol. It was at this point that Scotus was dropped. Had Willard not tried to justify a symbolic truth within a logical frame of reference he probably would have realized that imagination can capture in symbols what logic cannot comprehend, but Willard was neither a poet nor an artist.

The religious mind, as distinct from the merely logical mind, has, ever since the Greco-Roman period, constantly shifted back and forth between the incommensurables in thought by attempting to make discursive language do the work of symbolism. Since ancient times thinkers have tried to bring together Greek speculation and Christian revelation.

It is particularly significant to note that after having abandoned Scotus, Willard picked him up once again and wrote,

> God cannot make a Creature of such Capacity as to know him in the latitude of his being; and hence flows the impossibility for a man, or any other second being, to put an adequate Name upon him. . . . IF God should reveal himself to any second being fully, and make his name perfectly known, it must be to a Creature that *is able to receive this revelation*, and apprehend what he declares concerning himself; but there cannot be a Creature capable of this; it is inconsistent with a Created Nature; to fit a second being for this, God must make such another as himself not only in his Image and likeness, but equality; Infinitely wise, Eternally knowing, which would imply a contradiction: for he should not make a Creature but a God.[83]

After abandoning Scotus why did he resurrect him? In spite of the fact that Christian mystery asks that logic be transcended in symbolism, the Puritan mind returned time and time again to reason. This is the indomitable core of Puritan rationalism. It is the same rationalism which allowed the poet Taylor to return to "mere words" after having called them croakings of a toad. It is the same core rationalism which made Willard embrace Scotus after having abandoned him. He abandoned him when he had to hold God's communicable and incommunicable glories apart and embraced him when skirting the dangers of unintelligibility. Only through Scotus could Willard attain the symbolic blend he desired but only through Scotus was the distinction between God's communicable and incommunicable glory blurred. It is in the sense that Willard both accepts and rejects Scotus that he becomes the true religious thinker adhering to his symbolic blend rather than a philosopher building an airtight coherent system. Measures of internal truth were not so important to Willard as correspondence to a higher truth, the truth of religious symbolism. It is only when we face these fundamental problems of Puritan symbol making do we realize that Willard was working his symbols in much the same way that the poets and stonecarvers were working theirs.

Willard's arcane speculations seem rather remote from practical affairs in our eyes, yet it would be a modern prejudice to see him as only a crabbed thinker in a dusty study writing about things that few would care to read. Nothing could be further from the truth. Each argument was in point of fact cast into the form of a sermon to be read aloud to his congregation who looked carefully for any crack in the structure of orthodoxy. The concern the average Puritan had for such ideas is another indication of the profound rationalism of Puritanism for it is not every congregation which will listen and take notes enthusiastically by the hour on a subject as dry as philosophical theology. Willard was aware of how easily any chance remark could provoke a controversy just as a few anti-Arminian sermons read by John Cotton in the early days of the settlement stirred up the whole community. Verbal symbols, especially those purporting to deal with man's knowledge of God, had to be handled very carefully in Puritan circles.

The variety of Puritan symbolic experience in religion was enormous. We have seen it range from the erection of symbolic gravestones to thoughts about man's knowledge of God. Later we will see symbolic ideas operating on the level of religious practices. The dialectical nature of these symbolic experiences has never been adequately studied.

The three major issues which engaged the affairs of men on a symbolic level were Antinomianism, Arminianism, and Revivalism. It is to them that we must turn to see Puritan symbol making in action.

II. PURITAN SYMBOLISM IN RELIGION UNTIL 1800

THROUGHOUT the Puritan epoch in America the forces of religious orthodoxy attempted to limit the enthusiasm of the multitudes for fear that zeal would overstep the bounds of sense and become heresy. The history of religious controversy (excepting disputes over polity) could be written in terms of the attempted suppression of almost all immediacy in religious affairs. Hence the use of symbolism in formal theology from *ca.* 1637 until well into the 18th century championed measure, reason, mediacy, and propriety while the imagery which began to develop in Essex County, Massachusetts,[84] after 1668 was so enthusiastic and exuberant that the visual and the verbal symbols of Puritan religion stand at odds with one another.

The backgrounds of the use of Puritan symbols in theology may be reviewed as follows. The first indication of controversy was the Antinomian heresy. This was historically followed by the problems of Arminianism and then the Great Awakenings. All attempted to shortcut mediate logical thought or at least to expand the use of verbal symbols so that communication could be opened up between the finite and the infinite orders without the passivity desired by orthodoxy (for fear of the taint of free will). All were aware that the use of religious art could soon turn into the veneration of idols and the forces of orthodoxy did not want to expand the use of religious symbolism in that direction any more than they wanted the Arminian controversy or the Antinomian heresy. They were more successful in putting down the latter two than they were in controlling the visual symbols or the passion which the rural Puritans had for the Great Awakenings of the 18th century. Samuel Willard was a rigid iconoclast and as orthodox a theologian as New England ever produced. He wrote,

> HENCE *how very unsu[i]table it is to represent the Divine Nature by any Corporeal similitude:* I mean in Pictures or Images of any visible and bodily substance, and that whether it be for civility or devotion, *i.e.,* either merely as Ornamental, or as some pretend, to encreate devout Affections in any; how is it possible to rightly shadow a Spirit? Who ever was able rightly to decypher the form or shape of a being which is invisible! It is folly to pretend to afford us the Portraiture of an Angel, but it is madness and wickedness to offer any image or Representation of God: How many solemn cautions did God give his people against this by *Moses,* besides the express forbidding of it in the second Command; and God declares it to be a thing *Idolatrous.*[85]

In spite of the iconophobia of Willard, the Puritans persisted and created thousands of images of souls and angels. What is still to be answered is why they did so. And why did the ministers often have the most elaborate stones?[86]

It seems that it was because the visual imagery opened up the possibility of communication between contrite man and a beneficent, forgiving God. In sharp contrast to Puritan theology, which left no room for supplication, the gravestones are rich in these possibilities. The emerging formula concerning the use of symbols in New England seems to have amounted to this: the more transcendent the God, the greater the need for visual imagery. As the avenue of subjectivity in religion narrowed, a boulevard of symbolic imagery appeared. The more verbal the formulas of the institutionalized church the more the multitudes strove to express the "nouminal" immediacy of spirit in their stone icons.

The major controversies over how much immanence the Puritan would allow into the affairs of religion began with the Antinomian heresy. Antinomianism has had a long history. In brief, it was the belief that the Christian was freed from the moral law of the Old Testament by the irresistible dispensation of grace. It existed in antiquity in the Gnostic sect. They believed that sin was an incident of the body and that the "saved soul" could not err no matter what it did. In the Reformation the same doctrine was used by John Agricola[87] to deny the doctrine of good works of the Roman Church. According to Agricola, man was saved by faith alone regardless of his obedience or disobedience of the moral law. Such an extreme position, no matter how close to the logic of the situation, was fraught with cultural dangers. No community could be run according to its principles and survive in this less than perfect world. For the New Englanders, the extreme position of Agricola became tantamount to an admission of social nihilism. During the 1630's the controversy broke out in the Massachusetts Bay Colony but was soon crushed. So difficult was the balancing act that while avoiding Antinomianism, even Governor Winthrop seemed to be slipping toward Arminianism.[88] Charles Francis Adams, in his *Antinomianism in the Massachusetts Bay Colony*,[89] has grouped all the documents together along with an illuminating introductory text. The brilliant Ann Hutchinson was the prime mover of the affair and the target of the orthodox counterattack.[90] In her evening study sessions, which became as popular as the sermons of ordained ministers, she flatly stated that sanctification was no indication of justification. Man's works and displays of outward piety and striving were not evidence of true sainthood. Apparently it all started with the spark of John

Cotton's anti-Arminian sermons which urged people to turn away from the belief that striving could in any way alter man's eternal estate.

Ann seemed to have acted upon this conventional Calvinist formula and wrung yet another heresy from it. Working these propositions so carefully that they soon became absurd in the light of daily practices, Ann was soon covertly claiming that not only was sanctification no indication of justification, but that the truly justified person could winnow out the hypocrite from the Church of God. It seems that she believed that in some way special revelations were granted to the justified saints which would allow them to judge their fellow men. The new result was that it soon became a common Boston practice to speak about people under a doctrine of grace or works. The normative function of the visible church and its ministers was undermined and a ground swell of amateur opinion began to gain more and more force within the town. Her weekly study sessions grew until the Hutchinsonite faction seemed to be strong enough to propose that John Wheelwright be made a teacher in the Boston Church.[91] Nevertheless, through a series of intricate political moves by ex-Governor Winthrop, the Hutchinsonite faction was rebuked, but its members remained the majority in Boston itself. Governor Vane was championing the Hutchinsonites. But by May, Winthrop was re-elected governor, and the days of the heresy were growing short. By November Ann Hutchinson was brought to trial in Cambridge (the stronghold of orthodoxy), and conveniently outside Boston itself. During the trial of 1637 Mistress Ann proved superior in wit and wisdom to the legalistic and theological bumbling of the prosecution and had all but vindicated herself when suddenly, and without apparent reason, she blurted out,

> I will give ye one place more which the Lord brought to me by immediate revelations, and that doth concern you all, it is in *Dan. 6* when the Presidents and the Princes could find nothing against him, because he was faithful, they sought the matter against him concerning the Law of his God, to cast him into the Lions denne; so it was revealed to me that they should plot against me, but the Lord bid me not to feare, for he that delivered *Daniel,* and the three children, his hand was not shortened. And see this Scripture fulfilled this day in mine eyes, therefore take heed what yee go about to do unto me, for you have no power over my body, neither can you do me any harm, for I am in the hands of the eternall Jehovah my Saviour, I am at his appointment, the bounds of my habitation are cast in Heaven, no further doe I esteeme of any mortall man, then creatures in his hand, I feare none but the great Jehovah, which hath foretold me of these things, and I do verily believe that he will deliver me out of your hands, therefore take heed how you proceed against me; for I know

that for this you goe about to doe unto me, God will ruine you and your posterity, and this whole state.

When she had thus vented her mind, the Court demanded of her, how she
expected to be delivered, whether by miracle as *Daniel* was, to which she answered yes, by miracle as *Daniel* was. Being further demanded how she did
know that it was God that did reveal these things to her, and not Satan? She
answered, "how did *Abraham* know that it was the voyce of God, when he
commanded him to sacrafice his sonne?"

The Court answered by an immediate voice. Mistress Ann then admitted
that God had spoken to her too by an immediate revelation. By the voice of His
spirit to her soul.[92]

Here was everything orthodoxy feared. In the wrong hands anti-
Arminianism led to Antinomianism and the latter to ecstatic visions
of revelation, secret whisperings between God and man, and the ability
to soothsay man's eternal estate. Mistress Ann was banished in March,
1638. The forces of orthodoxy had met and mastered the challenge.
The forces of nihilism stood rebuked. John Cotton, the minister who
may have started it all, was made to recant. It was not a happy tale no
matter how we look at it.

But though bitter retribution was meted out to those who carried
logic to an illogical social extreme; from the point of view of using
symbols the controversy was highly informative. The forces of orthodoxy were doing nothing more than making certain that revelation
could come only through Scriptures in the mediate form of reason;
and that it could come only in one direction, from heaven to earth. The
error of the Hutchinsonite faction was their premature attempt to extend the process of communication between time and eternity. This
expansion of knowledge, even if thought to be freely given by eternity
itself, was heresy because the last immediate revelation of God was in
the last chapter of the Apocalypse. Once the gates of religious experience were flung open to visions and voices, however faint, it would not
be long before private whisperings went on between time and eternity.

The growing concern over Arminianism, the villain of New England theology, was equally interesting.

Arminianism was the name given to a modified version of reformed
theology in honor of its founder, Jacobus Arminius,[93] a Dutch theologian. From his doctrines emerged the anti-Calvinist Reformed Remonstrant church in Holland. Arminius said that the will of man was
free and thereby limited Calvin's belief in the absolute sovereignty of
God. In the hands of his successor, Simon Episcopius, it received its
most coherent form. The New Englanders did not like it because it

meant that man was free to will his own salvation and free to prepare himself for it. The covenant between man and God was thus conceived to be a true contract with both sides freely choosing to follow and honor it.

In theology, if not in practice, the Puritans always attempted to follow most carefully Calvin's doctrine of predestination. But it was often very difficult for the thoughtful Puritan to know just how much effort the individual could make, just how much sermons helped, and just how much preparation was necessary before orthodoxy toppled over into Arminianism. During the 18th century the radical New Lights of the Connecticut Valley were certain that the orthodox formula of "preparation" was nothing more than a covert form of Arminianism. Orthodoxy was convinced that without preparation, the logic of Christ's Logos revealed in Scripture, and painfully extracted by man's reason, would have little or no place on the theological horizon. And finally, if the Holy Ghost were present during "preparation," all would be saved anyway when Spirit supervened over the natural order. At a "Thursday Lecture" in 1731 in the Massachusetts Bay Colony, Jonathan Edwards charged orthodoxy with Arminianism and began a whole century of ecclesiastical controversy which was to echo down through the history of New England long after Edwards was dead. Somehow the Puritan was expected to preach like an Arminian and pray like a Calvinist.

Once again the use of symbols was in the center of the controversy. The New Lights wanted to restrict the function of verbal symbols even more while the Old Lights felt that the doctrine of preparation, if it was ever really developed in a systematic rather than a practical form, was limitation enough. While the forces of orthodoxy used the device of preparation ostensibly to allow a would-be saint to feel that human will and effort were needed, when pressed by their peers they always retreated into the position that the Holy Ghost was present at that stage as well. The hard, young, analytical minds of the recently graduated Yale clergy in the 18th century thought that the position of orthodoxy was too "spongy" at best and too Arminian at worst. But if irresistible grace descended from infinite to finite, and could not even ascend in the cloak of orthodox preparation, precious little communication was left. The New Lights, however, merged their hard doctrine of God's irresistible grace with evangelical preaching and thus added a new dimension to the problem. Without the evangelical spirit which seemed to permeate many of them, their message was little more than gloom and doom. But Jonathan Edwards and the New Lights who followed him were by no means so simple. While closing the vertical path to heaven through preparation through the Scriptures, they attempted to open up, through their preaching, that immediacy of spirit which would transform the heart and mind.

The orthodox doctrine of preparation left ample room for the human will to prepare the soul for a flood of grace from above. The symbols were, of course, mediate, but there was never any real question that the sermons and the Scriptures had efficacy in molding the new saint. All of this was suspiciously Arminian as far as the New Lights were concerned. Their formula was to shortcut preparation and expand the role of what Edwards called the "Religious Affections."[94]

The New Divinity was profoundly unhappy with the wholly mediate workings of reason and preparation outlined by their more orthodox peers in the orbit of Harvard and Boston. The latter men, during the 18th century, liked their religion "proper" and "respectable." The goal of the fiery New Lights, who naturally prospered in the rural Connecticut Valley and other pockets of "unsophisticated" life, was to introduce evangelical immediacy into the affairs of religion. To many this meant simply scaring the hell out of their congregations. To Jonathan Edwards and his followers it meant a great deal more, although he did preach his most famous sermon, "Sinners in the Hands of an Angry God," at Enfield, Connecticut.[95] As we shall see when we glance at the ideas of Edwards, this was but half the coin.

Jonathan Edwards wanted to keep Arminianism out of Puritanism. On the other hand, he wanted to open up symbolic activity in another way by replacing mediacy with immediacy in the affairs of the religious heart.

Once again the function of verbal symbols was re-examined. The formulas of orthodoxy were felt to have greatly limited the religious heart from ascending to God. The New Lights following Edwards tended at once to be more conservative because they wanted to eliminate any last vestige of preparation and, hence, Arminianism from Puritanism. They were bolder because they attempted to replace preparation with their own brand of evangelical preaching which affected the heart as well as the mind.[96] The moment for the injection of immediacy into the affairs of the religious community had arrived when the majestic figure of Jonathan Edwards strode upon the stage.[97]

The Great Awakenings, which were so much a part of the early program of the New Lights, had their beginnings long before the

1730's when Solomon Stoddard[98] five times harvested souls in North-ampton between 1679 and 1718. But by the time of Edwards' harvest of 1734–1735 in Northampton, the experiment had begun in earnest. Between 1734 and 1746 he wrote at least three works concerning the Awakenings, but his *Religious Affections* of 1746 was his most systematic effort.[99]

According to John E. Smith, in his introduction to the *Affections*, Edwards' aims were three.[100] He attempted to distinguish between Christianity and mere morality with emotional overtones. Nineteenth century "liberalism" would have had little place in his analysis. Religion had to do with the inner man and his relation to God rather than his relations with society. Second, he attempted to inject the direct and relevant experiences of the individual into the process of salvation.[101] Any understanding which excluded intimate personal experience had no meaning for religion. This attitude may have been a product of his exposure to British empiricism, which in the form of the writings of John Locke[102] may have also influenced his thought. Smith (one of the Cambridge Platonists, 1618–1652) believed that along with thought "spiritual sensations" were also generated. This latter notion might have influenced Edwards' writings on the religious affections which bear a strong similarity to Smith's "spiritual sensations." Edwards wanted to preserve the rationality of orthodoxy while enriching it with a "New Sense" which distinguished the merely sanctified from the truly justified. Throughout his career Edwards never sanctioned the suppression of reason. If that is what took place during the Great Awakening it was not what Edwards had originally expected.

Edwards believed that rationality and immediacy could and must be blended together in the religious consciousness. He also believed that the "affections" had rules and regulations which so transformed the soul and the will that it was possible to tell the true from the spurious saint. We need not be concerned with these rules and regulations which Edwards treated at some length in his book on religious affections. Suffice it to say that almost every minister in New England wanted his congregation composed of regenerate souls alone. Throughout the long history of Puritanism in New England the problem was never satisfactorily solved because in fact it never really could be resolved. There are no tests of justification. Many approaches were tried ranging from admitting only "True Saints" (those who had an inner experience of regeneration and had made a public profession) through the intermediary stage of admitting members' children to Baptism but not Communion until they had experienced regeneration and had made a public profession, to the Stoddardian approach of throwing the doors of Church membership open to all because it was too difficult a business to distinguish the saints from the sinners.

Today there still remains a question concerning Edwards' relation to the Great Awakenings and how much "enthusiasm" he would allow. It seems to me that John E. Smith was right when he said,

> Edwards has declared himself for the heart religion and against a narrow rationalism; to many this meant full support for revivalism even if it reached the bounds of enthusiasm and immediate revelation. But Edwards rejected enthusiasm and branded as false much of the popular piety resulting from the high tide of revivalist preaching. The heart, he contended, must be affected, for genuine religion is power and more than the verbal acceptance of doctrines. But the change of heart is not in the convulsion or the shout, the flowing tears or the inner voices.[103]

Nevertheless, Edwards was concerned with liberalizing the use of symbols and for our purposes that is why Edwards and the Great Awakenings loom so large in the study of Puritan mediate and immediate symbols. According to Edwards, true religion consisted of "holy affections."[104] These affections were the exercise of "the inclination and will of the soul." Edwards said,

> God has imbued the soul with two faculties; one is that by which it is capable of perception and speculation, or by which it discerns and views and judges of things; which is called the understanding. The other faculty is that by which the soul does not merely perceive and view things, but is some way inclined with respect to the things it views or considers; either is inclined to 'em, or is disinclined, and averse from 'em; or is the faculty by which the soul does not behold things, as an indifferent unaffected spectator, but either as liking or disliking, pleased or displeased, approving or rejecting. This faculty is called by various names: it is sometimes called the *inclination:* and, as it has respect to the actions that are determined and governed by it, is called the *will:* and the *mind*, with regard to the exercises of this faculty, is often called the *heart*.[105]

Orthodoxy, according to Edwards, was too filled with arid intellectualism which committed the soul to nothing, because the soul was a spectator rather than an actor. Putting commitment back into the religious formula meant opening up the definition of verbal symbols only to the degree that something more than understanding was involved. I imagine that orthodox Puritans thought that in their formulas something more was involved, but Edwards obviously thought that they were wrong. The question is not whether Edwards had characterized intelligence and understanding too narrowly, but whether Puritan mediate symbols were being remolded to embody a degree of sensible, immediate directness which they lacked prior to that time. We must not, however, be too quick to associate the affections with the passions. Edwards was very clear in distinguishing between the two. He said,

> The *affections* and *passions* are frequently spoken of as the same; and yet, in the more common use of speech, there is in some respect a difference; and affection is a word, that in its ordinary signification, seems to be something more extensive than passion; being used for all vigorous lively actings of the will or inclination; but passion for those that are more sudden, and whose effects on the animal spirits are more violent, and the mind more overpowered, and less in its own command.[106]

According to Edwards the affections and the understanding go together. The former do not snuff out the latter.

But hell-fire Evangelism did not go well with such a subtle doctrine, and by 1746 Edwards had for some time been disenchanted with the wailing, tearful, croaking kind of religion which he and Whitefield had seen[107] when Davenport and Tennant invaded New England.

Edwards' use of language tells us a great deal about what he expected from the affections. He said,

> As all the exercises of the inclination and will, are either in approving and liking, or disapproving and rejecting; so the affections are of two sorts; they are those by which the soul is carried out to what is in view, cleaving to it, or seeking it; or those by which it is averse from it, and opposes it.[108]

No longer does reason hold apart love and the loved, the affections melt the one into the other as the soul cleaves to the object it seeks. Here is the fundamental difference between Edwards' formulation of how symbols should be used and that of orthodoxy. Orthodoxy never explicitly granted that anything could pierce the veil of mediate reason between finite and infinite. Edwards, on the other hand, was convinced that the affections could reach out and grasp the Word without running the risk of completely melting together the finite and infinite orders. If the forces of orthodoxy were saying the same thing about love, it was still perfectly clear that they had not as yet formulated so modern an epistemology.

That the message of Edwards was misunderstood may have something to do with his cryptic style and his inability to engage in the Church politics of the times with success. But that his message was an attempt to inject immediacy into the religious experience of the time is beyond question. By 1750 he was forced to leave his church in North-ampton, Massachusetts.[109] While the New Lights ostensibly grew in power in the Connecticut Valley after 1750, Edwards' plight showed the increased estrangement between community and clergy which marred the religious affairs of New England until the beginning of the 19th century.

Thus far I have attempted to trace quickly many of the more important attempts to remold verbal symbols, so that more of the eternal would filter down into the affairs of this world. With the failure of the Great Awakenings and the growing anticlericalism of the laity during the 18th century it would seem that orthodoxy won a pyrrhic victory. It had stemmed the tide of the immediate. Wherever the New Lights had taken over, they had quickly estranged the multitudes. A verse from the *Connecticut Courant* of July 16, 1771, summed it up:

> Would God that all Christ's ministers would cease
> Their paper war, follow the prince of peace,
> Forebear to wrangle with their scribling pens,
> And show the world that christians can be friends.[110]

III. PURITAN THEOLOGY, SYMBOLISM, AND IMAGERY

IN sum, we have seen how religious symbols were used by the forces of orthodoxy to restrain rather than to encourage enthusiasm. Verbal symbols were thought of as lenses through which the mysteries of Christianity could be refracted through measure and reason via Scripture with the authority of the Holy Ghost. Reason distinguished clearly between the transcendent order of things and combined the just amount of immanence with the proper degree of transcendence. God was conceived of as both transcendent and immanent, or partially revealed and partially cloaked in the traditional manner.

The combination of such an arid intellectual theory of how theology ought to be conceived with the severity of religious practices in Puritan New England was often too confining a formula. Now and again forces within the community attempted to find formulas for opening up Puritan symbols but their efforts were suppressed. The Antinomian and the Arminian heresies were put down and it never became clear to the Puritans that their own doctrine of preparation could be and was interpreted as quasi-Arminian. Later, when the Awakenings quickened the pulse of New England and attempted to replace orthodox mediate symbols and abstractions with the immediate, felt affections of the heart, the multitudes and certain demented preachers soon managed to engulf the whole noble experiment in excesses so obvious and odious that the principle of revival was discredited in New England just before the middle of the 18th century. It seems that as often as attempts were made to modify the normative religious symbols of orthodoxy, just as often were they rebuked.

But if we turn to their devotional poetry, their religious art, and their burial rituals, an entirely different picture of Puritanism emerges; a picture composed of image after image of heaven-borne souls traversing the mysterious passage between time and eternity, a picture which seems to be a countermovement to the dogmas of their organized religion.

Why did these images, the last and most permanent acts of Puritan burial rituals, exist side by side with the official doctrine of iconoclasm? Many answers have been given ranging from statements that the art was meaningless to citations of the symbols as evidence of the corruption of true piety which began with the second generation. Neither extreme position seems plausible. The final demonstration of what the symbols may have meant to the Puritans can only come out of a study of the symbols themselves. Religious symbols exist only in so far as they are recognized as such and as yet no study has been made of Puritan visual imagery. The problem of whether or not the themes the Puritans cut upon their gravestones functioned as symbols or decorations depends upon how the Puritans read them, not upon how we might choose to read them. By looking at Puritan imagery through the eyes of the modern world we are not measuring Puritan symbolic art, we are simply seeing the images as our fancy dictates. Thus the Puritan soul dove, an ancient soul symbol, becomes to us a modest decoration because we fail to read the meaning behind the image.

The idea that the American Puritans would brook no religious art is derived not only from what the Puritans said and did and what historians have discovered, but what the English Puritans did to their own art. In 1550 in England whole shiploads of religious statuary were exported to France.[111] In 1559 two great bonfires in London consumed the wooden rood images from St. Peter's and elsewhere. Almost a century later during the Civil War of 1642, Puritan troops visited destruction upon other "graven images." The great cathedrals of Exeter, Canterbury, and Winchester recoiled under the relentless hammerings of the Puritan iconoclasts.

But in spite of what the zealots might have done in England, when they arrived in New England they rapidly changed their minds about imagery and began as early as 1668 to fill their burial grounds with emblems and symbols. This complex movement from iconophobia in England to iconography in New England is one of the most neglected transformations in our cultural history.

The Puritans did not, to be sure, fall to decorating their meeting-houses with paintings and sculptures of departed saints, but when they came to bury their wives and husbands and children, they could not be satisfied with the colorless doctrines their ministers intoned at the grave. Their love could not be reduced to the cold incision of a name on a boulder, and so, the Puritans fell back upon symbols often older than Christianity itself to express their hopes and fears in the face of the mysteries of death and Resurrection.

IV. SYMBOLIC MEDIACY AND IMMEDIACY IN NEW ENGLAND: RELIGION AND ART

THE dialectic of symbol making ranges from mediacy to immediacy in Puritanism; immediacy when the image of the soul in bliss soars heavenward and mediacy when verbal symbols are restrained by the reflective nets of reason anchoring the soul in the bondage of the corporeal and defining the spiritual world as almost wholly transcendent. The immediacy of symbolic art makes the beauty of salvation immanent in the mystical symbol rather than in the written word which was too carefully watched by the forces of orthodoxy to be allowed such freedom.

The terms "mediacy" and "immediacy" have had currency in philosophical studies since at least the time of Hegel whose notions on the subject were surprisingly modern for a 19th century thinker. According to Hegel the first mode in which the mind apprehends the Absolute is in immediacy, or in the guise of external sense objects. The shining forth of the Absolute in the world of chaos and illusion is beauty. Beauty is manifested in art. Long before the mind makes notions it has general images of objects and it is by recourse to these images of immediacy that mind can comprehend in a thinking manner. Feeling, perception, and mental images, precede thought proper in consciousness. According to Hegel these images and feelings give rise to thought, but reflection itself is thought about thought.

Hegel's critique of empiricism in the shorter logic allows us an insight into what he hoped to accomplish by bringing together once again what analysis had broken apart. In the rich activity of sense impressions we have a plurality of elements which analysis peels off like the skin of an onion. In the process we add nothing but our own act of disintegration, and create only rubbish. We gain clarity, according to Hegel, in the movement from the immediacy of sensation (which is by nature without distinctions) to thought (which points out the layers). The attributes which we name and which are in union in the sense object, acquire a universality by being separated. But empiricism does not leave the object as it was. It transforms the concrete image into an abstraction and in consequence the living thing is killed. To the extent that discursive language never attempts to put together what it has torn asunder, Hegel proposed that the job of reconstruction remained to be accomplished. Hegel's invention of the dialectic is the synthetic agent which puts the onion back together again, so to speak. Through the dialectic the estrangement of man from the absolute can be bridged. Mediacy and immediacy melt together in the final stages; but for the multitudes the trail blazed by Hegel was impenetrable. Nevertheless, all were aware of how analysis chopped up the simple unity of feeling or sense impressions.

The Puritans were certainly aware of how mediate thought limited them to a severely circumscribed understanding of Spirit. The Puritans were certainly aware that by virtue of their analysis what they then thought was heresy had been rebuked, but the path toward a willed reconciliation with Spirit was destroyed in the process. To entertain immediacy is precisely to bring together the possibilities of heaven and earth and this is exactly what the Puritans did not want to do. But the extent to which they used symbolic art forms on their graves indicates that under certain circumstances they were ready to allow the fact of immediacy into their religious lives. The symbols we have yet to review did not place a screen or lens of reason between the symbols and the symbolized. Puritan symbols seemed to replace the screen of analysis with aesthetic and religious immediacy which is the constitutive element in all religious art. Because of this special function Puritan visual symbols seem to have had a cultural significance quite beyond their existence in the aesthetic mode of apprehension.

V. SYMBOLIC STONECARVING: A STUDY IN REALIZED ESCHATOLOGY

THE Western religious heritage has traditionally revolved around the persistent belief that there are two orders of reality, one sensuous and finite, and the other essential, eternal, and infinite. The latter is necessary, substantial, immutable, and eternal in contrast to the flux and flow of sublunary things. Moreover the flickering lights of the forms of heaven are never wholly dimmed by imprisonment in the flesh. Time itself is the moving "likeness" of eternity according to Plato.

The same ordering of the universe into two spheres may be found in the Old Testament of the Jews, although not in particularly philosophical terms. It was left to the Greek tradition to take this fundamental stream of religious consciousness, and attempt to reason out the connections between the two orders of things and to reduce religious beliefs into a series of coherent and comprehensible propositions concerning the principles of the universe. Although there is a great deal of scholarly disputation concerning the degree to which Platonic and Aristotelian thought were concerned with "rationalizing" the religious, by our standards it seems clear that any system of transcendental forms (or even forms within things, involved with the metaphysical principles of substance predicate logic) is fairly well bound up with a "religious" view of the universe whether the final principle is a mind or an angry God with a beard.

From at least Plato onward, part of the Western heritage was the Orphic belief that alienated man had to attain his destiny in the stars and return to the immutable forms from which he sprang. Although there was no doctrine of the Fall and original sin, the estrangement of man from the divine was clear. The "Symposium" is perhaps the best account of how man can hope to achieve this bliss. The "Apology" may have been an Orphic allegory with Socrates caged in the jail of his body and finally through choice returning to eternal rest in death. Plotinus, in late antiquity, was the last important Platonic philosopher to attempt such a synthesis before pure Greek speculation was engulfed by the onrushing tide of Christianity.

Early in its course of development Christianity inherited more from the Jews than from the Greeks, although even during Philo's lifetime, which overlapped that of Jesus Christ, Judaism itself was Hellenized to a degree unthought of before Goodenough embarked upon his series of remarkable books. From what I have gathered from the Scriptures there was, in spite of the Hellenization of Judaism, little philosophical in what the disciples of Jesus said He said, but of course as in everything philosophical principles were inherent. Later, when the followers of Christ met head on with the sophisticated thought of the Greco-Roman world, they began to attempt to tell their story in the language of Greek speculative thought, which was of course the way in which those with education were taught. Hence at a very early stage Christianity was faced with organizing a metaphysical-theological order which could compete with the riper Greek tradition. The object of all this effort was not to create a mere metaphysics, but to get back into heaven. Like the Orphics before them, the Christians wanted to assert their original birthright, although in this case they had original sin to overcome. There were many ways in which the Christian could attempt to accomplish this awesome task. For the multitudes the institutionalized Church, then as now, acted as the defender of orthodoxy (whatever orthodoxy happened to be at the moment) and mediated between man and God. Because the problems of sin and redemption were so great, a clergy was needed to sort out the ideas and help to dispense the proper means of effecting fusion to the multitudes who otherwise would merely drift, then as now.

Even after the Reformation, which was a struggle to clear away the apparatus of the Roman Church from the path between man and God, the Church itself and the preaching clergy could not be dispensed with for obvious reasons. Although sanctification was no longer an indication of justification, there would be those who could manage nothing more than to live according to the lower law of simply doing as they were told and hoping for the best. An institution was still needed for those who required the comfort of Protestant ethics in the hope that it might lead them to a richer vein. But this was by no means the only way, either in the Roman Church or in the multitude of denominations that the Reformation spawned.

Among the most potent weapons in the Christian arsenal was philosophical theology. Intellectuals attempted to hone and sharpen Christian dogma and metaphysics throughout the medieval and modern epochs so that the more contemplative could come to some understanding of what their faith was all about. Explanation aided those with minds as the mere following of the lower law had helped the multitudes.

While the motto *credo ut intelligam* was never doubted, there was yet another path to the eternal. With all the brilliance of reason, mediate symbols between man and God were still the result, and like the Orphics before them some Christians preferred a more mystical approach. Christian mysticism shortcut both the lower law of the institutionalized Church and the speculation of the philosophers. Even Aquinas in his old age admitted that his labors in the garden of philosophical speculation were just so much straw in relation to the mystical encounters he was able to experience later in his life. But in spite of the fruits of mystical experience its nature is to transcend polity and theology. Hence it has never been truly popular with ecclesiastical authorities. It undercuts the very foundation of their function. Although Christianity can do little to prevent the mysticism of the truly pious, authority does little to encourage it. The Great Awakenings in New England are good examples of what happens when the multitudes are allowed to savor some of the heady wine of immediacy. Things have a way of soon getting out of hand and eccentric preachers like Gilbert Tennant and James Davenport took every opportunity to challenge the authority of the established Church.

From what we have learned from the Great Awakenings it would be foolish to believe either that the itinerant preachers or the vast multitudes got anything more than a glimpse of mystical truth, if that. It would again be foolish to believe that piety could be completely satisfied with the lower law of Puritan ethics; or with the difficult reasonings of the ministers. Neither would they long be satisfied with the pseudo-mystical extravagances of the Great Awakenings.

Nevertheless it would be wise to look at the similarity between mystical practice and symbolism for a moment because they are indeed similar in many ways. Both are attempts to circumvent the lower law and reason-drenched theology. Both attempt to communicate with the divine. To be sure the mystic encounter is personal and transformal, while the symbols are couched in the forms of paint or stone and external to the self; but the goal seems to be the same, namely, to realize some sense of eschatology whether in the here and now of the mystics, or after death in the case of our symbols.

It may be that the multitudes, not capable of the rarified heights of mystical experience, and unhappy with their wholly mediate theology, attempted through their carved symbols to savor some of its flavor and to instill some of its meaning into their hearts. Goodenough has defined mysticism as realized eschatology.[112] We will see how gravestones may have brought the New Englander some of the comforts of realized eschatology without the social opprobrium of mystical practice. So too it was with their devotional poetry.

Mysticism is first of all a method of behavior rather than a series of comprehensible propositions knitted together by the mind into a system. The goal of mysticism has always been to transcend the cage of the flesh so that the soul will be free to return to the transcendent world from which it came. Unlike Puritan doctrines of eschatology, this journey was to take place during life, not after the death of the body. The methods of attaining this goal and the nature of the goal itself have been as diversely seen as there have been different cultures and mystics within them yearning for release. But on several fundamental issues they agree. First off, reason has to be transcended simply because it stands in the way of the infinite order of things. In transcending reason almost all mystics agree that love is a necessary element. But what love is and what is meant by the term seems to elude even the most sensitive philosophical and psychological thinkers. Perhaps our methods of thought destroy the delicate petals in the very process of probing into the flower. Even so, all but the most perverse will admit that mature men have some vague notions of what love is all about and that the term is not totally devoid of meaning. Nor is the mystics' use of it wholly incomprehensible, although most of us could not attempt to follow them.

But love alone is not sufficient for mystical experience, for mental discipline is involved: not the kind that students are taught at great universities, namely the ability to make their ideas clear and to interpret clearly the published ideas of others, but a discipline involving the emotions and their intimate connection with things spiritual.

The great mystics of India, for example, were convinced that mind had to be consciously emptied in order to prepare the way for the great flood of mystical experience. Such an endeavor could take many years of effort and self denial. In Japan, Zen Buddhism has become an institutionalized form in which a devotee can put himself under a master so that the mysteries will eventually be opened for him. To be sure, such practices involve an element of barbarity, extending from self-inflicted punishment to the abandonment of all worldly concerns, but for the few it may be worth it.

Mystical union seems to occur only a few times in a lifetime. Always the mystic re-enters the world of ordinary experience. Many have attempted to put their experiences into words. It would of course be absurd to believe that the experience could be transformed from feeling to words intact, but the following citation is probably fairly representative in summing up what many mystics have said about these encounters. It reads,

> For silence is not God, nor speaking is not God; fasting is not God nor eating is not God; nor yet any of all the other two such quantities, He is hid between them, and may not be found by any work of thy soul, but all only by love of

thine heart. He may not be known by reason, He may not be gotten by thought, nor concluded by understanding; but He may be loved and chosen with the true lovely will of thine heart. . . . Such a blind shot with the sharp dart of longing love may never fail of the prick, the which is God.[113]

What was not fully understood during the Great Awakenings in New England was that inner discipline was involved. Mysticism was a method or methods which relied primarily upon inner experiences rather than the social frenzy created by demented preachers. Mob hysteria has never been an element in mystical experience because the stimuli are false. The stimuli of mob hysteria reside in the crosscurrents of activity aroused by group emotions and have no bearing on the flooding of purified consciousness with ecstatic visions of an otherworldly character. In many cases it is difficult to tell where mysticism ends and self-delusion begins, but in the grosser cases of delusion even the most humble soul can easily tell the one from the other. Evelyn Underhill[114] suggests that the mystical path may be thought of as having three stages: the awakening of the self, the purification of the self, and the illumination of the self. This is perhaps a good way to envision the role that preparation plays in the making of a mystic. Once the stage of the illumination of the self is reached it is clear that the mystical union has bridged the gap between time and eternity and dwells for a moment suspended above thought in the frozen gardens of religious bliss. The silver threads of immediacy lace the experience together.

Mysticism attempts to transcend the world in the here and now. Eschatological religious symbols attempt to capture some of the power of the divine and make it immanent in the world in order to savor some mystical flavor. Both attempt to transcend the finite order by the injection of immediacy. For the traditional mystic, external sense objects were unnecessary. A less socially dangerous method was to embody these eschatological themes in the forms of religious sculpture. Time and eternity are thus fused in the symbol, but the emerging symbol has been objectified in form to the extent that rules of symbolism could be and were applied. No gravestone I have seen makes anything more than the claim that it hopes for a blessed Resurrection in Christ and that the symbols are present to encourage that encounter in whatever way possible. While the true mystic enjoys the bliss of union in the here and now, the New England symbol users seem to have hoped that with the encouragement of their images a degree of protection and a cessation of anxiety would be granted. Symbolism in New England thrived possibly because it was the most acceptable method of passionately realizing the fruits of eschatology without running the risk of yet another crude outburst of subjectivity, and because it took place outside the institutionalized Church.

The idea that religious art could produce elements of mystical revelation was nothing new in Christianity and certainly not something dreamed up to "explain away" the symbols. During the Middle Ages many theories were rampant and New England in its cosmology and piety were closer to the sentiments of the Middle Ages than to the European Enlightenment (in spite of the desire of her intellectuals to keep abreast of all the new knowledge). Suger, 1081–1151,[115] the Abbot of St. Denis, saw the religious symbol in precisely this context. Concerning the erection of a set of expensive cast and gilded doors, Suger said,

> Whoever thou art, if thou seekest to extol the glory of these doors, Marvel not at the gold and expense but at the craftsmenship of the work. Bright is the noble work; but, being nobly bright, the work should brighten the minds, so that they may travel, through the true lights, To the True Light where Christ is the true door. In what manner it be inherent in this world the golden door defines:The dull mind rises to truth through that which is material And, in seeing this light, is resurrected from its former submersion.[116]

The mystical notion of the light stream which man might traverse from the material to the immaterial world had a deep influence on the Middle Ages through the Pseudo-Dionysius, Dionysius the Areopagite, who wrote between *ca*. A.D. 354 and 430. Originally thought to be the Areopagite mentioned in Acts 17:34, a follower of Paul, his writings came to have particular meaning for Hilduin, Abbot of St. Denis, 814–840. He identified him with St. Denis, martyr and patron saint of France, in his *Areopagitica*. Hellenistic in sentiment, neo-Platonic in theory, and Judeo-Christian in spirit, the Pseudo-Dionysius naturally influenced the symbolically oriented Middle Ages.

Suger's dependence on the Pseudo-Dionysius and through him upon Plotinus and the Hellenistic world is more than apparent when Suger saw in the religious symbol the means by which the finite might be transcended into the "true light." Later we will see how the notion of light mysticism was not only part of the literature of Puritanism but of her symbolism as well. Symbols of Christ as the sun illuminating and warming the souls and bodies of the faithful appear throughout New England on her gravestones, although it was by no means the most popular theme.

By creating symbolic gravestones and the rituals surrounding them, the Puritans wanted to take a more dramatic role in bringing the eternal closer to a realization in form and thereby infusing the symbol with some of its power. They did so in an act of piety which significantly took place outside the apparatus of the institutionalized church.

The Puritans institutionalized the affairs of the heart as few other people have ever attempted to do and to the degree that the all important profession of sainthood became nothing more than a stylized recitation concerning the travail of the soul and its final redemption. While it might have been true that such mechanical formulas quelled the babbling of the merely enthusiastic they did little to assuage the anguish of the heart.

The turn from stylized forms within the framework of the institutionalized church to a deeply symbolic art was an obvious attempt to escape from the confines of empty gesturing before the face of death. But the turn toward visual symbolism, a stylized form of expression in itself, was not something held over and against normative Puritanism but something appropriate to it. Symbols must be conceived in form and form itself demands not only discipline but social acceptability as well. The genius of Puritanism was its ability to institutionalize man's subjective feelings and thus avoid social anarchy. Image making was institutionalized just as surely as it was in Medieval Europe centuries before, but not by ecclesiastical authorities but by conventions springing out of what was proper and fit to the popular community as a whole. The most interesting feature of Puritan symbol making was its growth and change without any apparent control from the ministerial or intellectual classes. The patterns of Puritan symbolic life were so strong at every level that what almost certainly began as a protest against the stifling verbalism of Puritan doctrine found its own doctrinaire level and in the end became little different from orthodoxy itself. What began as an act of deep piety and reverence for the dead ended as another Puritan institution.

VI. ENGLISH BURIAL RITUALS

THE setting up of the symbolic gravestone was the last in a series of acts which surrounded death in New England. Many of the rituals had their origin in the old country but vital changes were made almost immediately to meet the needs of the new world. John Weever's *Ancient Funerall Monuments*, published in London in 1631, reveals English practice just at the moment of emigration to America. Weever thoroughly lamented the iconoclasm of the Puritans and set before his audience the laudable example of the Europeans by writing,

> And also knowing withall how barbarously within these his Majesties Dominions, they are (to the shame of our time) broken down, and utterly almost all ruinated, their brazen Inscriptions, erazed, torne away, and pilfered, by which inhumane, deformidable act, the honorable memory of many virtuous and noble persons deceased, is extinguished, and the true understanding of divers Families in these Realms (who have descended of these worthy persons aforesaid) is so darkened, as the true course of their inheritance is thereby interrupted: grieving at this unsufferable injurie offered as well to the living, as the dead, out of the respect I have bore to venerable Antiquity, and the due regard to continue the remembrance of the defunct to future posteritie; I determined with myselfe to collect such memorials of the deceased, as were remaining yet undefaced.[117]

By building this sturdy wall of opinion about him he hoped to stay the flood of Puritan image smashing and rallied to his cause Horace, Ovid, St. Jerome[118] Homer, Virgil, Lucian, and upon occasion the Prophets.

Weever was aware that many of the earliest burials in England were "extra mural," or took place outside city walls and attributed this precedent to the second law of the twelve tables of Rome.[119] According to the historian Tacitus,[120] the tribes of England supposedly laid their battle slain out in rows and covered them up with large mounds of earth or "baroes." Weever and the 17th century continued to associate these "baroes" with the remarks of Tacitus and believed that all such burial mounds marked battle sites. Weever even believed that neolithic Stonehenge was in reality a Saxon funeral monument for the dead under the "baroes" on Salisbury plain.[121] Other examples of ancient tombs were found by the author throughout Scotland and Ireland.

Weever believed that burial outside city walls continued to be practiced until the time of Gregory the Great, 530–604, when it became proper for those well connected with the Church to be interred within its body.[122] Gregory himself was buried on March 12, 604, and interred in the porch of St. Peter's in front of the sacristy only to be subsequently moved time and time again until his remains finally came to rest under the altar of the chapel of Clement VIII. During the 7th century and perhaps even before, it was commonly believed that the soul's progress toward heaven was immeasurably aided by the number of masses chanted over it. It became popular to afford the deceased this additional advantage by placing their remains within the body of the church proper or immediately adjacent to it in a yard which eventually became the church-associated burial grounds which were so popular up until the last century in Europe.[123] Weever wrote,

> This order or custome of buriall without cities, continued amongst Christians, until the time of Gregory the Great, for as then the Monkes, Friers, and Priests (saith my foresaid Author [Durandus]) began to offer sacrafice for the soules departed; so that, for their more easie and greater profit, they procured first, that the places of sepulture should bee adjoining unto their Churches, and afterwards they got license to burie within Churches.[124]

In point of fact burial within the body of the church was still of even older origins and was apparently practiced during late antique times only to become less and less common until the revival of the practice by Gregory when it assumed new importance. Heretofore it apparently was reserved for the select few and did not as yet include churchyard burial. Weever noted this point by commenting that Constantine was buried within his temple,[125] Honorius within the walls of St. Peter and Paul's, and "Austine" the first Archbishop of Canterbury, in the porch of his cathedral just outside Canterbury, which subsequently housed six other archbishops.[126] Weever credited Cuthbert with first obtaining papal approval for burial in church related grounds where heretofore the honor had apparently been reserved for only those of rank.[127]

From the time of the Cuthberts it became popular to practice burial within city walls, and churchyards began to grow. The English continued to use the churchyard until the overcrowding of the 19th century forced speculators to invest in private cemeteries which were not connected with any ecclesiastical authority.[128] From the start the New Englander did not invest the church with powers over the burial ground but passed authority on to civic hands where it remained until the late 19th century when private cemeteries began to become fashionable in America. It was in this area that burial practice in old and New England took different paths and it will come as a surprise to many to discover that in spite of the fact that many New England burial grounds are adjacent to the sites of old meetinghouses and more modern churches, they were and are legally unrelated. Until this day they remain in the hands of the civil authorities who are charged with their upkeep and who more often than not do an indifferent job.[129]

During the time of Cuthbert another custom arose which can be traced intact to New England until the end of the 18th century. Weever wrote,

> This order of buriall being thus begun here in England, it likewise followed,

that Grave-stones were made, and Tombes erected with inscriptions engraven upon them, to continue the remembrance of the parties deceased, to succeeding ages; and these were called Epitaphs: now an Epitaph is a superscription (either in verse or prose) or an astrict pithie Diagram, writ, carved or engraven, upon the tombe grave, or sepulchre of the defunct briefly declaring (and that sometimes with a kinde of commiseration) the name, the age, the deserts, the dignities, the state, the praises both of body and minde, the good or bad fortunes in the life, and the manner and time of death of the persons therein interred.[130]

New England epitaphs followed the precedent set in the time of the Cuthberts, although by the beginning of the 19th century erosions of the original formula were already apparent and by the 20th century what was a medieval formula had vanished forever.

Having established the history of tomb making in England from earliest times, Weever turned his attention to the social rules surrounding burial in England, which were as strict in death as they were confining in life. Graven images should, according to the author, be erected in memory of the dead only in relation to his "qualitie and degree" in life.[131] Weever wrote,

that by the Tombe every one might bee discerned of what rank he was living: for monuments answerable to men's worth, states and places, have always been allowed, and stately sepulchres for base fellowes have always lien open to bitter jests; therefore it was the use and custome of revered antiquitie, to interre persons of the rusticks or plebeian sort, in Christian buriall, without any further remembrance of them, either by tombe, gravestone, or epitaph.[132]

One gathers from the text that it was unwise to cross the monumental barrier separating the classes. Those below the gentry were obviously quietly disposed of in charnel houses until a rather late date. For those lucky enough to be born above the plebeian level interment usually meant a flat tombstone and it is to this social convention that we can trace the Boston and Newport, Rhode Island, preferences for table and tombstones as marks of social class.[133] One fared better as a gentleman, in which case it was proper to have a bust or effigy carved in the round to be set upon a pillar or against a carved background and, I presume, set within the body of the church where it would not only be safe from the depredations of both nature and man but establish the rank of the deceased as well. One fared still better if noble blood could be claimed in which case one could properly ask for and get a full effigy cut almost in the round,[134] and a very important tomb. The materials suitable for the carving of an aristocratic tomb ranged from marble to alabaster and included porphyry and polished brass and copper while gentlemen had to be content with stone and, I presume, the lesser gentry with even a baser and less durable material such as wood, although the latter point is by no means certain.[135]

Status in death did not end with the selection of a proper monument. In a certain sense position, as in all things, was far more important. The place where the monument was to be housed was perhaps more significant in the establishment of class than the size, the iconographic type, or the materials from which it was made. The very best people naturally tried to get into the abbey, but barring that almost as many points could be scored in a cathedral and presumably fewer still in a parish church. Once inside, and it was no mean task to make it indoors,[136] it was best to be placed near the chevet, in an eastern apse, crypt, or possibly within a radiating chapel or, barring that, beneath an important altar. If one could not afford or justify such a placement the family could still gain a degree of social satisfaction from placing the monument on the inside walls on either side of the nave; although in this case a flatter monument was necessary giving one to reflect as to whether or not this type of interment was desirable. Running close in popularity to burial in the chevet was interment in the porch which could cite antique precedent on its side but which involved the construction of a less pretentious monument. Such interments nevertheless still retained immense popularity. A position far less glamorous and elevating, but still to be considered as a last resort was burial under the floors of the nave and aisles themselves in which case flat monuments were required. This was obviously an *ad hoc* solution for those who could not command a better position in death, and brought with it the additional indignity of being walked upon so many times that many of the shallow inscriptions are no longer legible. For those either too late or too poor or too plebeian in origins it was still possible to avoid being placed in the churchyard with the common folks by obtaining permission for the fastening of a monument to the outside aisle walls of the parish church. Plate 129 is a good example of such a monument which afforded a maximum of elevation above those placed in the churchyard, intimate connection with the body of the church, and protection from the elements. As a last resort burial in the churchyard was acceptable, and we must not denigrate this location. The space was so hotly competed for that long debates went on as to who should and who should not be admitted.[137]

The practice of placing the deceased became so much an issue that some famous epitaphs were written about the subject, such as the one for Robert Philip, a parish gravedigger cited by Burgess. His was,

> Here lie I at the chapel door,
> Here lie I because I'm poor
> The farther in the more you'll pay,
> Here lie I as warm as they.[138]

And again, at Corcham, Wilts, "In this Church porch lyeth ye body of William Tasker Gent, who chose rather to be a doore-keeper to the house of his God than to dwell in the tent of wickidness."[139] It seems that if in life one was well connected then in death one could be assured of being well placed.

Of less complexity to the picking and placing of monuments was the preparation for the trip to the church or churchyard. Weever sagaciously told his audience that only those of notable blood could ride to their burials in a hearse while those of a more lowly class had to be content to be carried upon the shoulders of their servants.[140] For those without servants the trip to the graveyard presented insurmountable problems. On the way to a noble burial it was proper for a whole orchestra to bleat out a mournful dirge but gentlemen were allowed but a solitary trumpet.[141]

Having set the norms for a proper death Weever went on to mock those who would die above their stations. He called such people tradesmen but was obviously referring to the newly rich merchant classes in general whose monuments so enraged the author that he often found them more fitting a potentate than a shopkeeper.[142] Indeed, it often becomes difficult to tell which Weever disliked more, the richly clad monuments of the merchant class which encouraged tailors to learn the latest fashions in church while thwarting the truly pious from worship, or the classical nudes which were flooding into England from Europe. Weever fulminated,

> And which is worse, they garnish their Tombes nowadays, with the pictures of naked men and women; raising out of the dust, and bringing into the church, memories of the Heathen gods and goddesses, with all their whirligiggs: and this (as I take it) is more the fault of the Tombe makers, then theirs who set them aworke.[143]

It is to the everlasting credit of New Englanders that they left the majority of these odious practices behind them in England. The shift in practice is all the more remarkable considering how slow burial customs are to change. In New England there was no instrumental music save for the tolling of a bell, and everyone rode to his burial in a hearse, regardless of class, in egalitarian uniformity.[144] If the Puritans did not practice democracy in life there was equality in death. Indeed, the monuments of any one period were usually of about the same size save for those cut for children which were smaller;[145] and there was no particular pattern of placement within a burial ground which denoted special status.

It is ironic to note that as democracy took root in America, class and station became far more important in death. During the closing decades of the 18th and during the entire 19th century burial grounds in New England slowly began to lose their egalitarian uniformity and simplicity and became showplaces under the sun where it was common for the better families to gobble up large tracts of land upon which outlandish monuments were erected. In the process, Americans created reflections of their cities and towns with good neighborhoods of monuments for the rich and tenements of crowded stones for those less well pursed. Thus did burial practices come full circle as America fast approached rituals over which Weever would have nodded in approval.

VII. BURIAL RITUALS IN NEW ENGLAND

Only in the rituals surrounding death did the Puritan community as a whole indulge in image making ranging from emblems of death to symbols of Resurrection. Many of the funeral rings and most of the stones still exist but the trappings which went along with them have been lost because of their impermanent nature.[146] Some of the emblems which were used in conjunction with the trip to the burial ground may be found on contemporary broadsides complete with their leering skulls and grim imagery.[147] Mourning rings carry out these devices and as we shall see presently were given out to immediate family and friends. At many a Puritan funeral the horses were draped and the robes painted with winged death's heads and coffins.[148]

But only in the burial ground could the average Puritan see an impressive quantity of visual art, hence the impact of the symbols must have been a good deal stronger then than now because imagery itself was so much more uncommon. In rural New England, where the symbolism was strongest in the 18th century, the average citizen had even less opportunity than his coastal cousins of seeing works of art.

The precious symbols which crowned the Puritan funeral were an important and costly ritual act in a community which otherwise had little affluence and could ill afford to indulge its tastes on art for art's sake. But no matter how costly the gravestone itself was, the burial rituals were even more costly. For example, in 1720 a Boston schoolmaster named Ames Angier was paid £100 for a year's work.[149] In 1722, John Flagg, a doorkeeper to the governor of Massachusetts, was paid £20 for six months' service.[150] In that same year a minister in Arundell was paid £40 and another in Dartmouth £100 for a year's work. But in 1723 it cost as much as £100 for a not immoderate burial in Boston. Samuel Sewell, 1652–1730, a prominent Boston judge and diarist, noted the following expenses for the funeral of Bridget Usher,[151]

June	5 To James Williams, Pass. Bells. & c	1	8	6
	To Michael Haverblaton (?) & Compy, Porters	2	15	0
June	10 To John Blake, for three Coaches to Braintree, in service of the Funeral, May 30	3	15	0
June	11 To Elisa. Hatch to 12 Duz. Gloves at 4s	28	16	0
June	12 To Mr. John Edwards, 23 rings	23	2	0
June	15 To Nathaniel Morse, Madm. Grove's Ring. 2p. wht. 18 grains	1	13	0
June	15 To Aema Salter, service for the funeral		6	
June	17 To William Pain, for the Coffin	3	0	0
June	26 To John Marshall of Braintree for the Grave and Monument	24	10	0
July	6 To Jno. Clark Esq. Embowelling and Ceros	4	0	0
July	11 To Printer Green, for inserting the Advert, three weeks succesively, and 3N Letters		5	9
July	16 To Col Checkley, Recording her Death and Burial		1	0
Aug.	9 To S. Kneeland, printing Mr. Foxcroft's Sermon, 4½ sheets	4	12	0
Sept.	20 Paid Mr. Edward Bromfield, Junr. particulars out of his shop, for the last sute		17	
Jan	20 To Mr. Samuel Gerrish, for paper to print Mr. Foxcroft's Serm. 4 Reams, 4 quires	4	90	0
	folding and stitching 500	4	0	0

Twenty-four pounds for the grave and monument were spent. This was not often the case. Gravestones ranged in price from simple stones at a few pounds to elaborate tombstones at over £40.[152] More usual would be an expense between £3 and £10 outside the urban centers. Nevertheless funerals were neither inexpensive nor simple in ritual as the list of expenditures makes clear. For the 1720's over £100 was a lot of money to spend on death. As late as 1768, £300 per year was considered a good living and could provide a fine house on the fashionable Boston Common.[153]

Spending on funerals became so excessive in Puritan Boston that in 1720–1722 and again in 1741–1742, the colony passed laws prohibiting the giving of scarfs, gloves, wine and rum, and rings at funerals.[154] Things certainly had gotten out of hand, and from what one can gather from executors' accounts of expenses, the law did little to curb the Puritan's desire to leave this world with fanfare and ritual. Burial rituals cannot be altered by the passing of a law, they are too deeply ingrained in the beliefs of the multitude. But according to the authorities of the general court, such practices were "a great and unnecessary expense, and, while practiced, will be detrimental to the province, and tend to the impoverishing of many families."

The burials themselves were even more interesting than the amounts of money spent on them. As the funeral procession of coaches and wagons wound its slow way through the streets of New England, bells sounded to signify the "translation" of the flesh into spirit. The epitaph on the Gamaliel Ripley stone Scotland, Connecticut, reads,

Oft as the Bell with sollemn toll,
Speaks the departure of a soul;
Let each one ask himself am I,
Prepar'd should I be called to die?
Then when the Solemn bell I hear,
If sav'd from guilt I need not fear;
Nor would the thought distressing be,
Perhaps it next may toll for me.

Many bells appear carved into gravestones. Given this epitaph it would be foolish to assume that the symbol was merely ornamental.

The burial procession itself was a spectacle as grand as the Puritans could offer. The horses pulling the coffin were often draped with cloth painted with the "scutcheons" of death,[155] probably winged death's heads, crossed bones, picks and shovels, imps of death, and coffins. The same motifs may be found on innumerable late 17th and early 18th century stones in and around the Boston area.[156] In some cases the emblems were armorial. The mourners were equally resplendent. Many of them wore long black "Mourning Cloaks,"[157] with large white scarfs around their necks,[158] and "good gloves" on their hands.[159] Often gold rings were worn under the gloves. Many of these mourning rings still exist. They are sometimes ornamented with coffins, angels, or winged death's heads and engraved with names or initials.[160] The funeral procession moved from the meetinghouse where a sermon was read to the burial ground where more orations and prayers were read.

In certain cases the funeral sermon was printed up and distributed to friends in the community. The cost of printing at Bridget Usher's funeral was over £15. While the coffin was still at the meetinghouse it was usual for it to be surrounded by six mourning women traditionally garbed in black. After the burial the family conducted an "open house" for friends where large quantities of food and wine were consumed. From the documents I have come across so far it is not clear if the feast had any of the profound religious connotations of the antique refrigarium. I would guess that the feast had less significance than antique burial banquets, but certainly more than just another meal. When further work is done in this area perhaps we shall be able to judge more clearly.

Before the day of the funeral itself, the rituals of invitation were hard and fixed and certainly symbolic. Gloves were traditionally sent as invitations to funerals. In 1723 they cost 4 shillings per pair and were usually sent to over one hundred people. Samuel Sewall said,

> Went to Funeral of Mrs. Sprague, being invited by a good pair of gloves.[161]

Gold rings were also sent out. Rings often cost as much as 19 shillings.[162] At the Usher funeral twenty-three were bought. This probably means that they were distributed only among the immediate family and close friends.

Gloves were also distrbuted as invitations for marriages. Sewall said,

> Visited Mrs. Betty Cooke now, Benning, upon her marriage last Thorsday. They sent us gloves and Bride-cake.[163]

Rings, of course, were traditional at marriages. But the interweaving of rings and gloves and feasts at both rituals leads one to the conclusion that death was conceived of as a spiritual marriage between Christ and the soul, while corporeal marriage was its earthly counterpart. The rituals show how close were the symbolic practices. Puritan literature supports such an interpretation. The poetess Ann Bradstreet, 1612–1672, said,

> In Power 'tis raised by Christ alone.
> Then soul and body shall unite
> And of their maker have a sight,
> Such lasting joys shall there behold
> as ear ne'er heard or tongue e'er told
> Lord make me ready for that day!
> Then, come, dear bridegroom, come away![164]

Thomas Hooker, 1586?–1647, a Puritan minister and the founder of Hartford, Connecticut, said,

> Secondly, I say this is a total union, the whole nature of the Saviour, and the whole nature of the believer are knit together; first, that it is a reall union, all the places of the Scriptures doe intimate as much: what the branch is to the vine, the Soule is to Christ: now they are more than imagination; so what the husband is to the wife, the soule is to Christ. Now they are more than in understanding; for a man may conceive of another women, as well as of his wife; but this is another union, whereby the person of the one is knit into another: the bond of matrimony knits these two together. This is the frame and guise of knitting the Soule to Christ, it is no bare apprehension but wee feed upon Christ, and grow upon Christ, and are married to Christ.[165]

Such interpretations of spiritual and corporeal marriage were "metaphorical" rather than "typical." Jonathan Edwards interpreted the Canticle of the Old Testament in a more traditional manner. He said,

> Marriage signifies the spiritual union and communion of Christ and the Church in the perfection of this union and communion forever.[166]

Both interpretations could and did live side by side. But they lived not only in the literature of the educated elite, but in the practices of the religious community as well. When we have probed more deeply into the meaning of Puritan art the notion that it too describes the mystical marriage of Christ and the soul may become clearer.

At the conclusion of the burial services the body was buried, either in a family tomb or in the ground. In 17th century Boston it seems that tombs were sometimes alloted to leading families, but by the end of the century individual burial in the ground became the more common practice for all. It seems that there was just not enough room to construct more tombs, which were usually in mounds at the side of the burial ground, but ample room in the center for individual burial. The practice of burial in the ground was founded not only upon dimly felt traditions but upon the living belief that the saint must be buried in sanctified soil. A Christian dictionary of 1655 defined the place of burial in the following words,

> in that Abraham bought a place of burial in the land promised him showeth his faith.[167]

For the Puritans the symbols and rituals surrounding death were almost certainly thought of as acts of faith. How seriously this belief was taken may be glimpsed by Cotton Mather's utter contempt for an epitaph which claimed that all ended in death.

The symbols and emblems surrounding death in Puritan times carried with them a great deal of authority because the impact of the imagery itself was not vitiated by incessant secularization. Indeed, the imagery carried so much authority that at times iconoclastic families had offensive symbols exorcised from the gravestones of their loved ones.[168] Society only defiles images when symbols become idols or when the truths revealed become too powerful for the community to realize in conscious terms. The multitudes who wanted soul effigies cut into their graves believed that they were acceptable means of realizing the fruits of an eschatological vision of eternity without the social stigma of what in New England was called "enthusiasm" while those few who exorcised the images felt that they were too dangerous or perhaps even too idolatrous to allow to exist on the stones of those dear to them.

Except for the devotional poetry, Puritan literature was not excessively Platonic but tended toward a more Scholastic and Aristotelian view of the universe. Both the erudition of the late Scholastic Puritan tradition and the official iconoclasm concerning religious imagery combined to make the surfacing of conscious thoughts on solar and light mysticism, like those found in Suger, improbable. What exists is a vast storehouse of visual imagery in burial ground after burial ground. Given the evidence of the symbols it cannot but be suspected that the multitudes were attempting to put into visual form old Christian sentiments which had more to do with the Orphic-Platonic-Augustinian thread in Christianity than with the Aristotelian-Thomistic tradition. The symbols, like those on the Allen and the Lane stones (plates 93A and B), revealed a part of Puritan life and belief about which the discursive literature had little to say.

In a world on the threshold of the 19th century, stonecarving and its symbolism was the end of something old in Western civilization rather than the beginning of something new. The carved symbols were as outdated as Jonathan Edwards' dream of a new theory of types and tropes. For 19th century sensibilities it was too crude to carve an effigy of a soul in heaven, or within a shrine or under a bower of grapes. Christianity in New England had already begun to move away from such primitive notions and symbols. From a glance at the neoclassical stones of the late 18th and early 19th centuries, it was evident that nobody wanted to retain the older sentiments when shiny new ones were so readily available. The older symbolism became nothing more than a curious relic of one of the last efflorescences of Reformation piety in the West. The older symbolism became nothing more than a mode of visualizing a cosmology and an eschatology which were fast becoming engulfed by the secular sentiments of the Enlightenment. The older symbolism was nothing more than an archaic dream symbolizing the smashed hopes the Puritans had had for creating a New Zion in the New England wilderness. As the older beliefs gave way to the technological concerns of the 19th century the symbols of Puritanism quietly faded into the burial grounds of New England where they have remained undisturbed until this day.

Iconography

I. NEW ENGLAND FUNERARY ART

FUNERARY art has been one of the most persistent functions of burial rituals for centuries and it is not surprising that less affluent but deeply religious peoples should turn to it first as the base upon which to build a more complex religious art. Art began in the tomb in both antiquity and Christianity and there is evidence that it began the same way in prehistory.

Because funerary art in New England never had the opportunity to emerge out of the vernacular tradition, the scope of the imagery was limited. It ranged in theme from emblems of death to Resurrection. Complicated allegories and narratives, although they did exist, played a minor role in the development.

Narrative and allegorical cycles as developed in the cultivated religious art of Europe could not carry the message of Resurrection as easily as could the emblem, another Catholic invention. The simple emblem had the additional virtue of not being associated with privilege and with Rome as did the monuments of high church art. The New England mind was never drawn to complexity where plainness of means would suffice. Much rich imagery was lost in the process, but an art of vivid simplicity was often attained.

The object of the emblem was to extoll the virtues of paradise and the transformation of flesh into spirit but not to describe the process in naturalistic detail. Scriptural narratives, although known and loved as sacred literature, were thus not appropriate sources for the stonecarver. For example, scenes from the Passion were popular gravestone themes in Catholic Ireland[1] in the 18th century, but in New England they would have been suspect because high church art was tainted with "Popery." In Protestant England allegories of the sacrifice of Isaac became fashionable in the 18th century, but not one can be seen in America.[2] The New England emblem had a blunt freshness about it which was apparently much favored throughout the 17th and much of the 18th centuries.

The shift from the high style of narrative and allegory to the vernacular style of the emblem may be thought of as a loose parallel to the art of the Christian catacombs in Rome. The Betsey Tracy stone, 1792, Norwichtown, Connecticut (plate 42A), is a good example of a paleo-Christian survival in New England. Like catacomb art the iconography of New England was often lacking in specific Christian content.[3] Except for the use of the Communion service,[4] the cross,[5] and a variety of inscriptions naming Christ, the emblems themselves were not specifically Christian. It is impossible, for example, to tell one denomination from another by looking at the carved symbols. Doctrinal disputes dissolved at the grave and the symbols simply suggested the rewards of the just. Christ never appeared directly and God the Father only once,[6] although the cross was more popular than we would have imagined from a reading of religious tracts and from the secondary literature on the subject.

Despite the verbal conflicts over theology and polity which enlivened New England life for over two centuries there is nothing in New England art which would indicate anything but a complete uniformity of interest in religious matters.

In investigating the meaning of Puritan symbols I shall follow the traditional iconographer's method and attempt to connect a pictorial device with a contemporary literary source; by a contemporary literary source will be meant any work of Puritan letters written between 1650 and 1815 or roughly the period covered by this study. In some cases I shall cite English material when it is meaningful to do so and on occasions when symbols remain mute I shall turn to the source of all Christian metaphor, Scripture itself. I shall not, however, cite Scripture in all cases because Biblical metaphors were constantly being reinterpreted and consequently often need elaborate criticism.

The symbols are discussed here in thematic units ranging from emblems of death to the final flight of the soul to paradise. The more enigmatic geometric symbols will be reviewed at the end.

II. THE REPERTORY OF SYMBOLS

1. Symbols of Transformation

DURING the 18th century New England produced a unique group of stones for which there is little historical precedent.[7] Called symbols of transformation,[8] they seem to depict the voyage of the soul through death toward new life in terms of becoming rather than being. As soul image after soul image voyages through the grey voids of becoming on the stones of New England the imagery slowly reveals an eschatology of spiritual transition conceived in motion intellectually, but pictured stylistically in static moments. At the harbors of death and life, the beginning and the end of the symbolic voyage, the imagery crystallizes first into the forms of the winged death's head and then into the equally clear effigy of the glorified soul, but between the two are numerous images which seem to represent neither. Taking these puzzling stones in their proper context they appear to me to be representations of souls "fossilized" in frozen stillness between time and eternity. They seem to me to be nothing less than mystical transfigurations in stone. These complex themes are made doubly ambiguous by the crude simplicity of their execution which often deceptively suggests an equally crude and simple meaning. Such seems not to have been the case, although it is impossible to tell if these remarkable representations were consciously conceived or not.

It was far more usual for the carver to picture the transition from life to death by juxtaposing the symbols of each within a single design. For example, the skull on the Nathaniel Jackson stone, 1743, Plymouth, Massachusetts (plate 8A), is being pierced by a living tendril while the coffin on the Bridget Snow stone, 1768, Mansfield Center, Connecticut (plate 9B), is being encoiled by a mystical vine.[9] In neither case do the symbols of life and death involve themselves in the picturing of the myriad stages between death and new life.

Edward Taylor wrote,

> The Painter lies who pensills death's Face grim
> With White bare butter Teeth, bare staring bones,
> With Empty Eyeholes, Ghostly Lookes which fling
> Such Dread to see as raiseth Deadly groans,
> For thou has farely Washt Death's grim grim face
> and made his Chilly finger-Ends drop grace.
>
> Death Tamde, Subdude, Washt fair by thee! Oh Grace!

Made Useful thus! thou unto thine dost say
Now Death is yours, and all it doth in't brace.
The Grave's a Down bed now made for your clay.
Oh! Happiness! How should our Bells hereby
Ring Changes, Lord, and praises trust with joy.[10]

The epitaph on the stone of Reverend Richard S. Storrs reads,

Religion, her almighty breath,
Rebuked the winds and waves of death;
Amidst that calm and sweet repose
To Heaven his gentle spirit rose.[11]

Both writers content themselves with simple symbolic contrasts of images standing for life and death, for sweet grace, and grim death rebuked. The stonecarvers used the same technique when they juxtaposed the shell and the skeleton or the hooped snake and a symbol of Death triumphant in the form of a garlanded skeleton (plates 6 and 7). The effect of each symbol is enhanced by their marriage. Indeed, such simple symbolic juxtapositions were the fountainhead of Puritan thought. Edward Taylor wrote,

How sweet is this: my Death lies buried
Within thy Grave, my Lord, deep under ground
It is unskin'd, as Carrion rotton Dead
For Grace's hand gave Death its deadly wound
Deaths no such terror on th' Saints blesst Coast
Its but a harmless Shade: No walking Ghost.[12]

According to Thomas Foxcroft,

Rom. 8.17 "Now He took the Grave in His Passage to Heaven." "As *Christ* that pure prolific Corn of Wheat fell into the ground and died, and arose again; so (the Grave being made fertile by His dead body lying in it) the Saints shall be impregnated, and Spring up; sprout upon his Stalk, and (being ripe to the Harvest of Glory) be gathered into the Garner of Paradise."[13]

The same marriage of symbolic opposites took place on the Gershem Holmes stone of 1739, Plymouth, Massachusetts (plate 1A), where a profile effigy has been superimposed over a conventional winged death's head. The meaning of this stone is to contrast the effigy with the death's head and by conjunction symbolize the triumph of the soul over death, although a variant reading might be a picturing of the product of grace washing away the grim face of death. By the time of the Elizabeth Bradford stone of 1741, Kingston, Massachusetts (plate 1B), the profile effigy has been so placed as to appear directly over the serrated row of teeth of the death's head suggesting that the soul of the deceased is being disgorged from the mouth of death. The passage of the soul from its body toward heaven in the form of a naked baby slipping forth from the mouth of the deceased was a common theme in medieval art and the Bradford stone might be the New England variant. By the time of the Wilborah Washbun stone of 1743 in Kingston, Massachusetts (plate 1C), the profile effigy of the Bradford stone of two years before had become a heart palmette. The symbol of the heart was a common one in Europe after the Counter Reformation and among other things it symbolized the Trinity and the love of the soul for God.[14] In New England the symbol of the heart had associations with the soul triumphant and is often seen in conjunction with scenes of glorification.[15] In spite of the change of symbols the death's head is still being played off against a symbol of new life, but after *ca.* 1750 on stones such as the Sarah Hall Marker, 1756, Kingston, Massachusetts (plate 1D), the central symbol of the death's head itself has been transformed into what is probably a soul effigy.[16] The symbolic contrast between life and death has been eliminated but there are still many anachronistic stylistic "archaisms" which so clearly link this new image with what it had just replaced. Notice, for example, the similar feathering of the wings, the cleft in the cranium, the splayed-out nose and the vacant eye sockets. Changes occurred when the lower jaw of the earlier skull was transformed into a neck and when the serrated row of teeth (on the 1739 Holmes stone, plate 1A), was transformed into an ornamental T-cross suggestive of a mouth rather than the brittle hardness of glistening teeth. Stones of this type completely replaced the older imagery after *ca.* 1750 in Plymouth County and there is hope that further study will reveal the all important effigies cut between 1743 and 1756. But even without these connecting links it is still clear what happened. The image of death triumphant in the form of the winged death's head was slowly eroded away by the superimpositions of symbols of new life until it was itself transformed, thus eliminating the need for the profile effigies or the heart palmettes.

The shift in symbolic values in Plymouth County was mirrored in the Connecticut Valley during the same years, although there was no ostensible connection between the two traditions. While the Plymouth County stones after *ca.* 1750 reveal their pedigree in the light of comparative stylistic evidence, we have only seen the simple oppositions of symbol versus symbol and the completed transformation. We have not as yet seen a symbol in transition. The Connecticut Valley provides

A.

B.

C.

D.

PLATE 1. A. Detail of the Gershem Holmes stone, 1739, Plymouth, Massachusetts. Slate. 15½ x 19¾. B. Detail of the Elizabeth Bradford stone, 1741, Kingston, Massachusetts. Slate. 17¼ x 16¾. C. Detail of the Wilborah Washbun stone, 1743, Kingston, Massachusetts. Slate. 18½ x 23½. D. Detail of the Sarah Hall stone, 1756, Kingston, Massachusetts. Slate. 18¾ x 24.

PLATE 2. A. Detail of the Joseph Hickox stone, 1725, Durham, Connecticut. Red sandstone. 19 x 28. B. Detail of the Jacob Strong stone, 1749, South Windsor, Connecticut. Red sandstone. 29½ x 32½. C. Detail of the Sarah Skiner stone, 1753, South Windsor, Connecticut. Red sandstone. 20¼ x 31. D. Detail of the William Wolcott stone, 1749, South Windsor, Connecticut. Red sandstone. 31½ x 40½.

many such examples. On the Joseph Hickox stone, 1725, Durham, Connecticut (plate 2A), the carver has borrowed a conventional winged death's head and simplified it while retaining the original meaning. By the time of the Jacob Strong stone of 1749 in South Windsor, Connecticut (plate 2B), the death's head has become crowned, the lower jaw eliminated, and serrations of teeth appear on the upper row, a characteristic of carving in the Connecticut Valley. By 1753 on the Sarah Skiner stone, South Windsor, Connecticut (plate 2C), if it were not for the telltale serrations of teeth on the upper jaw it would be difficult to associate the image with the conventional death's head of 1725 (plate 2A). Indeed, the foliage just below the Skiner effigy suggests symbols of Resurrection such as the ones which appear on the Wolcott example of 1749 in South Windsor, Connecticut (plate 2D), where a proper mouth has replaced the serrated row of teeth and the image has been almost entirely transformed. On the Wolcott stone an iconographic type had emerged which was to be clarified and refined for the next half century.[17] But during the 1740's and 1750's it was far more common to see enigmatic images such as the one on the Skiner stone until the new imagery became fully entrenched. The Skiner example is an image in transition while the Wolcott example of 1749 is a symbol having completed the cycle of transformation.

On the Phebe Strickland stone of 1750, South Windsor, Connecticut (plate 3A), the older image of the death's head has vanished almost entirely but there are still certain telltale marks such as the thin, serrated row of teeth set in a vestigal jaw. Setting the old and the new imagery apart is the animation in the eyes which in New England was characteristic of the soul effigy rather than the winged death's head. The eyes on the Strickland stone have been set closely together and are in small scale, suggesting that they are no longer to be taken as empty sockets such as the ones on the Jacob Strong stone (plate 2B). On the Elijah Sadd stone, 1756, South Windsor, Connecticut (plate 3B), an effigy similar to the 1750 Strickland example appears but this time without the serrated row of teeth or the vestigal jaw, while on the Reverend Isaac Chalker stone, 1765, East Glastonbury, Connecticut (plate 3C), the vestigal jaw and the serrated teeth surface again in the context of what is almost certainly a crowned soul effigy in victory. On the Deacon Daniel House stone, 1762, East Glastonbury, Connecticut (plate 3D), the serrated row of teeth is visible, only in this case they do not appear with the vestigal jaw and the effigy is again envined in grapes and hearts suggestive of new life through the sacraments.[18] In

A.

B.

C.

D.

PLATE 3. A. Detail of the Phebe Strickland stone, 1750, South Windsor, Connecticut. Red sandstone. B. Detail of the Elijah Sadd stone, 1756, South Windsor, Connecticut. Red sandstone. 15 x 19. C. Detail of the Reverend Isaac Chalker stone, 1765, East Glastonbury, Connecticut. Red sandstone. 25¾ x 26½. D. Detail of the Deacon Daniel House stone, 1762, East Glastonbury, Connecticut. Red sandstone. 23½ x 24¾. Signed by Peter Buckland.

all but the Sadd marker the effigies suggest themes of life rather than death and are related to the older imagery only by stylistic carry-overs.

A similar process took place in Massachusetts, but the symbolic cycle was never fully closed and the imagery remained ambiguous and never achieved a great deal of popularity. The Abigail Chamberlain stone of 1760, Chelmsford, Massachusetts (plate 4A), contains elements of the older death's head as well as confusing new accretions. For example, the thin elongated lower jaw is almost certainly a carry-over from the earlier winged death's head symbolism but in this case it is enigmatically unserrated with rows of teeth while a single slash for a mouth appears directly under the abstract splayed-out nose. The absence of the serrated teeth and the inclusion of the mouth suggests the very real possibility that we are dealing with a symbol in transition, as yet iconographically unresolved, rather than a simple superimposition of one symbol upon another. On the Thomas Prentice stone of 1760, Lexington, Massachusetts (plate 4B), the same characteristics of ambiguity are combined. The contour of the effigy is that of a skull with a clearly defined lower jaw but there are no serrations of teeth and the eyes have become animated, given almond-shaped lids with round pupils, transforming the older formula of empty eye sockets on the more conventional death's heads. Once again we are dealing with a symbol of death in the process of being revitalized, rather than with an image of a skull revealing within it an animated allegorical figure of Death himself.

The subtle differences between a patently clear image of death and one in transition may be seen by comparing the Susannah Fitch stone, 1748–1749, East Hartford, Connecticut (plate 5A), with the William Buckland stone of 1758, East Hartford, Connecticut (plate 5B). In the former the vacant eye sockets, the tapering of the jaw, and the serrations of teeth all indicate that we are dealing with a variant of the 1725 winged death's head formula of the Connecticut Valley; but by 1758, on the Buckland stone, the eyes have become animated, eyebrows added and the serrated row of teeth reduced to mere notching. All that remained to transform this image in transition into a proper soul effigy was the addition of a mouth in which case it would look like the House stone of 1762 (plate 3D). The image at this stage, like the Skiner marker of 1753 which it resembles, is not yet ready to become stabilized as it seems to hover in conscious ambiguity between the meaning of life and death.

A.

B.

PLATE 4. A. Detail of the Abigail Chamberlain stone, 1760, Chelmsford, Massachusetts. Slate. 28½ x 35. B. Detail of the Thomas Prentice stone, 1760, Lexington, Massachusetts. Slate. 21¾ x 31. Signed by Abel Webster.

A.

B.

PLATE 5. A. Detail of the Susanna Fitch stone, 1748/49, East Hartford, Connecticut. Red sandstone. 21½ x 26.
B. Detail of the William Buckland stone, 1758, East Hartford, Connecticut. Red sandstone. 23 x 32½.

Turning our attention to those symbols which suggest the journey of the soul from death to life through the simple opposition of symbols it may be noted that the Thomas Faunce stone, 1745–1746, Plymouth, Massachusetts (plate 7), shows a skeleton sitting upon a winged hourglass with the scythe of Time in hand. Directly above the figure of the skeleton a large shell has been cut. The shell has, from prehistoric times, been associated with burials and in historic times with the principle of Resurrection.[19] Whether or not the carver knew of this meaning is difficult to ascertain without the aid of documents but we can see from the composition that the shell is being played off against the skeleton and winged hourglass and raised up above them. It would seem then that the point of Resurrection is being stated in plastic rather than verbal terms. On the Jayne stone (plate 6), a similar point has been made in plastic terms, only in this variant the serpent with its tail in its mouth has replaced the shell. Death triumphant is embraced by the hooped snake, a Renaissance symbol for eternity. Death's giving way to new life may be seen in two formulations on the Nathaniel Jackson stone, 1743, Plymouth, Massachusetts (plates 8A and 8B). In the first variant a skull is pierced by a living tendril while in the second a cinerary urn bursts forth with flowering life. On the William Hooker stone, 1782, Farmington, Connecticut (plate 9A), a coffin sprouts a bud while on the Bridget Snow stone (plate 9B), a coffin with an effigy of the deceased within is entwined in a mystical vine symbolic of the sacraments.[20]

2. The Triumph of Death

MODERN sensibilities shrink from the Puritan's use of coffins, skulls, picks, shovels, and hourglasses; but the Puritans of the 17th century were doing nothing more than following the mortuary tradition handed down to them in England.[21] For the Puritans these symbols held less dread than for us today because for them the passing away of the flesh was as much a part of life as birth and the renewal of life after the death of the body.

Death for the Puritan was, however, more than the mere extinction of the flesh. It also meant the dreaded shadow of eternal death which even the gracious passed through. Jonathan Edwards wrote,

> Death temporal is a shadow of eternal death. The agonies, the pains, the groans and gasps of death, the pale, horrid, ghastly appearance of the corps, its being laid in a dark and silent grave, there putrifying and rotting and become exceeding loathsome and being eaten with worms (Isa. 66.24) is an image

PLATE 6. Detail of the Susanna Jayne stone, 1776, Marblehead, Massachusetts. Slate.

PLATE 7. Detail of the Thomas Faunce stone, 1745, Plymouth, Massachusetts. Slate. 22¾ x 32.

A.

B.

PLATE 8. A. Detail of the left side of the Nathaniel Jackson stone, 1743, Plymouth, Massachusetts. Slate. 25½ x 27. B. Detail of the right side of plate 8A.

A.

B.

PLATE 9. A. Detail of the William Hooker stone, 1782, Farmington, Connecticut. Red sandstone. 28¼ x 38. B. Detail of the Bridget Snow stone, 1768, Mansfield Center, Connecticut. Granite. 27¾ x 38.

of hell. And the body's continuing in the grave, and never rising more in this world is to shadow forth the eternity of the misery of hell.[22]

Many New England epitaphs echo Edwards' horror. The James Hickox stone, 1796, Durham, Connecticut, reads,

> Great God, how oft thy wraith appears
> And cuts off our expected years
> Thy wraith awakes our humble dread
> We fear the Tyrant which strikes us dead.[23]

Samuel Willard wrote,

> And remember, it is a cursed death you are going to; well may it be called a King of terrors. Read over the miseries that accompany it, and say whether it be not to be trembled at.[24]

The epitaph on the Sarah McKeon stone reads,

> How loved how Valued once avails thee not
> To whom related or by whom begot
> A heap of dust alone remains of thee
> 'tis all thou art and all the Proud shall be
> Survey this well, ye fair ones and believe
> The Grave may terrify but can't Deceive
> Yet Virtue still against decay can arm
> and even lend mortality a charm.[25]

The terrors of death are graphically depicted on the Susannah Jayne stone, 1776, Marblehead, Massachusetts (plate 6), in which a skeleton, crowned with the laurel of victory, holds orbs of the sun and moon in either hand while in the background the scythe, an attribute of Time, can be seen. In the four corners hover angels of heaven and bats of the underworld.

Less elaborate but far more common were the winged death's heads and skulls which became popular in greater Boston after *ca.* 1678. The Jonathan Poole stone, 1678 (plate 10A), the John Person stone, 1679 (plate 10B), and the Thomas Kendel stone *ca.* 1678 (plate 11), all in Wakefield, Massachusetts, are examples of the type. Notice that on the Kendel marker the skull is raised upon a pillar probably signifying the triumph of death.

3. Coffins, Tombs, and Cinerary Urns

THE death of the flesh was often suggested by the use of carved coffins with an effigy of the deceased within as on the Latimer child stone,

A.

B.

PLATE 10. A. Detail of the Jonathan Poole stone, 1678, Wakefield, Massachusetts. Slate. 18¼ x 20½. B. Detail of the John Person stone, 1679, Wakefield, Massachusetts. Slate. 17¾ x 20¼.

PLATE 11. Detail of the Thomas Kendel stone, ca. 1678, Wakefield, Massachusetts. Slate. 21¾ x 25¼.

1789, Bloomfield, Connecticut (plate 12). In this example the coffin forms the outer contour of the stone and is not surrounded by a grape vine such as the one on the Bridget Snow stone of 1768 (plate 9B). A coffin may be seen being lowered into the ground by two imps on the William Dickson stone, 1692, Cambridge, Massachusetts (plate 27B), while on the Hannah Badger footstone, 1735, Haverhill, Massachusetts (plate 56B), a coffin in profile can be seen superimposed upon a pedimented shrine. On the Pember children stone of 1773, Franklin, Connecticut (plate 153A), a row of three coffins with effigies appears, while on a stone fragment from Franklin, Connecticut, of the 18th century a mother and child cut within a coffin were surrounded by bands of clouds. Tombs may be seen on the Henry Roby stone, 1807, Copp's Hill, Boston, Massachusetts (plate 20), on the Nathaniel Jackson stone, 1743, Plymouth, Massachusetts (plate 21A), and a variant wall tomb on the Martha Green stone, 1770, Lexington, Massachusetts (plate 57A). Cinerary urns may be seen on the Nathaniel Jackson stone, 1743, Plymouth, Massachusetts (plate 8B), on the Michael Martyn stone, 1689, Copp's Hill, Boston, Massachusetts (plate 29A), on the John Briggs stone, undated, Copp's Hill (plate 29B), bursting with flowers on the Ruth Carter stone, 1697–1698, The Granary, Boston, Massachusetts (plate 62A), on the Reverend Edward Thompson stone, 1705, Marshfield, Massachusetts (plate 62B), on the Marcia Holmes stone, 1800, Kingston, Massachusetts (plate 192C), on the John Hurd stone, 1784, The Granary, Boston, Massachusetts (plate 192D), on the Betsy Russell marker, 1790, Stratford, Connecticut (plate 193A), and on the Oren Alley stone, 1822, Durham, Connecticut (plate 193B).

4. Death and Sin

ACCORDING to Christian doctrine death entered the world because of sin. On the Sarah Swan stone, 1767 (plate 13), Bristol, Rhode Island, is to be found the only extant version of the Adam and Eve story in New England. So that there could be no doubt that this was a symbol of mortality rather than a decoration the legend "For as in Adam all die even so in Christ shall all be made alive" was cut into the stone from 1 Cor. 15.22.

The origin of death was so well known that we wonder why Samuel Willard had to say,

Wherefore as by one man sin entered the world, and death by sin: and so death hath passed upon all men, for that all have sinned.

PLATE 12. The Latimer child stone, 1789, Bloomfield, Connecticut. Red sandstone. 16 x 25.

PLATE 13. Detail of the Sarah Swan stone, 1767, Bristol, Rhode Island. Slate.

Remember then, that Death, is not only a thing that your frail nature subjects you to, but that unto which you are sentenced by a righteous God, as a just punishment of sin; that is a curse of the law, which is fallen upon you.[26]

Thomas Foxcroft, a Puritan minister, wrote,

The Meritorious *Cause of Death affects the Saints as well as others. They have Sin in them as well as other Men, which deserved Death*. Sin is the meritorious cause of Mortality, Rom. 5.12. *By one man sin entered into the world, and Death by Sin; and so Death passed upon all men; for that all have sinned. . .*[27]

Puritan epitaphs took up the chant on stone after stone throughout New England. The Hull stone in Cheshire, Connecticut, reads,

Death which came on man by ye fall,
cuts down father child and all.[28]

Another verse popular both in England and America reads,

Life is uncertain, Death is sure
Sin the wound and Christ the cure.[29]

The Eliakim Hayden stone, 1797, Essex, Connecticut, reads,

As in Adam, all mankinde
Did guilt and death derive,
So by the Righteousness of Christ
Shall all be made Alive.[30]

The verse on the Anthony Levi stone, 1799, Providence, Rhode Island, reads,

Death like an overflowing Stream,
Sweeps us away, our life is a dream,
an empty tale, a moving Flower,
cut down and withered in an hour.[31]

The Eunice Colton stone, 1763, Longmeadow, Massachusetts, shows a flower cut down by the scythe of time (plate 61A).

5. Death and Time

STONECARVERS simply followed an emblematic tradition when they linked together Death and Time as on the Colton stone.[32]

For Francis Quarles, the popular English poet and emblem writer, Time was a partner of Death, a partner who brought a brief respite between coming to be and passing away. The following lines from Quarles' text are illuminating,

Time   Behold the frailty of this slender stuff Alas,
        it has not long to last. . . .
Death Time, hold thy peace, and shake thy slow pac'd hand;
        Thy idle minutes make no way;
        Thy glass exceeds her pow'r, or else doth stand,
        I can not hold, I can not stay.
        Surcease thy pleading, and enlarge my hand,
        I surfeit with too long delay:
        This brisk, this bold-fac'd light
        Doth burn too bright;
        Darkness adorns my throne, my day is darkest night.
Time   Great Prince of darkness, hold thy needless hand:
        Thy captiv's fast and cannot flee,
        What arm can rescue? Who can countermand?
        What pow'r can set thy pris'ner free?
        Or if they could, what close, what foreign land
        Can hide the head that flees from thee?
        But if her harmless light offend thy sight,
        What need'st thou snatch at noon, what will be thine at night.[33]

The engraving illustrating the poem was used by a Charlestown, Massachusetts, carver on the Joseph Tapping stone, 1678, King's Chapel, Boston, Massachusetts (plates 151A and B, and 14). It was used again in 1681 on the John Foster stone in Dorchester, Massachusetts (plate 15), and 18th century variants may be found on the Rebekah Gerrish stone, 1743 (plate 16A), on the Samuel Adams stone, 1728 (plate 16B), and on the Rebekah Sanders stone, 1745–1746, all in King's Chapel, Boston, Massachusetts. Notice that on the Adams marker of 1728 Death holds the scythe of Time. The interchanging of symbolic attributes between Death and Time was an old European tradition[34] carried over to the new world and may be seen on stones such as tomb number 85 in The Granary (plate 17) (where Death has been crowned with a laurel symbolic of victory) on the Nathaniel Jackson stone, 1743, Plymouth, Massachusetts (plate 21A), on the Polly Harris marker, 1787, Charlestown, Massachusetts (plate 21B), on the Thomas Faunce stone, 1745, Plymouth, Massachusetts (plate 7), and on the Edward and Joseph Richards stone, 1747, Copp's Hill, Boston, Massachusetts (plate 22B).

The hourglass, an attribute of Time, could be given over to Death or connected with him by juxtaposition. Hourglasses appear on the Thomas Faunce stone (plate 7), the Nathaniel Jackson stone (plate 21A), the Edward and Joseph Richards stone (plate 22B), and on the William Dickson stone, 1692, Cambridge, Massachusetts (plates 24

PLATE 14. Detail of the Joseph Tapping stone, 1678, King's Chapel, Boston, Massachusetts. Slate. 28 x 28½.

PLATE 15. Detail of the John Foster stone, 1681, Dorchester, Massachusetts. Slate.

A.

B.

PLATE 16. A. Detail of the Rebekah Gerrish stone, 1743, King's Chapel, Boston, Massachusetts. Slate. B. Detail of the Samuel Adams stone, 1728, King's Chapel, Boston, Massachusetts. Slate. 29¼ x 27+.

PLATE 17. Detail of Stillman and Binney Tomb no. 85, The Granary, Boston, Massachusetts. Slate. Mid-18th century.

PLATE 18. Detail of the Isabella Tawley stone, 1737, Marblehead, Massachusetts. Slate. Probably a re-cut inscription over a stone originally cut in the late 17th century.

PLATE 19. Detail of the right panel of the Tawley stone. See plate 18.

PLATE 20. Detail of the Henry Roby stone, 1807, Copp's Hill, Boston, Massachusetts. Slate.

A.

B.

PLATE 21. A. Detail of the central portion of the Nathaniel Jackson stone. See plates 8A and B. B. Detail of the Polly Harris stone, 1787, Charlestown, Massachusetts. Slate. 22¼ x 24¾.

A.

B.

PLATE 22. A. Detail of the Thomas Faunce stone. See plate 7. B. Detail of the Edward and Joseph Richards stone, 1747, Copp's Hill, Boston, Massachusetts. Slate.

A.

B.

PLATE 23. A. Detail of the Elizabeth Coggeshall stone, 1773, Newport, Rhode Island. Slate. B. Detail of the Mary Harris stone, 1744, Providence, Rhode Island. M.U. 16¼ x 18. (The abbreviation "M.U.," here and elsewhere, signifies "material unknown.")

and 25), where hourglasses are held by imps of Death. Hourglasses are often seen in simple symbolic conjunction with the winged death's head as on the Poole and Person stones of the late 1670's in Wakefield, Massachusetts (plate 10). Allegorical figures of Time and Death are usually pictured together as on the Tawley stone dated 1737 in Marblehead, Massachusetts (plates 18 and 19), but Time could also be seen alone as on the Henry Roby marker of 1807 (plate 20).

In Rhode Island in the 18th century, it was common to depict the attributes of Time by showing a scythe splitting an hourglass in two, such as on the Elizabeth Coggeshall stone of 1773, in Newport, Rhode Island (plate 23A), while on the Mary Harris marker of 1744 in Providence, Rhode Island (plate 23B), the scythe touches but does not split the hourglass. Suggestive of the flight of Time, these stones are similar to the Faunce marker (plate 22A), and the Richards stone of 1747 where winged hourglasses may be seen (plate 22B).

6. The Imps of Death

EVIL demons armed with the arrows of Death were common devices in the symbolism of Joseph Lamson, a Charlestown carver. On the William Dickson stone (plates 24 and 25), and on the John Stone marker, 1691, Watertown, Massachusetts (plates 26A and B), imps of the underworld may be seen with darts of Death, hourglasses, and a scythe. Symbols thus normally associated with the allegorical figures of Death and Time have now been given to the naked imps which go about the business of symbolizing Death. Imps are also to be seen carrying the pall on the Pierpont stone of 1709 in Wakefield, Massachusetts (plate 28A), a common device in greater Boston in these years.

The arrow, seen in the hand of Death on the Polly Harris stone (plate 21B), was commonly called the dart of Death. The epitaph on the Marcy Brown stone, 1736, Providence, Rhode Island, reads,

> Old age being come her race here ends
> When God ye fatal dart he sends[35]

A Christian dictionary of the 17th century called arrows,

> generally the instruments of God's wrath and judgment.[36]

Edward Taylor wrote,

> Oh! Good, Good, Good, my Lord. What more I Love yet.
> Thou Dy for mee! What, am I dead in thee?
> What did Deaths arrows shot at me thee hit?

PLATE 24. Detail of the left panel of the William Dickson stone, 1692, Cambridge, Massachusetts. Slate. 28¼ x
20½.

PLATE 25. Detail of the right panel of the William Dickson stone, 1692, Cambridge, Massachusetts. Slate. 28¼ x 20½.

A.   B.

PLATE 26. A. and B. Details of the left and right panels of the John Stone marker, 1691, Watertown, Massachusetts.
    Slate.

A.

B.

PLATE 27. A. Detail of the Zechariah Long stone, 1688, Charlestown, Massachusetts. Slate. 18½ x 22½. B. Detail of the central frieze of the William Dickson stone. See plates 24 and 25.

PLATE 28. A. Detail of the central frieze of the Reverend Jonathan Pierpont stone, 1709, Wakefield, Massachusetts. Slate. 30 x 27½. Signed with initials 'N.L.,' possibly Nathaniel Lamson, the son of Joseph Lamson.
B. Detail of the central frieze of the Sibyll Wigglesworth stone, 1708, Cambridge, Massachusetts. Slate. 20¾ x 18¾. c. Detail of the central frieze of the Hannah Hayman stone, 1684, Charlestown, Massachusetts. Slate. 24¼ x 24.

A.

B.

PLATE 29. A. Detail of the Michael Martyn stone, 1689, Copp's Hill, Boston, Massachusetts. Slate. B. Detail of the John Briggs stone, date below ground level, probably cut in the last decade of the 17th century or the first decade of the 18th; Copp's Hill, Boston, Massachusetts. Slate.

Didst slip between that flying shaft and mee?
Didst make thyselfe Deaths marke shot at for mee?
So that her Shaft shall flying no far than thee? [37]

The arrows of Death may be seen on the William Rogers stone, 1772, Newport, Rhode Island (plate 187A).

The imps of Death, now winged, may be seen on the Zechariah Long stone of 1688, Charlestown, Massachusetts (plate 27A), atop a winged death's head pressing their arrows into the skull. Notice in particular the inclusion of the hourglass in the emblem. On the central frieze of the Dickson stone (plate 27B), the imps without their arrows are seen in the process of lowering a coffin into the grave.

It is important to note that these imps of Death, the demons of New England symbolism, were never popular and are not to be seen after *ca.* 1710. In spite of all the emphasis the Puritan put on death he developed no deep interest in demons; an interest so common in Medieval and Reformation art in Europe. This tells us a good deal about the types of symbols the Puritans found appropriate for their graves and those which they discarded after a period of testing. The Puritan did not care to dwell upon the triumph of Death, hence he was not apt to popularize the triumphant imps of Death in his funerary art, although he momentarily tried them out between *ca.* 1690 and 1710. The fact that they were (after *ca.* 1710) excluded from the vocabulary of stonecarving is as important to remember as their previous inclusion.

It is evident that the Puritan had mixed feelings about giving up life for the uncertain pleasures of the next world. Samuel Willard wrote,

> *1. IT makes a Separation between the soul and body.*
> This is the very nature of it, and is in itself a misery; and for that reason the Godly themselves have a natural reluctancy against it: they would not pass through it if they could go to heaven without it. [38]

Jonathan Edwards wrote,

> Hence the reason why almost all men, and those that seem to be very miserable, love life, because they cannot bear to lose sight of such a beautiful and lovely world. The idea, that every moment whilst we live have a beauty that we take not distinct notice of, brings a pleasure that, when we come to the trial, we had rather live in much pain and misery than lose. [39]

These labored passages on the terrors of death indicate that no matter with how much zeal the Puritan pursued heaven, he was reluctant to die. No matter how much he despised the corporeal cage of his soul, he loved the humble beauties of life and feared to give them up.

The epitaph on the Elah Camp stone, 1787, Durham, Connecticut, reads,

> He who knows the worth of the Soul
> Prefers the Treasures of Heaven
> to those of the Earth and drops the world
> before the world drops him.[40]

The Puritan as both man and Christian loved and turned his back upon the world in order that he might say along with the epitaph on the Lemuel Garnsey stone, 1782, in Durham, Connecticut,

> We mourn not as wretches do:
> Where vicious lives all hope deny
> A falling tear is natures due:
> While faith looks up to joys on high.[41]

In the midst of darkness and confusion there was light, the triumph of Death was overcome by eternity. The fear of death gave way to the thrill of spiritual pleasures yet to come as archangels trumpeted the glorious day.

7. Symbols of the Resurrection

THE translation of flesh into spirit took place in two phases: at the time of death there was the immediate glorification of the soul and later, at the time of judgment, general Resurrection. In the latter phase the body joined the soul in heaven. Samuel Willard wrote,

> THE Souls of Believers are at their Death made perfect in Holiness, and do Immediately pass into Glory, and their Bodies being still United to Christ, do rest in their Graves till the Resurrection.[42]

Thomas Foxcroft agreed with Willard, when he wrote,

> Again Believers die, that their *Bodies* may partake of a Glorious Resurrection. . . . At the end of the present life God will have them in part (as to the *Soul*) admitted to the possession of it; yet as to the *Body*, He sees meet to refer the recompence of the just, till the great and last day, when there shall be more public and complete retribution.[43]

On the glorious day of resurrection the heavens were to be rent with flames and smoke and the glorious trumpet sounded. The epitaph on the Reverend John Keep stone, 1784, Sheffield, Massachusetts, reads,

> When Suns and Planets from their orbs be hurl'd

And Livid flames involve this smoking world;
The Trump of God announce the Savior nigh
And shining hosts of Angels crowd the sky
Then from this tomb thy dust shall they convey
To happier regions of eternal day.[44]

8. Trumpeting Figures

A trumpeting angelic figure appears from the left on the Margaret Cumings stone, 1790, Billerica, Massachusetts (plate 30A), while on the Elizabeth Nichols stone, 1778, Wakefield, Massachusetts (plate 30B), a similar figure wings in from the opposite direction. On the Cumings marker the legend "Arise Ye Dead" pours forth from a scroll with the lettering cut backward into the stone while on the Nichols version the legend is correctly lettered. Another trumpeting figure, this time with a fully carved and cloaked body, appears on the Elizabeth Clark stone of 1767, Chelmsford, Massachusetts (plate 31A), while on the Alexander Miller stone, 1798, Plainfield, Connecticut (plate 31B), two winged half figures bugle at one another announcing the Resurrection. Seminude reclining figures with modern bugles appear on the Major Jonathan Allen stone, 1780, Northampton, Massachusetts (plates 32 and 33), while on the Colonel Seth Pomeroy marker of 1777 in the same burial ground (plate 34), similar figures are winged and provided with horns rather than bugles and crowns rather than coifs.

On the Sarah Allen stone, 1785, Bristol, Rhode Island (plate 35), a sun blowing a horn of Resurrection appears. As musical sounds swirl out of the funnellike opening in a rush of wavy lines, smaller suns arise to either side.

9. The Tree of Life

THE tree of life has had symbolic significance since at least Sumerian times[45] and has been steadily used by a number of cultures to symbolize spiritual values until the present day. The New Englander borrowed the symbol from European sources and created a great many tree variants throughout the 18th century. The Holmes children stone, 1795, East Glastonbury, Connecticut (plate 36), reveals four profile heads (plate 196), and a tree of life divested of four branches. The epitaph reads,

But whilst you sleep the Lamb on Calvery slain,
Feeds the young branches which shall sprout again.[46]

A.

B.

PLATE 30. A. Detail of the Margaret Cumings stone, 1790, Billerica, Massachusetts. Slate. 23¼ x 29½. B. Detail of the Elizabeth Nichols stone, 1778, Wakefield, Massachusetts. Slate.

A.

B.

PLATE 31. A. Detail of the Elizabeth Clark stone, 1767, Chelmsford, Massachusetts. Slate. B. Detail of the Alexander Miller stone, 1798, Plainfield, Connecticut. Slate. 21¼ x 39.

PLATE 32. Detail of the allegorical figures on the Major Jonathan Allen stone, 1780, Northampton, Massachusetts. Red sandstone. 29¾ x 49.

PLATE 33. Detail of the allegorical figures on the Major Jonathan Allen stone, 1780, Northampton, Massachusetts. Red sandstone. 29¾ x 49.

PLATE 34. Detail of the Colonel Seth Pomeroy stone, 1777, Northampton, Massachusetts. Red sandstone. 24 x 47.

PLATE 35. Detail of the Sarah Allen stone, 1785, Bristol, Rhode Island. Slate.

Edward Taylor wrote,

> And in Gods Garden saw a golden Tree,
> Whose Heart was All Divine, and gold its barke.
> Whose glorious limbs and fruitful branches strong
> with Saints, and Angells bright are richly hung.
>
> Thou! thou! my Deare-Deare Lord, art this rich Tree
> The Tree of Life Within Gods Paradise.
> I am a Withred Twig, dri'de fit to bee
> A Chat Cast in thy fire, Writh off by Vice.
> Yet if thy Milke white-Gracious Hand take mee
> and grafft mee in this golden stock, thou'lt make me.
>
> Thou'lt make me then its Fruite, and Branch to spring.
> And though a nipping Eastwinde blow, and all
> Hells Nymps with spite their Dog's sticks threat ding
> To Dash the Grafft off, and it's fruits to fall,
> Yet I shall stand thy Grafft, and Fruits that are
> Fruits of the Tree of Life thy grafft shall beare.[47]

There can be little doubt that when tree symbolism is used both by the poets and the stonecarvers we are dealing with a widely diffused image familiar to all. Taylor's imagery suggested that the tree of life is hung with saints and on the Park family stone, 1803, Grafton, Vermont (plate 37), a tree of life hung with twelve anthropomorphic soul discs may be seen. The John Brooks epitaph, 1788, Stratford, Connecticut, reads,

> Farewell Bright Soul a short farewell
> Till we shall meet again Above
>
> In the Sweet groves where Pleasures dwell
> And Trees of Life bear fruits of love
> There Glory sits on every face
> There friendship smiles in every eye.[48]

The verse was widely used in New England and may be found on such stones as the John Rogers marker, 1809, Palmer Center, Massachusetts.[49]

Twin but barren trees of life may be seen on the Margaret Campbell stone, 1799, Rockingham, Vermont (plates 38A and B) while on another marker in Rockingham (plates 38C and D), a tree bears small buds. On the Muzzy stone, 1764, Lexington, Massachusetts (plate 39A), and on the Green stone of 1770, in Harvard, Massachusetts

PLATE 36. Detail of the Holmes children stone, 1795, East Glastonbury, Connecticut. Red sandstone. 48 x 45.

PLATE 37. Drawing of the Park family stone, 1803, Grafton, Vermont. Slate.

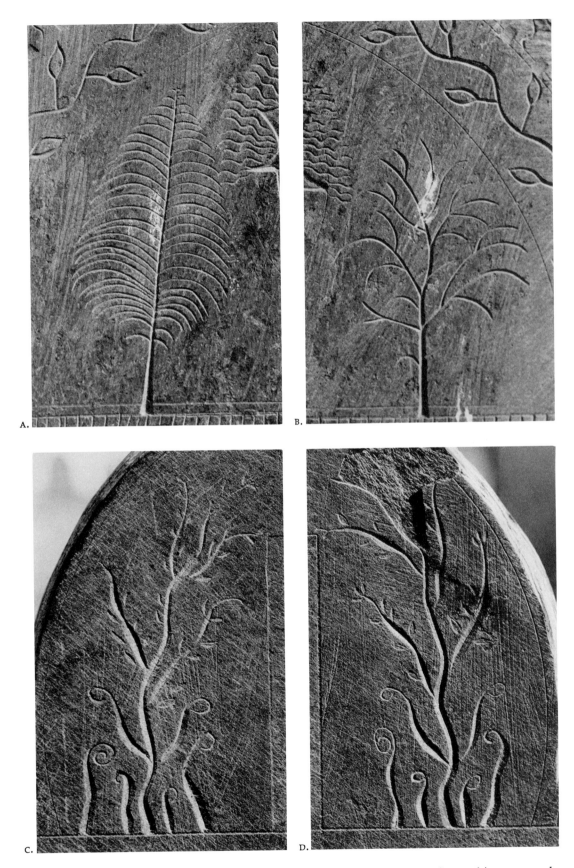

PLATE 38. A. and B. Details of the Margaret Campbell stone, 1799, Rockingham, Vermont. Slate. 20¼ x 38. C. and D. Details of the Read child stone, 1802, Rockingham, Vermont. Slate. 12 x 19¼.

A.

B.

PLATE 39. A. Detail of the Muzzy family stone, 1764, Lexington, Massachusetts. Slate. 32¼ x 41½. B. Detail of the Martha Green stone, 1770, Harvard, Massachusetts. Slate. 27 x 37.

(plate 39B), properly foliated trees may be seen. Four trees of life, now transformed into palms, may be seen on the Daniel Squier stone, 1783, Franklin, Connecticut (plates 40A and B), while on the Manning children stone, 1750, Norwichtown, Connecticut (plate 245A), twin trees *qua* palms may be seen topped with peacocks. More difficult to recognize are the twin birds topping the trees *qua* palms on the Martha Welch marker of 1775 in Storrs, Connecticut (plates 50 and 51), and on the James Luce stone, 1776, Scotland, Connecticut (plates 52A and B). A reed-thin tree, more like a vine, appears on the Whiting family stone, 1781, Rockingham, Vermont (plate 106B), while doves nestle in the sturdier trees on the Pamela Munro stone, 1770, Lexington, Massachusetts (plate 114A), on the Job Harris stone, 1729, (plate 115A), and on the William Harris stone of 1725 (plate 115B), both in Providence, Rhode Island. On the Ephraim Walker stone, 1777, Brookfield, Massachusetts (plate 89), an abstract tree of life within a disc at the base of the stone gives root to a grapevine springing up the sides of the stone and bowering the central soul effigy. On the Deborah Samson stone, 1769, Kingston, Massachusetts (plate 112A), a barren tree of life is set within a tiara crowning the soul effigy.

Trees being felled may be seen on the Mehitable Hull stone, 1747, (plate 41A), and on the Elizabeth Norton stone, 1751, (plate 41B), in Durham, Connecticut. In both a hand appears from a cloud and cuts down the tree. I assume that the hand belongs to God, although on the Hull variant He cuts down a solitary tree while on the Norton marker He fells only one tree of three, the center one probably standing for the Tree of Life, while the other two flanking it might represent the lives of Mr. and Mrs. Norton. John Calvin wrote,

> They are plainly told that all whom the heavenly Father hath not been pleased to plant as sacred trees in his garden, are doomed and devoted to destruction.[50]

A Christian dictionary defines trees as,

> Every person, man or woman good or bad.[51]

Layers of meaning are obviously involved when a tree can stand for the tree of life in the celestial paradise and for a human life as well. Trees abound on the carved stone markers of New England and during the late years of the 18th century they were taken over by the newer neoclassical stones when they were transformed into the still popular weeping willow seen so often on 19th century mourning pictures (plates 192C, 192D, 193A, and 193B).

A.

B.

PLATE 40. A. and B. Details of the Daniel Squier stone, 1783, Franklin, Connecticut. Granite.

A.

B.

PLATE 41. A. Detail of the Mehitable Hull stone, 1747, Durham, Connecticut. Red sandstone. B. Detail of the Elizabeth Norton stone, 1751, Durham, Connecticut. Red sandstone. 29¼ x 46½.

10. The Palm of Victory

A variant of the tree of life symbol, the palm of victory, is an ancient symbol signifying victory and it is strange that it should have survived intact upon the stones of New England when it seems to have gone out of fashion in Medieval, Renaissance, and Baroque iconography in the form in which it appears in America.[52] The New Englander quoted the theme with archaeological correctness more than a dozen times in the burial grounds around eastern Connecticut in the last half of the 18th century on such stones as the Betsey Tracy marker of 1792 (plate 42A), on the Russell Brown marker, 1795, (plate 42B), on the Whiting family stone, 1794, (plate 43A), all in Norwichtown, Connecticut, and on the King stone, *ca.* 1790, Norwich, Connecticut (plate 44B).

The New Englander probably associated the palm with the righteous man and with salvation. Psalm 92.12 reads,

> The righteous shall flourish like the palm tree: he shall grow like a cedar in Lebanon.

Rev. 7.9 reads,

> After this I beheld, and, lo, a great multitude, which no man could number, of all nations, and kindreds, and people, and tongues, stood before the throne, and before the Lamb, clothed with white robes, and palms in their hands.

On the Clough stone (plate 70A) an allegorical figure of Hope clutches a palm of victory to her. On the Durkee family stone, 1787, Norwichtown (plate 43B), and on the Sally King marker, 1791, Norwich (plate 44A), both in Connecticut, clouds appear from the left but the hand of God and the palm of victory motifs are omitted.

11. The Crown of Righteousness and the Cross

THE crown of righteousness was as common a theme in New England as the palm of victory was rare. A covey of crowns may be seen on the Jonathan Allen stone, 1780, Northampton, Massachusetts (plate 45A), on the Seth Pomeroy stone, 1777, Northampton, Massachusetts (plate 45B), on the Ann Goddard stone, 1760, Durham, Connecticut (plate 45C), on the Sarah Porter stone, 1775, Hadley, Massachusetts (plate 45D), on the Nathanael Sutlief stone, 1760, Durham, Connecticut, (plate 47A), on the Abigail Camp stone, 1769, Durham, Connecticut (plate 47C), on the Joseph Tibbals stone, 1774, Durham, Connecticut (plate 47D), on the John Hurlbut stone, 1778, East Hartford, Connecticut (plate 47E), on the Elijah Kellog stone, 1804, Marlboro,

PLATE 42. A. Detail of the Betsey Tracy stone, 1792, Norwichtown, Connecticut. Granite. 22 x 37. B. Detail of the Russell Brown stone, 1795, Norwichtown, Connecticut. Granite. 22 x 25.

A.

B.

PLATE 43. A. Detail of the Whiting family stone, 1794, Norwichtown, Connecticut. Granite. 33½ x 39¾. B. Colonel and Mrs. John Durkee stone, 1787, Norwichtown, Connecticut. Granite. 31 x 36.

A.

B.

PLATE 44. A. Detail of the Sally King stone, 1791, Norwich, Connecticut. White marble. 19½ x 22. B. Detail of the Mrs. W. King stone, Norwich, Connecticut. White marble. 24½ x 32.

Connecticut (plate 47F), on the Dorothy Walker stone, 1804, Brook-field, Massachusetts (plate 48A), and on the Joseph West stone, 1764, Tolland, Connecticut (plate 48B). Crowns came pointed, fluted, layered, ribbed, pierced, banded, and beaded, but in whatever guise they appeared they all seem to proclaim the same message when associated with the soul, Resurrection in Christ. 2 Timothy 4.8 reads,

> Henceforth there is laid up for me a crown of righteousness, which the Lord, the righteous judge, shall give me at that day: and not to me only, but unto all them also that love his appearing.

I Peter 5.4 reads,

> And when the chief Shepherd shall appear, ye shall receive a crown of Glory that fadeth not away.

James 1.12 reads,

> Blessed *is* the man that endureth temptation: for when he is tried, he shall receive the crown of life, which the Lord hath promised to them that love him.

A 17th century Christian dictionary defined the crown of glory as follows,

> The most excellent glory which the Saints have in heaven forever, shadowed unto us by a Kingly crown, which of all earthly things is most glorious.

> Eternall life which is given as a free reward to such as lead a righteous life, which the God who is most righteous, hath promised, and will also perform...[53]

The widespread use of the cross on gravestones is most unusual in the light of the following citations which show the degree of Puritan antipathy toward it. Samuel Sewall commented,

> Mr. Whetcomb buried. Coffin was lined with Cloth on the outside, and below the name and year a St. Andrew's Cross made, with what intent I can't tell.[54]

An English Christian dictionary defined the cross as follows:

> The Papists, without all reason adore Reliques of it, and attribute virtue to it being but a Creature, if it were extant.[55]

Crosses may be seen on the Jonathan Allen stone (plate 45A), the Seth Pomeroy stone (plate 45B), the Ann Goddard stone (plate 45C), the Sarah Porter stone (plate 45D), the Joshua Abell stone, 1725, Norwich-town, Connecticut (plate 45E), the Martha Welch stone (plate 45F), the Thomas Lovall stone, 1718, Ipswich, Massachusetts (plate 45G), the Mary Burpee stone, 1721, Rowley, Massachusetts (plates 45H and

PLATE 45. A. Detail of the Jonathan Allen stone, see numbers 32 and 33 for information. B. Detail of the Seth Pomeroy stone, see plate 34. C. Detail of the Ann Goddard stone, 1760, Durham, Connecticut. Red sandstone. 26 x 51¼. D. Detail of the Sarah Porter stone, 1775, Hadley, Massachusetts. Red sandstone. 28¼ x 51½. E. Detail of the Joshua Abell stone, 1725, Norwichtown, Connecticut. Granite. Schist. 13 x 9½. F. Detail of the Martha Welch stone, 1775, Storrs, Connecticut. Granite. 35½ x 58½. G. Detail of the Thomas Lovall stone, 1718, Ipswich, Massachusetts. Schist. 23¾ x 28½. H. and I. Details of the Mary Burpee stone, 1721, Rowley, Massachusetts. Schist. 21¼ x 19.

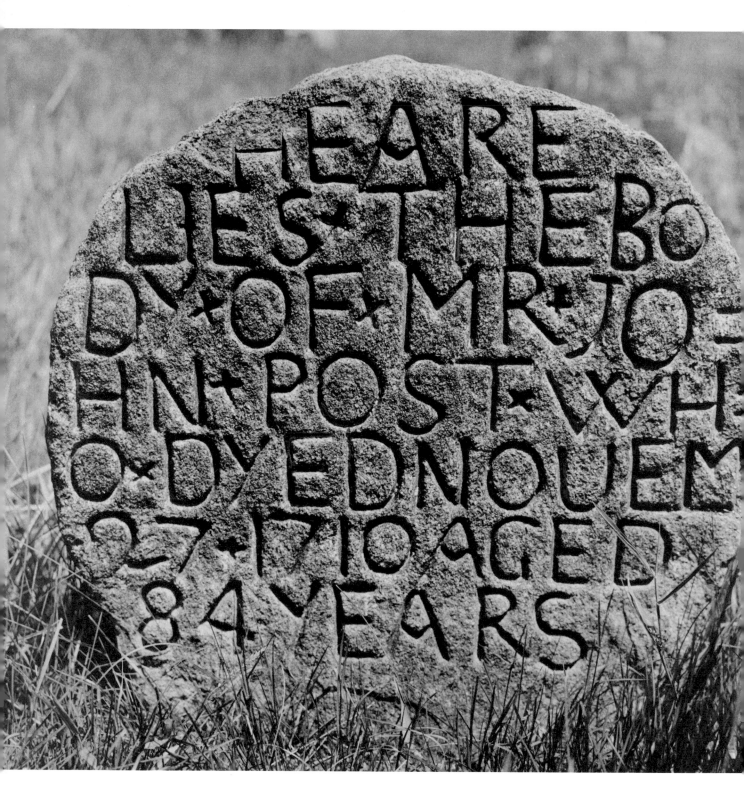

PLATE 46. The John Post stone, 1710, Norwichtown, Connecticut. Granite. 22¼ x 22½.

A.

B.

C.

D.

E.

F.

G.

PLATE 47. A. Detail of the Captain Nathanael Sutlief stone, 1760, Durham, Connecticut. Red sandstone. 27 x 54. B. Detail of the Abigail James stone, 1748, Durham, Connecticut. C. Detail of the Abigail Camp stone, 1769, Durham, Connecticut. Red sandstone. 21½ x 38. D. Detail of the Joseph Tibbals stone, 1774, Durham, Connecticut. Red sandstone. 30¼ x 52. E. Detail of the John Hurlbut stone, 1778, East Hartford, Connecticut. Granite. 25¾ x 51½. Signed by Rockwell Manning. F. Detail of the Elijah Kellog stone, 1804, Marlboro, Connecticut. Red sandstone. 29¼ x 51. G. Detail of the Simeon Terry stone, 1791, Enfield, Connecticut. Red sandstone. 23¾ x 36.

A.

B.

PLATE 48. A. Detail of the Dorothy Walker stone, 1804, Brookfield, Massachusetts. Quartzite? 24 x 33. B. Detail of the Deacon Joseph West stone, 1764, Tolland, Connecticut. Red sandstone. 25 x 49.

1), and possibly on the John Post stone, 1710, Norwichtown, Connecticut (plate 46). The symbol of the cross could appear emblazed across the face of a stone, hidden away in the corners, obscured by a circular band, cut in the shape of a Maltese cross, or like a rosette; but whatever way the New Englander chose to have his cross carved, there is no longer any question that it was a far more popular symbol than any historian of 18th century New England has hitherto supposed.[56] It still remains to be seen for whom these crosses were carved and why.

12. Peacocks and Cocks

THE peacock was a widely used funereal symbol in early Christian times and was a favored device on Byzantine sarcophagi.[57] St. Augustine probably gave impetus to the growing vogue for peacocks when he wrote,

> the peacock's flesh, immune from the putrification from which not even the flesh of Plato was exempt.[58]

Peacocks were used in the 18th century both in Massachusetts and Connecticut, although the metaphor of the peacock does not figure actively in the contemporary literature. The John Cleverly stone, 1703, Quincy, Massachuetts (plate 49A), shows twin peacocks flanking an hourglass. A variant form appears on the Manning children stone, 1750, (plate 245A) where a peacock is perched atop a tree of life *qua* palm, but on the Martha Welch marker of 1775 (plates 50 and 51), one can no longer clearly distinguish the bird as a peacock, although there is a strong suggestion in that direction. Other birds which might be peacocks were cut on the James Luce stone, 1776, (plate 52) Scotland, Connecticut.

Cocks may be seen on the Naomi Woolworth stone, 1760, Longmeadow, Massachusetts (plate 49B), on the Ruth Steel stone, 1758, (plate 53B), and on the Isaac Williams stone, 1781, (plate 53C), both in Tolland, Connecticut. An abstract design flanking an hourglass, but in all ways similar in outline to the cocks on the Ruth Steel stone, appears on the Captain Stephen Steel stone, 1749, (plate 53A), in Tolland.

The cock was not only a symbol of man's fall from grace but of his Resurrection as well. Jonathan Edwards wrote,

> The awaking and crowing of the cock to wake men out of sleep and to introduce the day seems to signifie the introducing the glorious day of the church by ministers preaching the Gospel. Many shall be awakened and roused to preach

A.

B.

PLATE 49. A. Detail of the John Cleverly stone, 1703, Quincy, Massachusetts. Slate. B. Detail of the Naomi Woolworth stone, 1760, Longmeadow, Massachusetts. Red sandstone. 21¼ x 37.

PLATE 50. Detail of the Martha Welch stone, 1775, Storrs, Connecticut. Granite. 35½ x 58½.

PLATE 51. Detail of the Martha Welch stone, 1775, Storrs, Connecticut. Granite. 35½ x 58½.

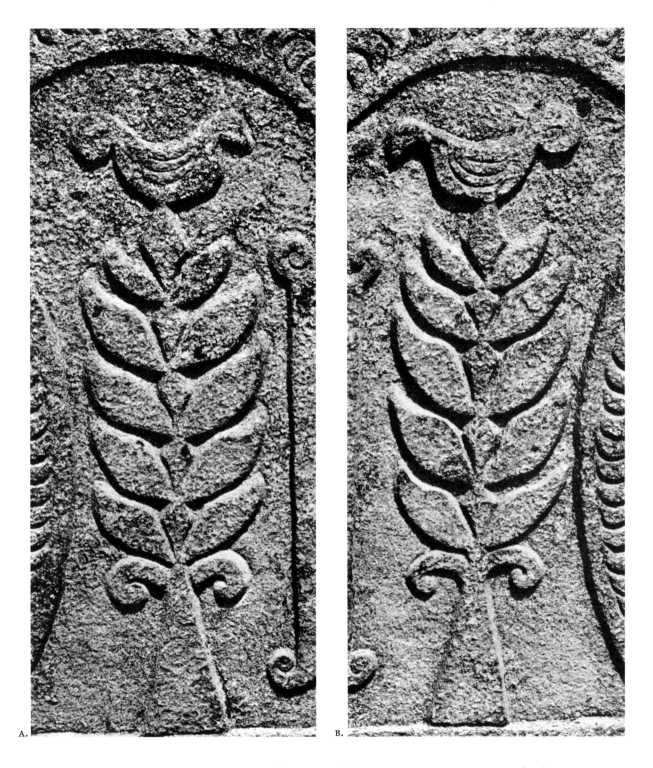

PLATE 52. A. and B. Details of the left and right panels of the James Luce stone, 1776, Scotland, Connecticut. Granite. 41¾ x 58¾.

A.

B.

C.

PLATE 53. A. Detail of the Captain Stephen Steel stone, 1749, Tolland, Connecticut. Red sandstone. 13 x 17. B. Detail of the Ruth Steel stone, 1758, Tolland, Connecticut. Red sandstone. 16½ x 26. C. Detail of the Isaac Williams stone, 1781, Tolland, Connecticut. Red sandstone.

the Gospel, with extraordinary fervency, to cry aloud and lift their voice like [a] trumpet. Peter's being awakened out of that deep sleep he had fallen into, and brought to repentance by the crowing of the cock at the break of day, signifies the awakening of Christ's church that is built upon Peter.... The introducing of the spring by the voice of spring birds signifies the same thing.[59]

13. Architectural Symbolism

MANY Puritans conceived of the journey to heaven in architectural terms. Samuel Willard commented,

Death is the portal to eternity, and carries men over to an unchangeable state.[60]

The epitaph on the Reverend John Sergeant stone, 1749, Stockbridge, Massachusetts reads,

Where is that pleasing form I ask, thou canst not show,
He's not within false stone, there's nought but dost below;
And where's that pious soul that thinking conscious mind,
Wilt thou pretend vain cypher that's with thee inshrin'd?
Alas, my friend's not here with thee that I find,
Here's not a Sergeant's body or a Sergeant's mind:
I'll seek him hence, for all's a like deception here,
I'll go to Heaven, and I shall find my Sergeant there.[61]

Although the soul of the deceased was enshrined in heaven, and earthly symbols were but cyphers, the majority of Puritans preferred the cypher or symbol to nothing at all.

The shrine is another symbol associated with antiquity[62] and European imagery which managed to survive in rural New England. The Arch of Titus in Rome (plate 109), symbolizes the victories in life and the final apotheosis of the emperor who is pictured being carried toward heavenly bliss on the back of an eagle. The arch itself is made of two supporting piers spanned by a barrel vault suggesting a passageway which must be traversed. The Puritan knew such symbols well and used them many times. The Neal children stone, ca. 1678, The Granary, Boston, Massachuetts (plate 54A), was cut in the shape of a classical temple façade within whose pediment a winged death's head appears while the lintel is supported by four columns and spanned by three vaults suggesting that death is a passageway or door into the unknown. On the Worthylake family stone of 1718 in Copp's Hill, Boston, Massachusetts (plate 54B), a similar motif has been cut but this time with two bays spanned by a lintel rather than an arch. The "archivolts" contain winged death's heads. On the Joseph Tapping stone of 1678 (plate 55), the lower half of the stone is composed of a

A.

B.

PLATE 54. A. The Neal children stone, ca. 1678, The Granary, Boston, Massachusetts. Slate. 53 x 20½+. B. The Worthylake family stone, 1718, Copp's Hill, Boston, Massachusetts. Slate.

PLATE 55. The Joseph Tapping stone, 1678, King's Chapel, Boston, Massachusetts. Slate.

central allegory flanked by gothic arches set within four thin columns on plinths. The gothic motif was to be the last to appear in New England until its revival in the 19th century. The Captain Samuel Dwight stone, 1763, Enfield, Connecticut (plate 56A), is formed like a doorway with fluted jambs at either side and a fan light above suggesting that the deceased was about to set forth through the portals of death. On the Hannah Badger stone, 1735, Haverhill, Massachusetts (plate 56B), a pedimented shrine may be seen with a coffin superimposed upon it while on the Martha Green stone, 1770, Harvard, Massachusetts (plate 57A), effigies are set within a brick shrine flanked by willows. On the Gamaliel Ripley stone, 1799, Scotland, Connecticut (plate 57B), a soul effigy may be seen within an architectural shrine of fluted pilasters set with a capstone at the top; the whole surrounded by bands of clouds suggesting the soul enshrined in heaven. On the Daniel Weever stone, 1801, Rockingham, Vermont (plate 58A), a similar representation appears while on the Reverend Abraham Nott stone, 1756, Essex, Connecticut (plate 58B), the winged soul effigy flutters toward heaven in the company of two columns and two pilasters, possibly symbolizing the architecture of bliss, although the meaning is not clear. On the Thomas Drury stone, 1778, Auburn, Massachusetts (plate 59), the sides of the stone are cut in the form of pilasters with capitals supporting an arch set with dentils while within the arch a soul effigy bursts forth from the ground flanked by twin blooming flowers symbolic of the Resurrection. Architectural symbolism may be found throughout New England and during the 19th century there was a sudden renewal of the imagery on stones such as the Captain and Mrs. Cargill stone, 1813, Palmer Center, Massachusetts (plate 60), on which two draped neoclassical cinerary urns are set within two flanking fluted piers, separated by two thin trees of life, and capped by a heavy entablature of white marble.

14. *Flowers, Conifers, and Garlands*

THE life of man has been associated with flowers since at least the time of the Scriptures. Job 14 reads,

> Man *that is* born of woman *is* of few days, and full of trouble. He cometh forth like a flower, and is cut down: he fleeth also as a shadow, and continueth not.

In Isaiah 40.6 the flowers of the field are compared not to the shortness of man's life but to the good,

> All flesh *is* grass, and all the goodliness thereof *is* as the flower of the field:

A.

B.

PLATE 56. A. The Captain Samuel Dwight Stone, 1763, Enfield, Connecticut. Red sandstone. 29 x 38. B. The Hannah Badger footstone, 1735, Haverhill, Massachusetts. Schist.

A.

B.

PLATE 57. A. Detail of the Martha Green stone, 1770, Harvard, Massachusetts. Slate. 27 x 37. B. Detail of the Gamaliel Ripley stone, 1799, Scotland, Connecticut. Granite. 29¾ x 48.

A.

B.

PLATE 58. A. Detail of the Daniel Weaver stone, 1801, Rockingham, Vermont. Slate. B. Detail of Rev. Abraham Nott stone, 1756, Essex, Connecticut. Red sandstone.

PLATE 59. The Thomas Drury stone, 1778, Auburn, Massachusetts. Slate.

PLATE 60. Detail of the Mary Cargill stone (Captain and Mrs.), 1813, Palmer Center, Massachusetts. White marble. 32 x 38.

The flowering of man's life is cut off by the scythe of Time on the Eunice Colton stone, 1763, Longmeadow, Massachusetts (plate 61A). This was a very popular emblem on English gravestones but quite rare in New England, this being the only extant example. Flowers sprouting from a chalice flanking a hovering crown may be seen on the Jonathan Allen stone (plate 61B). Lilylike flowers appear in the gadrooned urn of the Ruth Carter stone, 1697–1698, (plate 62A) while another variety of flower appears from the urn on the Reverend Edward Thompson stone, 1705, Marshfield, Massachuetts (plate 62B). Foliage and blossoms appear from the woven basket cut into the William Rogers stone, 1772, Newport, Rhode Island (plate 62C). Flowering vines coil up the Deborah Thomas and Edward Thompson stones in Marshfield, Massachusetts (plates 63A, B, C, D), while flowering palm branches appear on the Elisha Hurlbut stone, 1771, Scotland, Connecticut (plate 63E). A flowering branch is held aloft by the hand of the Mary Brown effigy, 1782, Plymouth, Massachusetts (plate 63F), while similar flowering branches are held by the seminude allegorical figures on the Sarah Porter stone, 1775, Hadley, Massachusetts (plate 63G).

A variety of conifers may be seen on the Mary Bliss stone, 1757, Longmeadow, Massachusetts (plate 64A) and on the Thomas Davis stone, 1760, Oxford, Massachusetts (plates 64B and C), where they blossom from the ground in clusters of three; while conifers flank thistles on the David Thurston stone, 1778, Auburn, Massachusetts (plates 64D and E). Bushy husked coniferlike forms appear from the top of the Ithamar Parsons stone, 1786, Durham, Connecticut (plates 64F and G), while on the Lemuel Garnsey stone, 1782, in the same burial ground (plates 64H and I), beetlike roots hang down over the head of the central effigy. The meaning of the latter symbol is as yet obscure. The symbol of the evergreen, however, is so patently clear as to need little amplification.

Garlands of victory, known from antique times,[63] were borrowed by the New Englanders from European sources and were quite popular. A garland of victory set above a winged death's head on the Sarah Marshall stone, 1689, The Granary, Boston, Massachusetts, (plate 65A), might symbolize either the victory of death or the victory of the soul over death if the two symbols were meant to form a simple opposition. I believe that in the vast majority of cases a simple juxtaposition of symbols of life and death was intended, although this cannot be demonstrated in this particular case except by the citing of comparative examples.

A.

B.

PLATE 61. A. Detail of the Eunice Colton stone, 1763, Longmeadow, Massachusetts. Red sandstone. 22 x 36¾.
B. Detail of the Jonathan Allen stone, 1780, Northampton, Massachusetts. See plate 32.

A.

B.

C.

PLATE 62. A. Detail of the Ruth Carter stone, 1697/98, The Granary, Boston, Massachusetts. Slate. 27 x 28¼.
B. Detail of the Reverend Edward Thompson stone, 1705, Marshfield, Massachusetts. Slate. C. Detail of the
William Rogers stone, 1772, Newport, Rhode Island. Slate. Signed by John Stevens, Jr.

PLATE 63. A. and B. Details of the Reverend Edward Thompson stone. See plate 62B. C. and D. Details of the Deborah Thomas stone, 1696, Marshfield, Massachusetts. Slate. E. Detail of the Elisha Storrs stone, 1771, Scotland, Connecticut. Granite. 38 x 52½. F. Detail of the Mary Brown stone, 1782, Plymouth, Massachusetts. Slate. 16¾ x 23. G. Detail of the Sarah Porter stone, 1775, Hadley, Massachusetts. Red sandstone. 28¼ x 51½.

A.

B.

C.

D.

E.

F.

G.

H.

I.

PLATE 64. A. Detail of the Mary Bliss stone, 1757, Longmeadow, Massachusetts. Red sandstone. 18¾ x 29. B. and c. Details of the Deacon Thomas Davis stone, ca. 1760, Oxford, Massachusetts. Slate. D. and E. Details of the David Thurston stone, 1778, Auburn, Massachusetts. Slate. F. and G. Details of the Ithamar Parsons stone, 1786, Durham, Connecticut. Red sandstone. 30½ x 52. H. and I. Details of the Lemuel Garnsey stone, 1782. Red sandstone. 27 x 46½, Durham, Connecticut.

PLATE 65. A. Detail of the Sarah Marshall stone, 1689, The Granary, Boston, Massachusetts. Slate. B. Detail of the left panel of the Nathaniel Jackson stone, 1743, Plymouth, Massachusetts. See plate 8. C. and D. Details of the left and right panels of the Ann Mumford stone, 1697/98, Newport, Rhode Island. Slate. E. and F. Details of the left and right panels of plate 65A.

Other garlands may be seen on the border panels of the Nathaniel Jackson stone, 1743, Plymouth, Massachusetts (plate 65B), where flowers, grapes, and a pear are combined, on the Ann Mumford stone, 1697–1698, Newport, Rhode Island (plates 65c and D), where gourds, pumpkins, and broad-leafed acanthuslike forms cascade forth from a geometric collar, and on the border panels of the Marshall stone (plates 65E and F), in variant form. On the Peter Tufts stone of 1702–1703, Malden, Massachusetts (plate 66), and on the Jonathan Remington stone, 1700, Cambridge, Massachusetts (plate 67), what I take to be soul effigies perch atop garlands composed of gourdlike fruits and wide-leafed acanthuslike foliage. On the Rebekah Bunker stone of 1710, Cambridge, Massachusetts (plates 68 and 69), the gourds appear as breasts. The gourd was a very popular symbol in the 17th and early 18th centuries in and around greater Boston and seemed to have been taken as a symbol of both life and death. Second Kings 4.39, 40 reads,

> And one went out into the field to gather herbs, and found a wild vine, and gathered thereof wild gourds his lap full, and came and shred *them* into the pot of potage: for they knew *them* not.
>
> So they poured out for the men to eat. And it came to pass, as they were eating of the pottage, that they cried out, and said, Oh thou man of God, there is death in the pot.

Jonah 4.6–10 reads,

> And the Lord God prepared a gourd, and made *it* to come up over Jonah, that it might be a shadow over his head, to deliver him from his grief. So Jonah was exceeding glad of the gourd.
>
> But God prepared a worm when the morning rose the next day, and it smote the gourd that it withered.
>
> And it came to pass, when the sun did arise, that God prepared a vehement east wind; and the sun beat upon the head of Jonah, that he fainted, and wished in himself to die, and said, *It is* better for me to die than to live.
>
> And God said to Jonah, Doest thou well to be angry for the gourd? And he said, I do well to be angry, *even* unto death.
>
> Then said the Lord, Thou hast had pity on the gourd, for which thou hast not laboured, neither madest it grow; which came up in the night, and perished in a night.

The gourd then, seems to have symbolized the coming to be and the passing away of earthly things. In early Christian art Jonah was often depicted as a typological symbol along with the gourd,[64] but in New England Jonah was omitted and the gourds retained, suggesting that the gourds of the Jonah story might have been more significant to the

Puritan than any complicated typological interpretation of the Jonah story.

The gourds on the Bunker stone could also be interpreted as breasts and it would be foolish to believe that the Puritans were too prudish to see the similarities.

15. Erotic Symbolism

In addition to the geometric heart symbol being an emblem of the soul's love of God and of the soul itself the Puritans symbolized the power of eros more directly both pictorially and in their literature. In literature, breasts could symbolize the Scriptures, the Church, the ministry, or the divine milk needed to nourish the soul. For example, Jonathan Edwards wrote,

> Milk represents the word of God from the breasts of the church, that is not only represented as a woman but of old was typified by heifers, the goats, etc. Milk by its whiteness represents the purity of the word of God; it fitly represents the word because of its sweetness and nourishing nature, and being for the saints in their present state, wherein they are children. That is, as it were, the natural food of a new creature or of the creature newly come into the world; by its whiteness and purity it represents holiness, that is the natural food and delight of the new spiritual nature, for it is the direct object of a spiritual relish and appetite.[65]

Edward Taylor was more graphic when he commented,

> Lord put these nibbles then my mouth into
> And suckle me therewith I humbly pray,
> Then with this milk thy Spiritual Babe I'st grow,
> And these two milke pails shall themselves display
> Like to these pritty twins in pairs round neate
> And shall sing forth thy praise over this meate.[66]

A Christian dictionary defined breasts as follows:

> *without breasts,* as having yet no established Ministry.[67]

According to Thomas Hooker,

> that which makes the love of a husband increase toward his wife, is this, *Hee is satisfied with her breasts at all times, and then he comes to be ravished with her love:* If a husband has a loose heart, and will not content himself with the wife of his youth, but hath his back doors, and his goings out; this makes a breach of matrimonial affection; but when hee is satisfied with her breasts, he is ravished with her love; so hope hath an expectation of mercy, and is satisfied herewith.[68]

PLATE 66. Detail of the left panel of the Peter and Mary Tufts stone, 1702/03, Malden, Massachusetts. Slate. 30¼ x 26.

PLATE 67. Detail of the right panel of the Jonathan Remington stone, 1700, Cambridge, Massachusetts. Slate. 24¾ x 19.

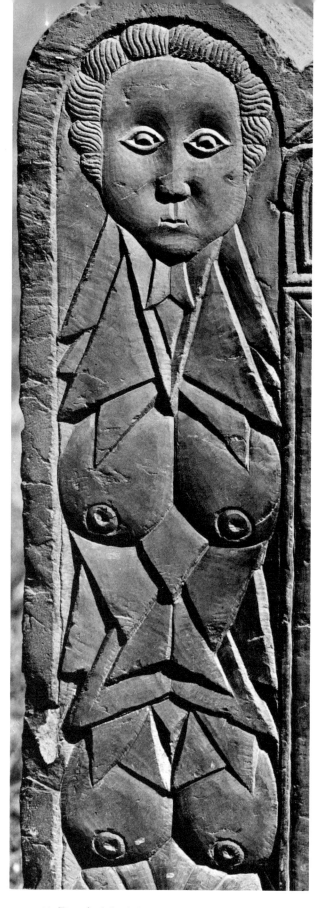

PLATE 68. Detail of the left panel of the Rebekah Bunker stone, 1709, Cambridge, Massachusetts. Slate. 19 x 16½.

PLATE 69. Detail of the right panel of the Rebekah Bunker stone, 1709, Cambridge, Massachusetts. Slate. 19 x 16½.

To the Puritan mind the love of God was conceived of in the most anthropomorphic terms, although the visual imagery was naturally more circumspect. Edward Taylor wrote,

> The Soul's the Womb. Christ the Spermodote
> And Saving Grace the seed cast thereunto . . .

> . . . Oh! let him kiss mee with his orall kisses.
> Should he but stop such acts of love and grace . . .
> Making dark Clouds mask up his brightsom face.[69]

Given these citations it is possible to interpret the pendantlike forms on the Bunker stone as either gourds or breasts. Certainly it can no longer be argued that the Puritan mind was too "Victorian" to indulge in such imagery.

An eros figure can be seen on the Clough stone, King's Chapel, Boston, Massachusetts (plate 70A), bringing a wreath of victory to an allegorical figure holding the anchor of hope and the palm of victory. Because the stone is badly damaged at the top, it is no longer possible to discover what, if anything, sat upon the fluted pilaster. Far more common was the use of the eros figure lofting toward heaven an emblem of the heart engraved with the name of the deceased. Such figures appear on the Lieutenant John Hunt stone, 1716, Rumford, Rhode Island (plates 70B, 71, 72, 73A), on the Captain Samuel Peck stone, 1736, Rehoboth, Massachusetts (plate 73B), and on the new Rebekah Tingley stone, 1790, South Attleboro, Massachusetts (plate 73C). A variant form where two eros figures flank a flowering urn may be seen on the Sarah Nisbett stone, 1698, Milford, Connecticut (plate 74). The emblem of the heart without the eros figures appears on the Sarah Long stone, 1674, Charlestown, Massachusetts (plate 75). This is the first extant heart emblem to appear on a New England gravestone. We know that in England and Europe[70] the emblem of the heart could have a variety of meanings, but in New England it appears to have been associated most closely with symbols of the soul in bliss and always in symbolic opposition to the imagery of death. On the John Holmes stone of 1728, Middleboro Center, Massachusetts (plate 76A), and on the Wilborah Washbun stone of 1743 in Kingston, Massachusetts (plate 76B), heart palmettes replace the mouth of death and seem to have been interchanged with the profile soul effigies superimposed over the face of death on the Gershem Holmes stone (plate 1A) and on the Elizabeth Bradford stone (plate

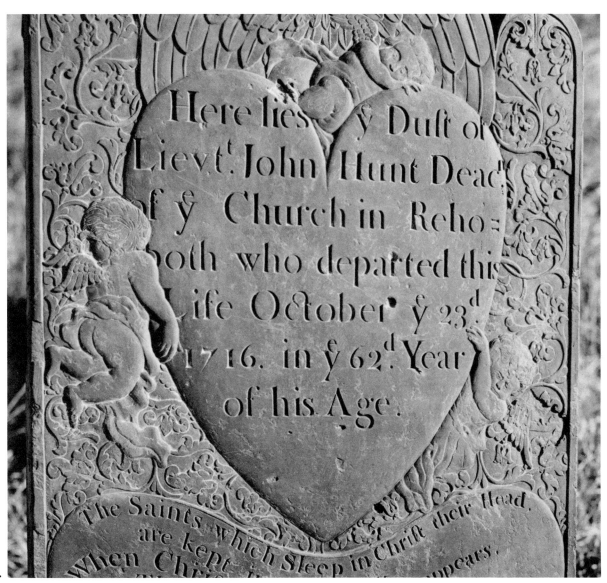

PLATE 70. A. Detail of the Benjamin Clough stone, King's Chapel, Boston, Massachusetts. Slate. 24 x 21½+.
B. Detail of the Lieutenant John Hunt stone, 1716, Rhode Island. Slate.

PLATE 71. Detail of putto on Hunt stone. See plate 70B.

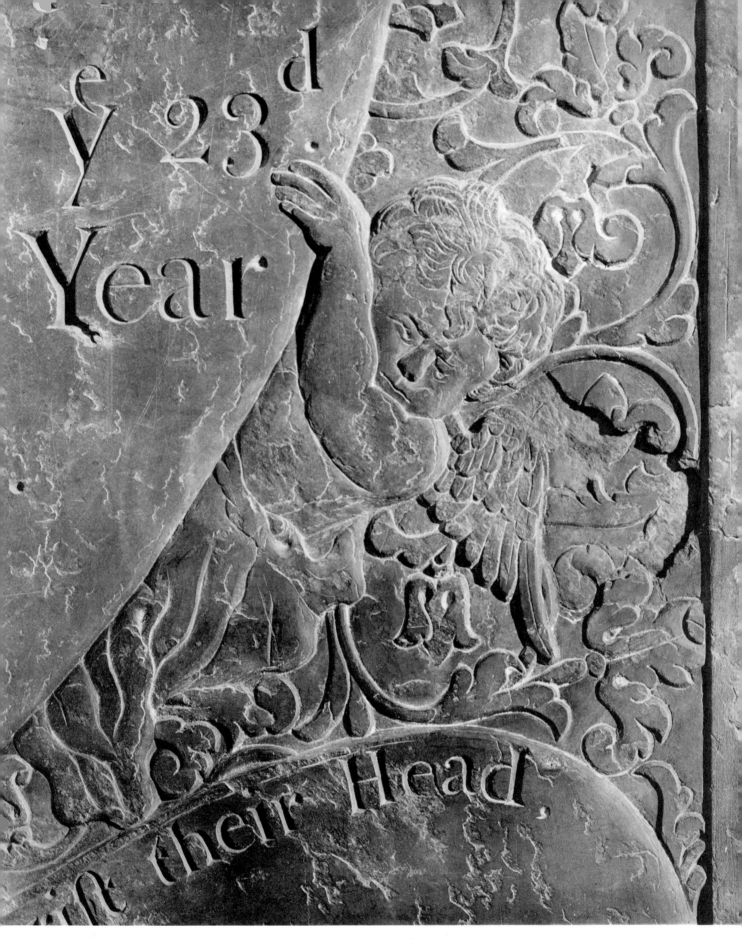

PLATE 72. Detail of putto on Hunt stone. See plate 70B.

A.

B.

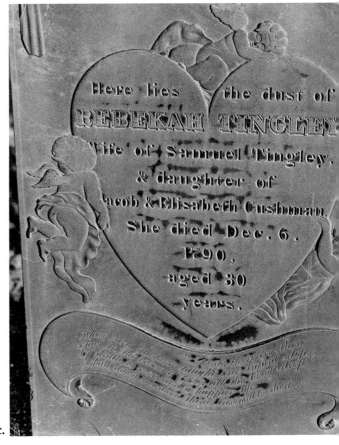

C.

PLATE 73. A. Detail of putto on Hunt stone. See plate 70B. B. Detail of the Captain Samuel Peck stone, 1736, Rehoboth, Massachusetts. Slate. c. Detail of the Rebekah Tingley stone, 1790, South Attleboro, Massachusetts. Slate. Stone probably cut in early 20th century after an 18th century model. Prototype probably the Peck stone in Rehoboth.

PLATE 74. Detail of the Sarah Nisbett stone, 1698, Milford, Connecticut. Slate.

SARAH LONG,
WIFE TO ZECHARIAH
LONG, AGED 38 YEARS
DECEASED JULY
TE 3
1 6 7 4

PLATE 75. Detail of the Sarah Long stone, 1674, Charlestown, Massachusetts. Slate. 27¼ x 24¼.

A.

B.

C.

PLATE 76. A. Detail of the John Holmes stone, 1728, Middleboro Center, Massachusetts. Slate. 18½ x 19. B. Detail of the Wilborah Washbun stone. See plate 1C. C. Detail of the Esther Sampson stone, 1782, Kingston, Massachusetts. Slate. 19¼ x 29½.

1B). On the Esther Sampson stone, 1782, Kingston, Massachusetts (plate 76c), a bower of hearts forms an arch over a winged death's head again suggesting an opposition of symbols.

It was far more usual, however, to find the emblem of the heart associated with soul effigies than contrasted to deaths' heads as on the John Felt stone, 1805, Rockingham, Vermont (plate 77A), where twin hearts embower a soul effigy, or on the Isaac Chalker stone, 1765, East Glastonbury, Connecticut (plate 77B), where a winged crowned effigy springs from a vine bent over with heart emblems. Moreover, on the Anna Hitchcock stone, 1795, Cheshire, Connecticut (plate 78), the body of the effigy is composed of a heart with another superimposed over it in line. On the Patience Watson stone of 1767, Plymouth, Massachusetts (plate 79), the effigy wears a heart-shaped locket as do the portrait effigies on the Elizabeth Morton stone, 1790 (plate 80A), and on the Mary Brown marker, 1782, (plate 80B) both in Plymouth, Massachusetts.

In summary then, the emblem of the heart was used as a shield within which the name of the deceased was cut, it was borne up toward heaven by eros figures, it was played off against the imagery of the death's head, it was used to flank and support effigies of the soul in bliss, it appeared as jewelry on portrait effigies, or finally, it sometimes formed the body of an effigy itself as on the Hitchcock marker of 1795 in Cheshire, Connecticut.

16. The Divine Fluid: Wine

BOTH the literature on and the visual symbols of wine are so abundant that it must be called one of the preoccupations of Puritanism. In the poetry of Edward Taylor the vine and the grape could either be the gracious soul or Christ, and in the visual symbols both variants are to be found. On the Nicholas Larrance stone of 1710, Charlestown, Massachusetts (plate 81), a soul effigy sucking upon a stem tops a foliated border panel made up of gourdlike shapes and heavy acanthus leaf forms. There is a similar stone in Copp's Hill, Boston, Massachusetts and another in Connecticut, the Captain James Lyman stone, 1769 (plate 82), which depicts three winged soul effigies sucking the end of a grapevine. What these symbols may have meant is not clear but they have something to do with the imbibing of wine or drink. On the same subject, Edward Taylor wrote,

> The Spirit of Grace is Graciously distilld,
> Thy mouth the Neck through which these spirits still.

A.

B.

PLATE 77. A. Detail of the John Felt stone, 1805, Rockingham, Vermont. Slate. 22½ x 33¼. B. Detail of the Isaac Chalker stone, 1765, East Glastonbury, Connecticut. See plate 3c.

PLATE 78. Detail of the Anna Hitchcock stone, 1795, Cheshire, Connecticut. Red sandstone. 33¾ x 50½.

PLATE 79. Detail of the Patience Watson stone, 1767, Plymouth, Massachusetts. Slate. 33 x 35.

A.

B.

PLATE 80. A. Detail of the Elizabeth Morton stone, 1790, Plymouth, Massachusetts. Slate. 22 x 27½. B. Detail of the Mary Brown stone, 1782, Plymouth, Massachusetts. Slate. 16¾ x 23.

PLATE 81. Detail of the Nicholas Larrance stone, 1710, Charlestown, Massachusetts. Slate. 26 x 19.

PLATE 82. The Captain James Lyman stone, 1769, Connecticut. Red sandstone.

My Soul thy Violl make, and therewith fill.[71]

Since it was a common belief that the spirit leaves the body through the mouth, and by the mouth Christ "distills" the spirit of grace into the just, it would seem likely that these difficult symbols make an oblique reference to wine symbolism, although the comparative and the literary evidence leave us little on which to base our opinions.[72] There are, however, areas of great clarity in wine symbolism. The symbolism of the vine was so important that Samuel Willard had to go to special lengths to clarify some of the basic issues,

> But though this union be truly spiritual, yet the Word of God gives us diverse carnal similitudes of it, for the help of our understandings, which we must warily apply to it; not grossly, but spiritually, remembering that every similitude hath something defective in it, and the spirit of God useth many, because no one can fully adumbrate it. It is compared to that of a *Vine* and its *Branches*, John 15. 1, 2, 4, 5, to note the closeness and connaturalness of it, and to let us understand, that by virtue of it, we derive all our life, and fruit from Christ, and receive the same sap of Grace from him, which is radicated in him. But yet there is this difference, the branches do grow naturally out of the Vine, and are of the same individual substance with it, whereas Christ and we are personally distinct, and we are put into him by an implanting, Rom. 6.5. *For if we have been planted together in the likeness of his death; we shall also in the likeness of his Resurrection.*[73]

Since the wine of Communion is pressed from the mystical vine, the matter was of prime concern for the Puritan and not to be taken lightly in the form of a similitude which could lead to error. Edward Taylor, however, was not so conservative when he wrote,

> This Spirituall Fare in Ordinances, and
> The Wine bled from the Holy Grape, and Vine
> Thats on the Table orderd by God's hand
> That Supper of the Lord, the feast Divine
> God's Gospel Priests this to that Table beare
> Where Saints are Guests and Angells waiters are.[74]

Wine symbolism was deeply rooted in New England. Edward Taylor knew and remembered John 15.1 when he wrote,

> Implant me as a branch in God's true vine
> And then my grape will yield thy Cup rich wine.[75]

John 15.1–5 reads,

> I AM the True vine, and my Father is the husbandman. Every branch in me that beareth not fruit he taketh away: and every *branch* that beareth fruit, he

purgeth it, that it may bring forth more fruit. Now ye are clean through the word which I have spoken unto you. Abide in me, and I in you. As the branch cannot bear fruit of itself, except it abide in the vine; no more can ye, except ye abide in me. I am the vine, ye *are* the branches: He that abideth in me, and I in him, the same bringeth forth much fruit: for without me ye can do nothing.

The mystical vision of Christ enlaced and coupled with the soul appeared time and time again in New England. Stones such as the Captain James Lyman marker, 1769 (plate 82), are very difficult to interpret. In this example, a crowned winged effigy releases the mystical vine from its mouth which then enlaces a cameo frame within which the name of the deceased has been carved. Twin heart emblems appear at the top and bottom of the cameo while to either side at the top of the stone twin crowned cherubim disgorge flowering plants from their mouths. Far more clear are the stones which develop the theme of sacramental symbolism such as the Deacon Matthew Rockwell marker, 1782, South Windsor, Connecticut (plates 83 and 84B), the Deacon Joseph Lothrop stone, 1788, (plate 84A) Tolland, Connecticut, and the Deacon Joseph West example, 1767, (plate 84C) again in Tolland. On the Rockwell variant two covered tankards are flanked by six cups. On the Lothrop example, a tankard appears with four cups, while on the West emblem no tankards appear at all but there are six cups flanking a rounded niche centered upon what I take to be a Communion table.

On the Rockwell stone, the meaning is further enhanced by the division of the stone into two horizontal tiers the bottom of which contains the tankards and the cups and the top a winged effigy with the initials "M. R." at either side, suggesting that the soul of Matthew Rockwell has been redeemed through the efficacy of the sacraments symbolized by the Communion service rendered below. It seems that stones cut for deacons, the men who cared for the meetinghouse silver, were the pretext for such symbolism and nowhere does an extant Communion service appear on a stone cut for anyone but a deacon. This fact does not diminish the power of the symbolism; it enhances it by demonstrating the carvers' conscious choice of the persons for whom such stones could properly be cut. A stone quite similar to the West marker (plate 85A), was cut for Timothy Williams, 1759, East Hartford, Connecticut (plate 85B), but in the latter case the Communion service has been omitted.

Symbols making a more direct reference to John 15.1 may be seen on the Deacon Daniel House stone, 1762, East Glastonbury, Con-

PLATE 83. The Deacon Matthew Rockwell stone, 1782, South Windsor, Connecticut. Red sandstone. 24¼ x 43.

A.

B.

C.

PLATE 84. A. Detail of the Deacon Joseph Lothrop stone, 1788, Tolland, Connecticut. Red sandstone. 23 x 45.
B. Detail of the Matthew Rockwell stone. See plate 83. C. Detail of the Deacon Joseph West stone, 1767,
Tolland, Connecticut. Red sandstone. 25 x 49.

A.

B.

PLATE 85. A. Detail of the Deacon Joseph West stone. See plate 84c. B. Detail of the Ensign Timothy Williams stone, 1759, East Hartford, Connecticut. Red sandstone. 25 x 41.

necticut (plate 86A), where a winged crowned effigy grows forth from a vine carved with emblems of the heart. It is significant to note that the grapes are conceived as part of the effigy rather than the vine suggesting that the mystical union between Christ and the soul is abiding together between the two. The soul has taken possession of Christ through the sacraments, and Christ of the soul through the vine in a picturing of the words "Abide in me and I in you." The symbolism is as profound as the carving is simple and naïve. On the Deacon Jonathan Smith stone, 1774, Hadley, Massachusetts (plate 86B), the mystical vine and a soul icon intertwine, but this time the hearts, the wings, and the crown formerly seen on the House stone have been omitted.

One need not assume that these most mystical symbols were reserved for deacons alone. The Elizabeth and William Hunt stones, 1797 and 1795, Northampton, Massachusetts (plates 87A and B), show two soul effigies bowered in a mystical vine. On the Elizabeth Hunt stone her arms reach out and clutch the vine to her while on the William Hunt variant the imagery is more passive and the arms remain at the sides. The Samuel and Mary Hinckley stones, 1792, Brookfield, Massachuetts (plates 88A and B), reveal further variants of the vine and soul icon theme. The soul image of Mary Hinckley is seen embowered in the mystical vine while the image of Samuel Hinckley is shown with the true vine bursting forth from his body. Another variant of the soul embowered in a vine may be seen on the Ephraim Walker stone, 1777, Brookfield, Massachusetts (plate 89), where the vine takes root at the base of the stone in a tree of life and snakes up the sides to canopy the effigy of the soul at the top. On the Pember family stone, 1783, Franklin, Connecticut (plate 90A), twin effigies are sheltered in a vine springing forth from what I take to be a palm tree. A more conventional interweaving of the soul in the mystical vine may be seen on the Sarah Hubbell stone. 1797, Bennington, Vermont (plate 90B).

In addition to appearing entwined with effigies of the soul, the vine theme was also used as a border panel on such stones as the Lieutenant John Hescy marker of 1689, Wakefield, Massachusetts (plates 91A and B), and on the Elijah Sadd stone, 1756, South Windsor, Connecticut(plates 91C and D).

A.

B.

PLATE 86. A. Detail of the Daniel House stone, 1762, East Glastonbury, Connecticut. See plate 3D. B. Detail of the Deacon Jonathan Smith stone, 1774, Hadley, Massachusetts. Red sandstone. 22 x 33.

A.

B.

PLATE 87. A. Detail of the Elizabeth Hunt stone, 1797, Northampton, Massachusetts. White marble. 22½ x 37½.
B. Detail of the William Hunt stone, 1795, Northampton, Massachusetts. White marble. 22 x 37½.

PLATE 88. A. Detail of the Samuel Hinckley stone, 1792, Brookfield, Massachusetts. White marble. 22½ x 37.
B. Detail of the Mary Hinckley stone, 1792, Brookfield, Massachusetts. White marble. 21¼ x 35.

PLATE 89. The Ephraim Walker stone, 1777, Brookfield, Massachusetts. Quartzite. 31 x 65.

A.

B.

PLATE 90. A. Detail of the Pember family stone, 1783, Franklin, Connecticut. Granite. B. Detail of the Sarah Hubbell stone, 1797, Bennington, Vermont. White marble. 27¾ x 56½.

PLATE 91. A. and B. Details of the Lieutenant John Hescy stone, 1689, Wakefield, Massachusetts. Slate. 27½ x 22.
C. and D. Details of the border panels of the Elijah Sadd stone, 1756, South Windsor, Connecticut. Red sandstone. 15 x 19. E. Detail of the Eliakim Hayden stone, 1797, Essex, Connecticut. Red sandstone.

17. Typological Symbols

AFTER Philo perfected the typological and allegorical interpretation of the Old Testament, Christians were not slow in picking up and using his method for their own purposes; thus many of the figures of the Old Testament became types prefigured in the New. The theory of types was refined throughout the Christian era until in the 17th century Benjamin Keach saw so many layers in the Scriptures that he had scarcely invented a category before another became necessary.[76]

The Puritans were not concerned about the theory of types, but Jonathan Edwards flirted with it[77] and the Eliakim Hayden stone, 1797, Essex, Connecticut (plate 91E), may be one of the indirect results. It is the only typological stone in New England.

In a shield the ark of Noah may be seen in the lower zone while in the upper portions a dove with a "green branch" is caught within the symbol of the cross. Topping the shield are two almond shapes which may be interpreted as the eyes of God. The epitaph reads,

As in Adam, all mankinde
Did guilt and Death Derive
So by the Righteousness of Christ
Shall all be made alive.[78]

Just as the symbol cites both the New and the Old Testaments, so does the epitaph. Noah was traditionally a type of Christ and since the direct symbolizing of Christ was improper in New England, the ark of Noah stood for the old vehicle of salvation as the cross stands for the new. The ark may be seen in the lower band and the cross in the top. The dove thus becomes both a theme of the Noah story and the symbol for the descent of the Holy Spirit. Adam brought death into the world of the Old Testament, and Noah saved mankind; but as mankind was still under the curse of death, Christ brought the hope of eternity.

18. Cosmological Symbols: The Sun, the Moon, and the Stars

ON the Susannah Jayne stone, 1776, Marblehead, Massachusetts (plate 92A), a skeleton laureled in victory and wrapped in a winding cloth holds the orbs of the sun and the moon in his hands, while on the Seth Sumner stone of 1771 in Milton, Massachusetts (plate 92B), two winged cherubim are flanked by celestial symbols of the sun, the moon, and the stars. Excepting these stones and several others like them, where the meaning of the cosmological symbols is not altogether clear,

A.

B.

PLATE 92. A. Detail of the Susannah Jayne stone. See plate 6. B. Detail of the Seth Sumner stone, 1771, Milton, Massachusetts. Slate.

the use of sun orbs and stars had a rather specific meaning on the gravestones. Jonathan Edwards wrote,

> The Different glory of the sun, the moon, and the stars represents the different glory of Christ and the glorified saints.[79]

On the Sarah Allen stone, 1785, Bristol, Rhode Island (plate 93A), a radiant sun blows a horn of Resurrection as smaller suns arise on either side. The legend carved into the stone reads "Saints Arising," suggesting that the smaller suns are to be taken as images of the true saints. If this interpretation of the Allen stone is correct then we have reason to associate the myriad carved New England suns with images of glorified souls. Souls as suns appear on the Lane family stone, 1791, Rockingham, Vermont (plate 93B) (note the association of the sun-soul symbol with the heart emblem), on the William Kentfield stone, 1777, Belchertown, Massachusetts (plate 94A), on the Theodotia Bard stone, 1790, again in Belchertown (plate 94B), on the Love Bakus stone, 1778, (plate 95A), on the Priscilla Huntington stone, 1742–1743, (plate 95B), both in Norwichtown, Connecticut, on the Margaret Campbell stone, 1779, Rockingham, Vermont (plate 96A), and on the Chad Brown replacement stone cut in 1792 (plate 96B), Providence, Rhode Island. In the latter case there is some question as to whether the image of the sun is a soul-sun effigy, or a more simple emblem of the Resurrection.

Stars were often associated both with sun-soul effigies or with the more common soul icons as backgrounds suggesting celestial abodes. The Anna Webb stone, 1805, Scotland, Connecticut (plate 97A), shows a soul effigy surrounded by bands of clouds with three stars further intimating a heavenly setting, while on the Samuel Walker stone of 1798, Rockingham, Vermont (plate 97B), the banked clouds are omitted, the stars remain in the form of six-pointed rosettes, and the soul effigy has been transformed into a sun-soul orb engraved with anthropomorphic features.

The symbols of the sun, the moon, and the stars were also grouped together with cosmological significance as on the Hannah Huntington stone, 1746, Norwichtown, Connecticut (plate 98). In this example a sun-soul effigy can be seen rising toward heaven while just beneath it a half-dome topped with a finial and engraved with emblems of the sun, the moon, and the stars may be seen flanked by grapevines. The verse cut into the stone reads,

> Death to fill this Narrow space in yonder Dome Made a Vast empty Place.

A.

B.

PLATE 93. A. Detail of the Sarah Allen stone, 1785, Bristol, Rhode Island. Slate. B. Detail of the Lane family stone, 1791, Rockingham, Vermont. Slate. 25¼ x 36¾.

A.

B.

PLATE 94. A. Detail of the William Kentfield stone, 1777, Belchertown, Massachusetts. Granite. 17 x 23½. B. Detail of the Theodotia Bard stone, 1790, Belchertown, Massachusetts. Slate. 19¾ x 21.

A.

B.

PLATE 95. A. Detail of the Love Backus stone, 1778, Norwichtown, Connecticut. Schist. 23¼ x 23½. B. Detail of the Priscila Huntington stone, 1742/43, Norwichtown, Connecticut. Granite.

A.

B.

PLATE 96. A. Detail of the Margaret Campbell stone, 1779, Rockingham, Vermont. Slate. 20¼ x 38. B. Detail of the Chad Brown stone re-cut in 1792, Providence, Rhode Island. Slate. 20¾ x 40¼.

A.

B.

PLATE 97. A. Detail of the Anna Webb stone, 1805, Scotland, Connecticut. Granite. 30¾ x 60. B. Detail of the Samuel Walker stone, 1798, Rockingham, Vermont. Slate. 23¼ x 36.

PLATE 98. The Hannah Huntington stone, 1746, Norwichtown, Connecticut. Granite. 30¾ x 32½.

I have little doubt that the epitaph and the symbols are making a crude reference to the principle of plenitude.[80]

The departure of a soul to fill a place in the heavens left an empty space in the world of becoming and perishing. The reference to the principle of the great chain of being makes these stones extraordinarily interesting. Aristotle said, and St. Thomas Aquinas provisionally claimed, that the goodness of the species transcended the goodness of the individual as form transcends matter. But according to Aquinas the perfection of the universe requires both a multitude of species and individuals.[81]

Although the Reformation was anti-Rome, Christian metaphysics were a fixture of New England well into the 19th century. The Puritans never abandoned a Medieval way of looking at the universe. Classical cosmology, although tempered by the Middle Ages and the Renaissance, and modified by Reformation thinkers, did not wither away in New England until long after the last symbolic stones were cut. Puritan divines like Cotton Mather read Newton's works and tried to incorporate the new physics into a cosmology derived from the Scholastics.

The belief in the great chain of being seems to have been so strong that it was quoted by a rural carver in vernacular form.

The loss of a single soul damaged the delicate links in the great chain of being. Jonathan Edwards was only voicing an opinion derived from the Scholastics when he said,

> Again it is apparent and allowed that there is a great and remarkable analogy in God's works. There is a wonderful resemblance in the effects which God produces, and constantaneity in his manner of working in one thing and another throughout all nature. It is very observable in the visible world; therefore it is allowed that God does purposely make and order one thing to be in agreeableness and harmony with another. And if so, why should we not suppose that He makes the inferior in imitation of the superior, the material of the spiritual, on purpose to have a resemblance and shadow of them? We see that even in the material world, God makes one part of it to agree strangely with another, and why is it not reasonable to suppose He makes the whole as a shadow of the spiritual world?[82]

Aquinas said,

> Since it belongs to the divine providence that order be preserved in the world, and since suitable order consists in a proportionate descent from the highest to the lowest, it is proper that the divine providence should reach the most distant thing according to a certain proportion.[83]

While the Puritan did not doubt the existence of the great chain of being, he followed Scotus rather than Aquinas when it came to a suitable theory of analogy. For our purposes it need only be stated that for the Puritans these truths were self-evident. Tedious proofs were not needed to convince the citizen of Norwichtown that the symbol on the Huntington stone was indeed appropriate. It would be foolish to claim that the citizens of Norwichtown misinterpreted the theory of plenitude, which applies to species and classes rather than to individuals within classes, and thereby forfeited meaning. An old idea was rather invested with new and sentimental meaning. Further, the symbol would have been unintelligible without a background in Christian cosmology, but cosmology was simply not enough to contain the feelings of New Englanders in the face of death and so they turned to the symbol. In a complicated shift of meaning an old theory burst forth in the language of form in rural Norwichtown, Connecticut.

19. The Scriptures and the Deity

THE Puritans believed that revelation came only through the Word and the Word was contained in the Scriptures. Like many of the denominations spawned by the Reformation, the Puritans believed that the descent of the Holy Spirit came only through Scripture and not separate from it. It would then seem likely that the importance of the Scriptures would be shadowed in the carved symbols, but this was not actually the case. Although we do find a book cut on gravestones from time to time, although we can safely assume that the book was the Bible, it was by no means a popular symbol and found only limited use. On the Colonel Jonas Clark stone, 1770 (plate 99), a winged angel holds a book up to an archangel who trumpets forth the Resurrection. The meaning of the stone seems to be clear: it is through Scripture that man may hope to partake in the Resurrection of the flesh on Judgment Day.

Twin portrait effigies appear on the Christiana Cook stone, 1796, Kingston, Massachusetts (plates 100 and 101), under canopies holding emblems of death and immortality.[84] In one, the hands hold an hourglass and a thick hoop which might represent a wreath of victory, while in the other representation the hands hold an hourglass and an opened book, probably the Scriptures. The hourglasses symbolize the corruption and decay of the flesh while the book and what I take to be a wreath of victory symbolize the victory of the soul over Time. On the Reverend Jonathan Pierpont stone, 1709, Wakefield, Massachusetts (plate 102), a carefully carved portrait effigy appears in clerical collar

PLATE 99. Detail of the Colonel Jonas Clark stone, 1770, Chelmsford, Massachusetts. Slate.

PLATE 100. Detail of the left cameo of the Christiana Cook stone, 1796, Kingston, Massachusetts. Slate. 27¼ x
42½.

PLATE 101. Detail of the right cameo of the Christiana Cook stone, 1796, Kingston, Massachusetts. Slate. 27¼ x 42½.

PLATE 102. Detail of the Reverend Jonathan Pierpont stone, Wakefield, Massachusetts. Slate. See plate 28A.

clutching an open book, probably a Bible. On the Lydia Peaslee stone, 1741, Haverhill, Massachusetts (plate 103), the body of the abstract effigy seems to be formed of two tablets which might represent the wisdom of the Old Testament, or perhaps arched doorways. The meaning here is by no means certain.

Only one direct representation of God the Father is known to exist in New England. It was cut on the Charles Bardin stone, 1773, Newport, Rhode Island (plate 104A). The stone is signed with the initials "J. B." for John Bull of Newport and Middletown. Indirect representations occur more frequently. The hand of God appears on about a dozen stones in Norwichtown, Norwich, Pachaug, Durham, and Middlefield Center, Connecticut. The almond-shaped footstones found in the Connecticut Valley with "pupils" of six-pointed rosettes facing in over the grave might be interpreted as the eyes of God; see the Abigail Lothrop stone, 1734, Norwichtown, Connecticut (plate 104B). Certainly the almond-shaped "eyes" on the Hayden stone in Essex, Connecticut (plate 91E), might be interpreted as the eyes of God. Christ himself never appeared directly but on the Allen stone (plate 93A) in Bristol, Rhode Island, the trumpeter in the guise of the sun might be interpreted as the Son of Righteousness calling the dead from their graves.

20. Symbols of the Soul's Flight to Heaven and the Soul in Paradise

THE Puritan died in the hope that his soul would rise to heaven and there be glorified.

The Betsy Shaw stone, 1795, Plymouth, Massachusetts (plate 105A), shows a brick-based slab tomb with a tree to the right. Hovering just above the tomb is a winged effigy of Mrs. Shaw leaving her earthly abode. On the Reverend Samuel Ruggles stone, 1749, Billerica, Massachusetts (plate 105B), a cameo portrait of Reverend Ruggles wings its way toward eternal bliss. On the Sarah Antram stone dated 1732 in Providence, Rhode Island (plate 106A), a host of angels escorts a soul to the bosom of Abraham. Samuel Willard had the following to say about the flight of the soul to heaven,

> THE soul shall have a Glorious Convoy to transport it to the place of its endless abode. It shall be honorably and safely Guarded thither by the Holy Angels. We read in Luke 16.22 And it came to pass that the beggar died and was carried by the Angels into Abraham's bosom.[85]

On the Whiting family stone, 1781, Rockingham, Vermont (plate

PLATE 103. Detail of the Lydia Peaslee stone, 1741, Haverhill, Massachusetts. Schist. 26 x 27½.

A.

B.

PLATE 104. A. Detail of the Charles Bardin stone, 1773, Newport, Rhode Island. Slate. Signed with the initials 'J. B.,' probably for John Bull. B. Details of the Abigail Lothrop footstone, 1734, Norwichtown, Connecticut. Granite. 21 x 14.

A.

B.

PLATE 105. A. Detail of the Betsy Shaw stone, 1795, Plymouth, Massachusetts. Slate. 22¼ x 36. B. Detail of Rev. Samuel Ruggles stone, 1749, Billerica, Massachusetts. Slate. 32¾ x 47¾.

A.

B.

PLATE 106. A. Detail of the Sarah Antram stone, 1732, Providence, Rhode Island. Granite? B. Detail of the Whiting family stone, 1781, Rockingham, Vermont. Slate.

106B), two sun-soul orbs pierce the heavens leaving "vapor trails" behind in their celestial wake, while on the Robert Cleave stone, 1730, Portland, Connecticut (plate 107), a puffy bald effigy soars heavenward on what can only be described as "bees" wings. On the unique Lucinda Day stone, 1800, Chester, Vermont (plate 108), the soul is carried toward eternal bliss in the belly of an eagle reminding us of a vernacular simplification of the famous apotheosis of the Emperor Titus on the inner central coffer of the arch of Titus in Rome (plate 109).

The epitaph on the Buckland White stone, 1806, East Hartford, Connecticut, reads,

> In life belov'd now lost to mortal Friends
> The Soul Immortal instantly Ascends
> On Seraphs wings by rapid strides it flies
> Wafted to its God above the skies.[86]

The seraph-winged effigies on the Manning stone, 1750, Norwichtown, Connecticut (plate 110A), on the *ca.* 1730 Rowley, Massachusetts, fragment (plate 110B), and on the Olive Storrs stone, 1785, Mansfield Center, Connecticut (plate 110C), seem to be invoking the spirit of the White epitaph as they wing their way heavenward; while the orb-enclosed crowned effigy on the James Cowles stone, 1789, Farmington, Connecticut (plate 111), calls to mind the common poetic metaphor associating the graceful soul with the form of a perfect sphere or circle. Edward Taylor wrote,

> Three Shining Suns rise in thy Chrystall Skies
> Of Mankinde Orbs, and Orbs Angelicall.
> Whose Rayes out Shine all pimping Stars that rise
> Within these Spheres and Circuite through them all.
> These do evigorate all Action done
> By men and Angells right, wherein they run.[87]
>
> In that thy hands this golden Orb is made
> This Orbe is emblem of the Sphere of Grace.[88]

Effigies apparently secured in celestial bliss may be seen on the Deborah Samson stone, 1769, Kingston, Massachusetts (plate 112A), by virtue of the tree of life tiara; on the Submit Lothrop stone, 1794, Vernon Center, Connecticut (plate 112B), by the addition of the torso and arms to the winged effigy suggesting the unity of body and soul in heaven; on the Mercy Buliod stone, 1771, Newport, Rhode Island

PLATE 107. Detail of the Robert Cleave stone, 1730, Portland, Connecticut. Red sandstone. 18½ x 23.

PLATE 108. Detail of the Lucinda Day stone, 1800, Chester, Vermont. Slate. 21 x 23.

PLATE 109. Detail of the central coffer of the Arch of Titus in Rome, ca. A.D. 81. Apotheosis of Emperor Titus.

A.

B.

C.

PLATE 110. A. Detail of the Manning children stone, 1750, Norwichtown, Connecticut. Granite. 28¼ x 49. B. Detail of a slate fragment, probably cut about 1730-1740 in Rowley, Massachusetts. C. Detail of the Olive Storrs stone, 1785, Mansfield Center, Connecticut. Granite. 28½ x 42½.

PLATE 111. Detail of the James Cowles stone, 1789, Farmington, Connecticut. Red sandstone. 24 x 49½.

PLATE 112. A. Detail of the Deborah Samson stone, 1769, Kingston, Massachusetts. Slate. 24 x 27¼. B. Detail of the Submit Lothrop stone, 1794, Vernon Center, Connecticut. Red sandstone.

(plate 113A); by virtue of the banded clouds, the inclusion of bodies, the incorporation of wings, and the use of a tiara; and on the Hannah Jackson stone, 1763, Plymouth, Massachusetts (plate 113B), by virtue of the portrait effigy appearing beneath a bank of stars and clouds.

The literature on the subject of the glorification of the soul and its subsequent flight to heaven is copious. Thomas Foxcroft said,

> Again believers die, that their *Bodies* may partake of a Glorious *Resurrection* . . . at the end of the present Life will [God] have them in part (as to the soul) admitted to the Possession of the Just, till the great and last Day, when there shall be a more public and complete Retribution.

> So hath God ordained that the Believers *Glorification* shall not be intirely perfected without the Intervening of a Temporal Dissolution; which, tho it not be any hindrance to His real Blessedness, yet is the Delay of it's proper perfection. This must not be expected till the Restitution of all Things, in the day of Judgment. When that arrives, then will our Declarative justification be complete in every point; and the Application of the Covenant of Grace receive its finishing Stroke, in the full Accomplishment of all the Promises.[89]

Cotton Mather wrote,

> But we are passing into an *Invisible World*. An Hades is to be looked into. But what then becomes of us? We then *Fly away to another world*. This expression, *we fly away*; it seems an Allusion to the Condition of a Bird, which has been hatching its full time. When the *Time* for it arrives, the *Shell breaks* and the *Bird* then does *Fly Away*. Our Death is the breaking of the *Shell*. And we have an Immortal Spirit in us, which is, *We*, and in this we *Fly away*.[90]

Mather calls the soul a bird and refers to the body as a shell keeping it captive. In another passage he refers to the soul escaping the fowlers of Satan who attempt to snare it. It reads,

> He is *flown* where he shall not only have all the Tears wiped from his Eyes, but also be *Free* from that which was the most bitter of all things that breached his *Tears*, never Sin any more; where the *Lusts of the Flesh* are dropt with the Flesh; where he may defy the Temptations of *Satan*, and sing with Triumph, *My Soul is escaped as a Bird out of the snare of the Fowlers; the snare is broken, and I am escaped*. He is flown *where he sits and feeds on the Tree of Life, and hears things that cannot be uttered*, and he does converse with God and *enjoy* Heavenly *Satisfactions* which no *Heart* on earth can soar high enough to conceive.[91]

The equating of the soul with the image of a bird was a common European metaphor in the 17th century and it is not surprising that the New Englander brought it to the new world with him.[92] For example,

A.

B.

PLATE 113. A. Detail of the Mercy Buliod stone, 1771, Newport, Rhode Island. Slate. Signed by John Stevens, Jr.
B. Detail of the Hannah Jackson stone, 1763, Plymouth, Massachusetts. Red sandstone. 20 x 23.

an emblem from Quarles illustrating Psalm 142.7 shows an angel releasing a soul from a wicker cage. The Pamela Munro stone, 1776, Lexington, Massachusetts (plate 114A), shows two soul doves seeking divine food from a flowering tree of life. The epitaph on the Elah Camp stone, 1787, Durham, Connecticut, mentioned the cage and implied an image of the flight of a bird. The verse reads,

> Death is to us a sweet repose;
> The bud was Op'd to show the rose;
> The cage was broke to let us fly
> and build our happy nests on high.[93]

The Mary Green stone, 1715, Newport, Rhode Island (plate 114B), shows two birds flanking a bowl in which spheroid objects are pyramided. Three birds nest in the trees of life on the Job and William Harris stone (plates 115A and B), Providence, Rhode Island, and we have already mentioned the birds resting atop the abstract palm trees on the Martha Welch stone (plates 50 and 51). Similar birds appear on the Doctor Benjamin Wheate stone, 1750, and on the Benjamin Lord tomb, 1784, both in Norwichtown, Connecticut. Doves formed in a series of delicate calligraphic strokes may be seen on the Ann Cunningham stone, 1775, Spencer, Massachusetts (plates 116 and 117), while on the Nathan Lester stone, 1773, Pachaug, Connecticut (plate 118A), they appear flanking a crown hovering above the head of a heavily coiffed effigy. On the Robert Cutler stone, 1761, Brookfield, Massachusetts (plate 118B), twin birds flutter down onto the shoulders of an effigy. The theme of the two birds flanking a soul effigy, such as the ones in plates 118A and B, first appeared in New England as early as 1674 on the Thomas Hart stone (plate 119B), Ipswich, Massachusetts, where they take the abstract form of double outlined birds touching beaks just above the central effigy. On the Sarya Wilcom stone of 1705 in Rowley, Massachusetts (plate 119A), they appear with heavier bodies flanking a crowned effigy. Such representations were quite common in northern Massachusetts and eastern Connecticut until at least 1730 (see plates 214 and 221).

21. Souls and Angels

IT is often difficult to distinguish between created angels and what we have been calling soul effigies, indeed, the Puritan did not always seem to keep his ideas about the two clearly distinguished and areas of vagueness naturally crept into the symbolism. For example, the epi-

PLATE 114. A. Detail of the Pamela Munro stone, 1770, Lexington, Massachusetts. Slate. 15 x 21. B. The Mary Green stone, 1715, Newport, Rhode Island. Slate.

A.

B.

PLATE 115. A. Detail of the Job Harris stone, 1729, Providence, Rhode Island. Slate. 24¼ x 27¾. B. Detail of the William Harris stone, 1725/26, Providence, Rhode Island. Slate. 23 x 25¼.

PLATE 116. Detail of the left panel of the Ann Cunningham stone, 1775, Spencer, Massachusetts. Slate. 22 x 25.

PLATE 117. Detail of the right panel of the Ann Cunningham stone, 1775, Spencer, Massachusetts. Slate. 22 x 25.

PLATE 118. A. Detail of the John Lester stone, 1773, Pachaug, Connecticut. Red sandstone. 32½ x 28. B. Detail of the Robert Cutler stone, 1761, Brookfield, Massachusetts. Slate or schist. 30 x 27.

A.

B.

PLATE 119. A. Detail of the Sarya Wilcom stone, 1705, Rowley, Massachusetts. Schist. 21¼ x 21¼. B. Detail of the Thomas Hart stone, 1674, Ipswich, Massachusetts. Schist. 17½ x 19.

taph on the Abigail Barber stone, Hebron, Connecticut, reads,

> In faith she died in dust she lies,
> But Hope pursues her to the skies,
> And sees her Angel spirit blest
> In mansions of eternal rest.[94]

It can thus be assumed that glorified souls become angelic bodies but they are by no means the equals of the created angels. Sometimes the two can be distinguished from one another but more often than not the stones themselves are equivocal. There is no real doubt that the angels bearing the Antram soul to heaven are not representations of glorified souls but of created angels performing their proper duties (plate 106A). There is also little doubt that the trumpeting figures in plate 30 are angels of the Resurrection rather than representations of glorified souls. Moreover, the seminude figures on the Allen stone (plates 32 and 33) are assuredly meant to be allegorical figures of the Resurrection rather than picturings of the soul in bliss. Conversely, there can be no question that the initials "M. R." cut into Matthew Rockwell stone (plate 83) just below and to either side of the winged effigy tell us in no uncertain terms that we are looking at the angelic soul of Mr. Rockwell rather than at a created angel. It is also clear that the four small suns arising on the Allen stone (plate 93A) are to be taken as representations of the soul as celestial suns. But between these clear-cut extremes of symbolization there are many images which are difficult to place in either camp except by reference to comparative data. Were it not for the fact that the figure of the guardian angel was a commonly held belief in the literary tradition of colonial New England, I would not hesitate to cast most of the imagery on the side of the glorified souls rather than on the side of the created angels.

We are lucky to have had in Increase Mather, 1639–1723, the Boston minister and author, a distinguished angelographer.[95] An angelography is a commentary on the function, hierarchy, and history of angels. According to Mather angels are,

> *Second Beings,* they receive whatever they are, their very Being, and all from another. Some of the Heathen philosophers supposd Angels to be co-Eternal with the Great God. But this is not so, nor is that possible to be true. There can be but one first, but one Eternal Being.[96]

Mather went on to say that angels were the creations of God and the instruments of His will,

Man is the most Excellent creature in this lower world; but he is Inferior to the Angels, and so was in his first and best estate. Psal. 8.5. "He *was made lower than the Angels.*"[97]

In addition there were both good and bad angels. Mather wrote,

> . . . there are Angels who are called *Evile Spirits and Devils.*
> . . . Hence the Scripture speaks of the *Devil and His Angels.*
> . . . there are *Evil Angels,* as well as good, and they are (though against their will) at the command of God.[98]

According to Mather, the function of evil angels was to tempt man while the function of good angels was to save him from temptation. He wrote,

> Now the Scripture is express and clear, that all the Angels of Heaven (not one excepted) are made use of to promote the Salvation and the Elect of God. Heb. 1.14, 33.[99]

Mather amplified the theme as follows,

> 11. The *Second Thing* to be inquired into is, *What benefit they that fear God, do receive by the Ministry of Holy Angels?*
> FOR ANSWER
> 1. *They are by them preserved from many Evils, that otherwise would befall them.* They do as a guard stand between them and many dangers, they are ready to overtake them. The Angels of Heaven are Nurses to the Children of God. Psal. 91.11, 12. *He shall give his Angels charge over thee and they shall bear thee in their hands, least thou dash thy foot against a Stone.* As a nurse holds the child she hath the care and charge of, in her armes; so they that fear the Lord, are kept from many a fall, preserved from many a hurt and blow, that would light upon them, did not the Angels look after them. Hence the fearers of God have a special protection in Journies, that they undertake according to His will. . . . Therefore the Angels of Heaven are always about them, to protect and preserve them, from the mischiefs, that their Spiritual and Invisible enemies are designing against them. The Devils are powerful enemies: but the good Angels are more powerful than they: Michael and his Angels are more powerful than *Satan* and his Angels.[100]

The Puritans were tempted from the cradle to the grave; but for the protection of the angels, some might have fallen. Mather wrote,

> . . . Throughout the whole course of their lives, from the Cradle to the Grave, Angels are Charged with them . . . The Devil doth romp about the Elect of God whilst they are in their swaddling cloths: But they have Holy Angels to protect them from the rage of Hell.[101]

According to Mather the guardian angels stayed with the elect until the day of general Resurrection which might mean that their use on New England gravestones would have been sanctioned by traditional belief. Mather wrote,

> Consider, if we fear God, the Angels will not forsake us at death. They will be with us all our lives long; yea, and at and after death too: when we must forsake all the world; when our Bodies and Souls must part for a time; when our Souls forsake our Bodies; the blessed Angels will not leave us, until they have brought us into the presence of Christ in Glory. . . . When ye fall, that is, when ye die, or cease to be in this world; *they may receive you*, that is to say, that they whose office it is to receive you, namely the Holy Angels, that they may receive your Souls into their Arms, and carry them upon their wings into everlasting Habitations.[102]

The traditional belief in the function of guardian angels was so strong in New England that from a review of the literary sources alone we would be tempted to interpret the imagery as this would indicate. It is my opinion, however, that the evidence of the stones themselves speaks as strongly as the literary data and we must take both sides of the argument into account. The problem is indeed a thorny one. I suspect that the imagery was in most cases a blend of angelic representations and that the stonecarvers and the patrons for whom they cut the stones did not often make any clear-cut distinctions between created angels and glorfiied souls and would have thought such distinctions quite academic.

22. *Geometric Rosettes*

ROSETTES appear on New England gravestones with such persistence that were it not for the internal evidence it could be assumed that they were used merely as space fillers. Such does not seem to have been the case, but the exact significance of the New England families of rosettes remains a vexing problem both because of their abstractness and the total lack of literary evidence pertaining to them.

Following the logic of the stones themselves we find that they were almost always used in conjunction with the image of the soul effigy and at times even replaced it.

Rosettes can be divided into a number of classes including the eight-, six-, and four-pointed variants, their cousins the wedges and webs, and the more distant but still related coils and whirls. Other relations, such as the simple disc and the bull's eye, surface only rarely. Most common of all are the six-pointed rosettes which appear on the Hannah Huntington stone, 1746, Norwichtown, Connecticut (plate

98), as geometric vines climbing the border panels and as large "wheels" buoying up the central winged effigy. On the Abigail Lothrop stone, 1734, again in Norwichtown (plate 104B), a six-pointed rosette forms the pupil of an "eye." Variants may be found in Palmer Center, Massachusetts. Rosettes set within rosettes appear on the Jonathan Worster stone, 1754, Harvard, Massachusetts (plate 219), while conventional rosettes may be seen on the Meriah Kilborn marker, 1710, Rowley, Massachusetts (plate 120B), on the Susanna Scott stone, 1719, again in Rowley (plate 121A), and on the Thomas Lovall stone, 1718, Ipswich, Massachusetts (plate 121B).

Sexpartite wedge rosettes appear on the Ephraim Walker marker, 1777, Brookfield, Massachusetts (plate 89), octapartite variants on the Hanah Johnson stone, 1717, Rowley (plate 221A). Quadripartite variations appear on the Joanne —— fragment ca. 1720–1730, Norwichtown, Connecticut (plate 221B).

Quadripartite web rosettes reveal themselves on the Susanna Scott marker, 1719, Rowley (plate 121A), and in octapartite form on the John White stone, 1668, Haverhill, Massachusetts (plate 209).

Coils appear on the Jonathan Worster stone, 1754, Harvard, Massachusetts (plate 219), in the form of vine tendrils climbing the border panels and on the Rebekah Worster marker of 1772 in the same burial ground (plate 220), as climbing tendrils set within leaves. Coils made up of double outlines may be seen on the Martha Fuller stone, 1785, Hebron, Connecticut (plate 124B).

On the Meriah Kilborn stone (plate 120A), a whirl rosette presses downward upon a distressed soul effigy while on the Abigail Merick footstone, Glastonbury, Connecticut (plate 123B), another whirl is borne heavenward on delicate wings.

Only the six-pointed rosette and the whirls had close associations with the motif of the soul effigy. On the Hulda Curtis stone, 1765, (plate 122A), and again on the Pixlee family marker, 1776, (plate 122B), both in Stratford, Connecticut, six-pointed rosettes are alternated with anthropomorphic discs of the same approximate size. We know from stones such as the Pecker family marker of 1727 (plate 122C), Haverhill, Massachusetts, that these small geometric discs were often meant to suggest the effigies of children, as the legend "twins" cut above the stone denotes. Indeed, we know from the epitaphs of the Curtis and Pixlee stones that the former was interred with one child while the latter was buried with two, and all three children are represented as anthropomorphic discs. Hence the six-pointed rosette could

A.

B.

PLATE 120. A. and B. Details of the Meriah Kilborn stone, 1710, Rowley, Massachusetts. Schist. 17¼ x 15.

A.

B.

PLATE 121. A. Detail of the Susanna Scott stone, 1719, Rowley, Massachusetts. Schist. 21 x 23½. B. Detail of the Thomas Lovell stone, 1718, Ipswich, Massachusetts. Schist. 23¾ x 28½.

A.

B.

C.

PLATE 122. A. Detail of the Hulda Curtis stone, 1765, Stratford, Connecticut. Red sandstone. 23½ x 47. B. Detail of the Pixlee family stone, 1776, Stratford, Connecticut. Red sandstone. 26½ x 34. C. Detail of the Pecker stone, 1727, Haverhill, Massachusetts. Schist. 23¼ x 18½.

A.

B.

PLATE 123. A. Detail of the Abigail Merick stone, 1773, Glastonbury, Connecticut. Granite. 28 x 48½. B. Detail of the above footstone, 18½ x 24½.

A.

B.

PLATE 124. A. Detail of the Philomena Smith stone, 1773, Glastonbury, Connecticut. Granite. 19 x 24½. B. Detail of the Martha Fuller stone, 1785, Hebron, Connecticut. Granite. 28 x 58.

be interchanged with the disclike effigy representations around Stratford, Connecticut with apparent impunity. On the Abigail Merick headstone, 1773, Glastonbury, Connecticut (plate 123A), a conventional soul effigy may be seen winging its way toward heaven while on the corresponding footstone (plate 123B), a whirl rosette has replaced the soul effigy and is being swiftly lofted toward heaven in its place. The suggestion here is that the geometry of the whirl rosette could and did upon occasion replace the more conventional anthropomorphic imagery when it suited the purpose of the stonecarver. Moreover, on the Philomena Smith marker, 1773, again in Glastonbury (plate 124A), the same carver has used the winged whirl rosette on the headstone rather than the footstone. The transformation from anthropomorphic soul effigies to totally abstract ones had been completed.

It would seem that from this interlocking network of internal visual evidence the rosette was used with some degree of consistency in New England, although in no case are the meanings literally spelled out.

III. MODALITIES OF MEANING

1. The Genesis of the Gravestone

THE typical New England gravestone was a late development out of the prehistoric menhir via the antique stela.[103] Tomb burial in New England was a development out of the stone cist of prehistory via the later form of the sarcophagus.[104] The sarcophagus, often formed with a gabled or coped roof, was in actuality a small shrine or sanctified house for the dead and was at times enlarged to monumental proportions. Venetian and Florentine tombs of the Renaissance often combined the forms of the stela with cists or tombs such as Rossellino's tomb of the Cardinal of Portugal in Florence (S. Miniato), which uses a sarcophagus to provide a house for the dead and a niche and background which gives the effect of a monumental stela or standing grave memorial.

The Puritans used both tombs and gravestones but they never combined the two. In addition, the forms were divided into headstones and footstones, tablestones, tombs, and slabstones. The headstone was a simple upright slab of stone set over a grave and completed by a smaller footstone at the other end of the grave. The tomb was a large brick or cut stone base over which a large flat carved slab was placed. There are few coped or gabled topped tombs of the 17th and 18th centuries in New England. The tablestone was much like the tomb but the flat carved slab was raised up over the ground by a series of four, six, or eight legs. The slabstone was a large flat stone carved on the top and placed flush against the earth on a bed of pebbles. By far the most popular memorial for the dead was the carved headstone or gravestone.

Normally, a house of the dead would be symbolized in art by a conventional carved or cut tomb, but the Puritans preferred to think of death as a translation of flesh into spirit hence a permanent house for the dead would not be as proper a Puritan symbol as would be a doorway through which the deceased passed on the way to glorification.[105] Thus symbols of portals and doorways such as the one on the Captain Samuel Dwight stone, 1763, Enfield, Connecticut (plate 56A), became some of the most conventionalized of all New England symbols. In reality the Dwight stone is nothing more than an early New England doorway complete with a fan arch and supporting fluted pilasters where the door jambs would normally be.[106] Doubtless the door was the portal through which the soul passed from the vision of mortal men into the realms of the "Invisible World." Many New England gravestones are themselves formed of tripartite divisions, traditionally the form of the triumphal arch through which the soul passed on the way to glorification, hence even without the addition of architectural symbols the stones themselves might very well be symbols of the portals to eternity. Such an interpretation would certainly help to explain the immense popularity of the tripartite gravestone in New England rather than the fence-post marker of wood which was common in England before *ca.* 1690 and therefore the type known to most Puritans.[107]

The gravestone would then be considered in the category of a triumphal arch or shrine rather than as a menhir from which they developed and which in prehistory often stood above or near burial grounds and had definite magical and anthropomorphic associations which the tomb or the shrine did not.[108] The menhir usually guarded a tomb complex and in later times became associated with individual burials and often simply stood alone guarding its mysterious treasures.[109] Two of the most famous examples are the Christianized menhir of St. Duzec in Brittany and the female statue menhir from St. Sernin.[110]

Veneration of menhirs was often connected with shrines or cults of the dead. In modern times peasants attribute dark powers to the monuments and there is no question that whether or not they have been carved with anthropomorphic features they are considered in the class of highly animate idols which combine attributes both of the symbol and the symbolized.

When the Puritan cut a gravestone with an image of the soul of the deceased upon it he was moving from the more placid symbolism of the tomb and shrine toward the creation of highly animate idollike stones.

2. Mutilated Symbols

APPARENTLY it was one thing to invest the gravestone with portal symbolism but quite another to animate the surface of the stone with icons of souls in heaven and thus transform the symbolism to a level close to that of the idol and the menhir of prehistory. The mutilated stones of New England testify to the fact that all Puritans did not accept the new imagery with enthusiasm. In addition to the problems created by these stones it is not always clear whether the excisions occurred before the monuments left the stonecarver's workshop, soon after, or sometime in the 19th or 20th centuries. If the image was chipped away before the stone was set up it would mean that the families who bought them were iconoclasts and directed the stonecarvers to excise the offending images. If the stone was mutilated after it was set up but still in Puritan times it might mean that someone other than the immediate family directed the work or that the family had had a change of heart. If the mutilation took place in the 19th or 20th centuries it would simply mean that we are dealing with a case of vandalism. The excisions were done so carefully, however, that the first interpretation seems most likely. The most important examples are the Martha Fuller stone, 1785, Hebron, Connecticut (plate 124B), the John Hurley stone, 1729, Haverhill, Massachusetts (plate 125A), and the Miriam Walton stone, Providence, Rhode Island (plate 125B). All bear identical excisions of the anthropomorphic soul image only. Thus far no such carefully mutilated stones have been found in the 17th century,[111] but 17th century imagery did not revolve around the picturing of a central soul image, if we accept the Haverhill, Massachusetts tradition.

The face was the seat of the soul according to an epitaph near Rockingham, Vermont, which reads,

> Here in this place of the human face
> Will in oblivion lie
> Till Christ on High shall rend the Sky
> And bid the dead arise.

In harmony with this belief the Puritans developed a style of cutting

PLATE 125. A. Detail of the John Hurley stone, 1729, Haverhill, Massachusetts. Schist. B. Detail of the Miriam Walton stone, 17—, Providence, Rhode Island. Slate. 14¾ x 18.

stones which emphasized the head and denigrated the importance of the rest of the body; hence the symbols of Resurrection were not masked in narratives and allegories as they were in England and thus made clearer targets for iconoclasts. There are very few portraits on 18th century English gravestones and nothing which in any way could be called a soul effigy.

The mutilated soul effigies, found in New England but not in England, suggest the possibility that the small body of iconoclasts who did the work felt that the imagery was offensive and idolatrous. This is yet another indication of the thin edge between symbol and idol in New England.

3. Patterns of Emphasis in the Development of Symbolism

THE first groups of stones with symbolic consequence appeared after *ca.* 1678 in Greater Boston and after 1668 in Haverhill, Massachusetts. Both developments were distinct iconographically and stylistically. The former was based upon provincial baroque formulas and conventional mortality emblems derived from English sources and the latter was concerned with the ornamental style and symbols of the soul in heaven.

The stones which became popular in Greater Boston were composed around a central image of a winged death's head derived from English funeral broadsides common since Elizabethan times.[112]

The John Watson stone, 1678, (plate 165A), shows a central winged death's head and a frieze of mortuary emblems. The William Dickson stone, 1692, (plates 24 and 25), shows imps of death, hourglasses, and darts. The Neal family stone, 1678, (plate 54A), shows a temple façade combined with a triumphal arch, and a winged death's head in the pediment. The Codman stone of 1708 (plate 174D), shows two flanking soul effigies in the border panels but the large central death's head and the imps carrying the pall are of much more importance, and many stones of this type escaped mutilation. In addition carving in Greater Boston now and then toyed with allegories as on the Tapping stone of 1678 and on the Gerrish stone of 1743 (plate 16A). Greater Boston also developed and borrowed the portrait stone from a variety of sources but this was more a vanity and a conceit than an idol. One of the first examples of the portrait effigy was the Rev. Jonathan Pierpont stone of 1709 (plate 102).

The emerging pattern moved stonecarving in Greater Boston and the areas it influenced (Map 5) from early emblems of mortality (which dominated the symbolism) to a few attempts at allegorical carvings (soon abandoned) to secular portraits like the Watson example in Plymouth (plate 151c) and the Barnard and Whitwell stones in Marblehead (plates 184 and 185). Throughout the 18th century in Greater Boston the older mortuary symbolism remained popular.

In contrast to the emblems of mortality which developed on gravestones in and around Greater Boston, the carvers of Essex County (Map 7) were more concerned with symbols of the soul in bliss than with a mere picturing of the terrors of death.

The first extant stone in the ornamental tradition, the John White example of 1668 (plate 209), already shows the shift both in terms of style and meaning. The central "lunette" instead of showing a conventional death's head reveals a winged anthropomorphic effigy, most likely a soul effigy. The style, in contrast to the provincial baroque carving of Greater Boston, has turned wholly ornamental and is composed of volutes and other schematic devices. By 1717 on the Hanah Johnson stone in Rowley, Massachusetts (plate 221A), the feathered wings of the 1668 White example have been transformed into chain ornament ending in birds' heads which touch beaks just above the central soul effigy. Banded bird ornament first appeared on the Thomas Hart stone of 1674 (plate 214A), in Ipswich, Massachusetts.

Through a series of complicated borrowings, which will be discussed later, the theme of the soul image was brought to Connecticut where as late as 1799 on the Ripley stone (plate 57B), a soul effigy may be seen within a shrine banded by a molding of clouds. On the Thomas Drury stone, 1778, Auburn, Massachusetts, a soul effigy arises from the ground flanked by flowers, supported by a pair of pilasters, and enclosed by a band of architectural dentils (plate 59). The theme of the soul effigy was brought to Massachusetts via another series of borrowings. Throughout the 18th century in rural New England the theme of the soul in Bliss remained the most popular in the repertory of stonecarving.

In summary, 18th century rural imagery differed from 17th century coastal imagery as the cist or tomb image differed from the menhir. Where the former symbolized a house of the dead or portals through which the soul passed toward immorality, the menhir was in itself an animate living idol or symbol saturated with the object symbolized. Hence the evidence of iconoclasm is found in New England only when the symbolism turns from the more circumspect and indirect shrine-portal symbols, or simple mortuary emblems, to the more animated and saturated fluttering soul effigies winging their way skyward. The difference between rural and coastal imagery and style is the basic difference between English and American stonecarving. The English were content to be more circumspect and indirect, hence they used symbols of the Resurrection borrowed from the allegories, narrative cycles and architectural devices long known in Europe. They never approached the seeming idolatry of carving an image of a soul, although crosses and guardian angels do appear. Nor did the provincial carvers of coastal New England often transform their emblems of mortality and their symbols of Resurrection into soul icons. The latter theme probably distinguishes New England from English stonecarving. In a larger sense it places the iconography of rural New England closer to the enthusiastic symbols of the primitive church than to the indirect emblems and symbols, narratives and allegories of the baroque period in England.

Sources and Definitions of the Major New England Styles

I. ENGLISH STONECARVING: 1550–1850

TOWARD the end of the Middle Ages the patronage for carved tombs widened so that for the first time many country gentlemen, priests, and professional men could afford monuments cut in the shape of coffin slabs and placed on coffin lids, on church floors, or in the garth as ledgers.[1] By the late 14th century the headstone, or gravestone, was used in hexagonal form as at Llanynys, Denbighshire, and was sometimes carved with the emblem of a bishop or that of Christ with extended arms.[2] A more common design for late Medieval headstones was the Maltese cross set within a disc.

In spite of the fact that patronage for carved monuments had broadened, the great majority within the professional and merchant classes had no monuments at all and faded into oblivion without suitable memorials marking their passage. There is little information about stonecarving in England between the late 16th and the late 17th century (if we except the church monuments which form a separate class).[3]

After about 1550 and during the reign of Elizabeth the use of carved memorials once again became popular, but there is little evidence in the monuments until the end of the 17th century. At that time thousands of stones cut in the manner of the English baroque were executed in almost every provincial burial ground where there had been few, if any, monuments before.

In England the popularity of the new style may be traced to the immigration of highly skilled craftsmen from the Low Countries into East Anglia as early as 1517, at which time native craftsmen revolted against the new competition.[4] Along with the immigrants from the Low Countries came the inevitable emblem books and thus England was launched into a new style. Emblem books were originally introduced into England from the Continent during the reign of Elizabeth and remained popular until the end of the 17th century. Drenched in allegory, they were the meeting ground between poetry and painting. Quarles' verse and the accompanying engraving, which have already been discussed, are illustrative of the type.

According to Frederick Burgess, by the middle of the 18th century,

> the repertoire of monumental types was wide, showing a good deal of ingenious regional variation particularly in such a new memorial as the pedestal tomb which had some pretensions to being minor architecture, consisting of one of more decorative plinths, supporting a pyramidion, sarcophagus or urn. The growing popularity of churchyard monuments, ranging from the humblest headstone to such edifices as this . . . encouraged a wide employment of craftsmen both in villages and towns, the latter including men of some local importance, who were statuaries and master masons engaged in building, often supporting more than one workship.
>
> This individually organized craft, along with the integrity of design that was its conspicious feature, gradually disintegrated in the course of the next century, a victim of the complex changes in social conditions that are conventionally described as the Industrial Revolution.[5]

By the middle of the 19th century the altered structure of the village could no longer support the craftsmen while the ownership of quarries, the backbone of the independent craftsmen, began to fall into the hands of industry.

It may be noted that the surviving monuments of the 16th and early 17th centuries are rare suggesting that wood might have been a major material.[6] According to Burgess,

> Georgian topographical engravings of churchyards often show monuments of wood, resembling a rail between two uprights, which at first sight seem part of a broken fence. In Surrey at least, during the 17th century, these were the sole means of commemoration, and it is evident that throughout the Weald, and in other wooded areas of the Home Counties, where the heavy clay-lands made transport of stone difficult, wooden memorials were once numerous, for in spite of their vulnerable nature, many still exist, albeit decrepit and illegible.[7]

Some were painted with emblematic designs.[8] The oldest extant wooden grave rail is lettered on both sides and was cut for Thomas Greenwood in 1658 in Sidlesham, Sussex.[9] At a later date these wooden monuments were imitated in stone by fixing a strut of metal or wood between the stone posts and such sockets have been found on a number of stones in Wrentham, Suffolk (1689), in East Grinstead (1703), and in Billingshurst, Sussex (1734).[10]

The first 17th century examples of headstones in England were small upright slabs no more than two or three feet high, and in the northern counties, worked both front and back,[11] an uncommon practice both in East Anglia and later in New England. Towards the close of the 17th century, scrolls and moldings became popular both in Kent and Surrey, but as yet there was no figural carving. Similar moldings are to be found in the old burial ground in Windsor, Connecticut, indicating a possible connection between the styles.[12]

The Baskervile tomb, 1641, Crypt, St. Paul's Cathedral, London, England (plate 126), was cut in an English variant of the Italian baroque style and is illustrative of the new tomb designs being brought to England from the Continent. The influence of these cultivated urban monuments had little opportunity of filtering down to the masses of yeomen unless carried by a large workshop tradition; and in 1641 there were not enough craftsmen conversant with the new style to make their marks felt. It was not until 1666 that the great fire in London created a situation conducive to the rapid diffusion of the new style. It brought about a need for ornamental wood and stone carvers to carry out the designs later planned for the new St. Paul's.[13] The rebuilding of St. Paul's Cathedral in London gave employment to craftsmen who executed the exterior and interior ornamentation, all coordinated under the direction of Wren in the English baroque style. The masonry was preponderantly of Portland stone, as were the majority of late 17th and 18th century gravestones. The master masons were at first Joshua Marshall and Thomas Strong (the latter being succeeded by his brother Edward). Other outstanding names among the craftsmen were Nathaniel Rawlins, Jasper Latham, Christopher and William Kempster, and the woodcarvers Jonathan Maine and Grinling Gibbons. The chief statuaries were Caius G. Cibber the Holsteiner, and Francis Bird, who carved, among other works, the conversion of St. Paul on the West Pediment.[14]

Both the Baskervile tomb and the south door bracket of St. Paul's (plates 126 and 127) were conceived in a fully plastic modelled manner

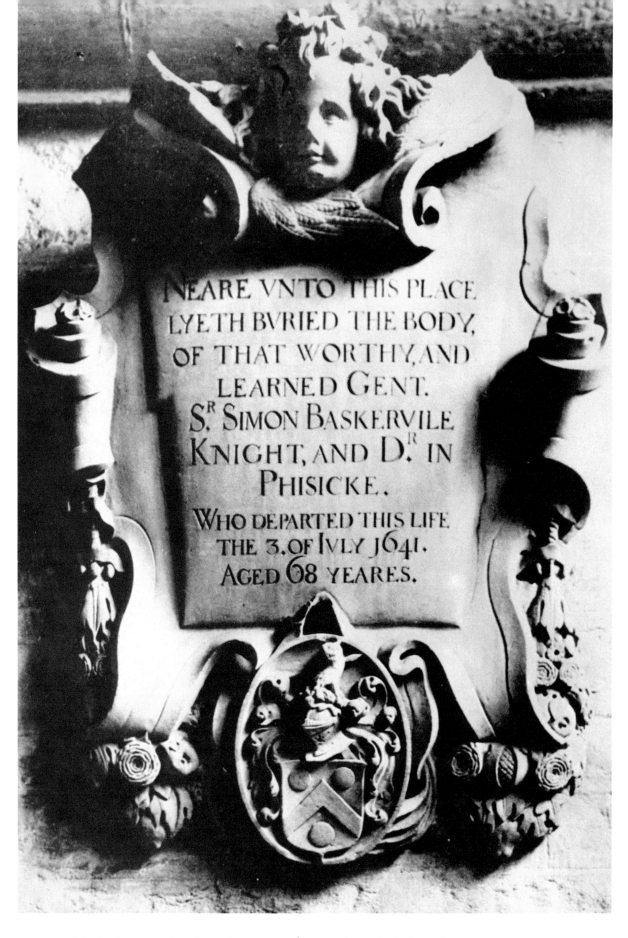

PLATE 126. The Sir Simon Baskervile tomb, 1641, crypt, St. Paul's Cathedral, London.

PLATE 127. Console bracket, south door, St. Paul's Cathedral, London.

emphasizing smooth naturalistic transitions and undulating surfaces, and together they reveal the basic grammar of the English baroque style from which less talented provincial carvers mined their motifs throughout the 18th century. The influence of the high style can be seen on the Bridget Webb tomb of 1715, in Stamford, Lincolnshire (plate 129). Excepting the variant scrolls and the cameo armorial crest, the stones are similar in motif. But as similar as they may be in principle, in execution they are far apart. While the Baskervile tomb moves through its complicated passages with a sense of smooth transition and mellow certainty, if not spontaneity; the Webb monument struggles to assume a posture of ease and elegance and ends with a totally inelegant formulation, interesting only from the point of view of its shifts from the "grammatical norm" of the Baskervile tomb. On the other hand, the Margaret Edwards stone, Linton, Herefordshire, 1764, is far more sophisticated (plate 128). Although a new sense of rococo aerial lightness has forced the ponderous baroque forms to become more brittle it is still far removed from the best examples of rococo ornament. While the technique of carving has been successfully mastered, making the stone look less rude than the Webb example of some years before, the forms still look oddly earthbound and lack that tension and attenuated linear rhythm which mark off the best formulations of the style. The work is, in a word, still provincial, but less so than the Webb example.

A far more obvious transformation of the high baroque style into the idiom of provincial art may be seen on the Mary Hubbard stone, 17——, Bourne, Cambridgeshire (plate 130). While it is surely an improvement over the Webb stone, it is still timidly conceived in relation to the Baskervile tomb. Indeed, the Sarah Herbert stone, 1710, Bury St. Edmunds, Suffolk (plate 131), is so far removed from the high baroque style that I refrain from even calling it a provincial example, and yet a provincial adaptation of the urban baroque style it surely is. It is complete with an undulating shield upon which the inscription is cut, volute and foliate side panels, and a horizontal frieze composed of twin skulls, a cherubim, and a draped swag, all motifs particularly evident in baroque stonecarving in England. But in spite of these obvious similarities, the carving plods through its rich passages weighted down with sodden mudlike areas everywhere apparent as the draped swag rests upon the head of the central cherubim like wet cement. Were it not for the fact that we know this to be a rural solution to a metropolitan problem it would look like a conscious parody of the baroque

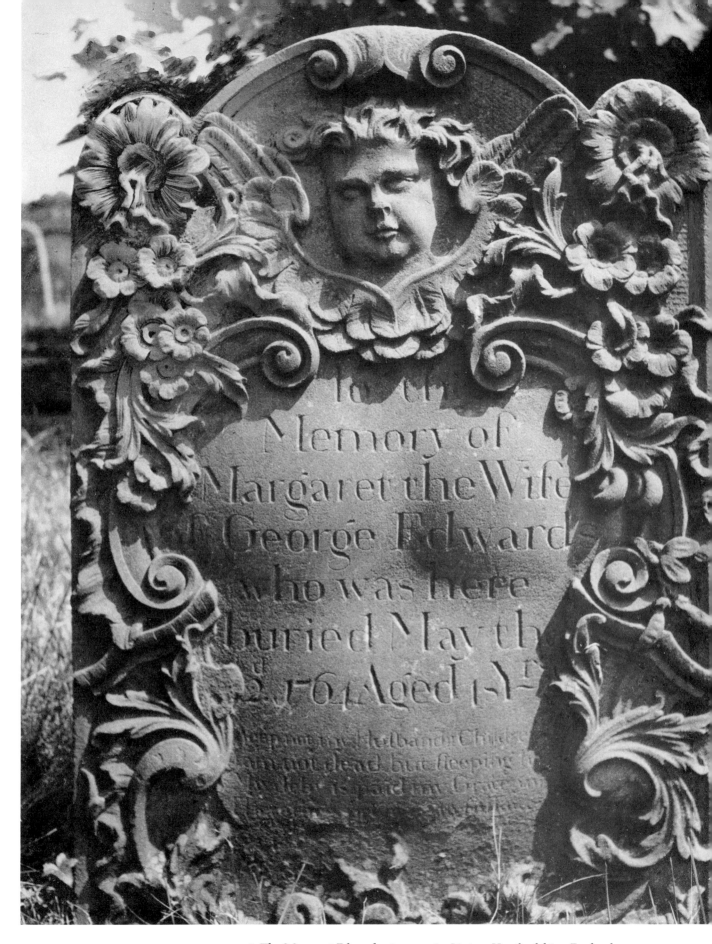

PLATE 128. The Margaret Edwards stone, 1764, Linton, Herefordshire, England.

PLATE 129. The Bridget Webb monument, 1715, Stamford, England.

PLATE 130. The Mary Hubbard stone, 17—, Bourne, England.

PLATE 131. The Sarah Herbert stone, 1710, Bury St. Edmunds, England.

style. In reality it is a rural vernacular transformation of a cultivated style into forms which could be coped with without vast workshop experience. Linguists have long studied the shift of language from a high style to a vernacular one and the structural changes thereby engendered. Art historians have yet to follow this lead, being chained as they are to the notion of "quality." The Herbert stone is instructive for our purposes because no matter how "rural" the English style became it rarely lost a sense of plastic volume, thus the connection with the urban styles was never lost and the carving almost never became totally flat, linear, and hieratic as in New England. Plates 132 and 133 are examples of English and Scottish rural types.

While certain rural English carving may be accused of barbarism, more often than not the borrowing was cultivated if not particularly stimulating. The Amy Cary Tomb of 1756, Hampstead, St. Andrew's, London (plate 134B), was almost certainly taken from a source similar to a detail of the south frieze of St. Paul's Cathedral (plate 134A). Both work with the same motifs but the Gibbons design for St. Paul's is not as inflexibly severe as the Cary example.

The John Rehbury stone, 1690, Bury St. Edmunds, Suffolk (plate 135A), is a common baroque theme to be found in many English burial grounds after *ca.* 1690 and before *ca.* 1750, when the formula became lighter. After *ca.* 1750 the ponderousness of the baroque formula began to quicken with the introduction of the more brittle, nervous, attenuated forms of the rococo. The Elizabeth Stokes stone, *ca.* 1730–1750, Bunhill Fields, London (plate 135B), is illustrative of the new trend which emphasized surface texture and movement rather than volume and shadow. Often the lightness of the rococo and the volumes of the baroque formula were combined on stones such as a 1770 example cut in Bunhill Fields, London (plate 135C). The rococo brought with it a hardness of line associated with metalwork and it is not surprising that on the Oldham stone of 1819, Thorney, Cambridgeshire (plate 135D), a brittle engraved effect had been achieved.

By the middle of the 18th century many new allegorical themes were introduced into English vernacular carving, and many endured well into the 20th century. According to Burgess the sources are difficult to trace down but it is well known that the pattern books of Dieterlin and De Vries were used.[15]

Among the most popular themes of allegorical and emblematic carving were the sundial, clocks, angels, urns, books, butterflies, caduceus, infants in prayer, columns, cornucopias, crowns, doves,

PLATE 132. Stone dated 1732 from Thorney, Cambridgeshire, England.

PLATE 133. Stone from Roseneath, Scotland, probably cut in the first half of the 18th century.

A.

B.

PLATE 134. A. South frieze, St. Paul's Cathedral, London. B. The Amy Cary tomb, 1756, Hampstead, St. Andrew's, London.

PLATE 135. A. The John Rehbury stone, 1690, Bury St. Edmunds, England. B. The Elizabeth Stokes stone, ca. 1730/50, Bunhill Fields, London. C. Stone cut ca. 1770, Bunhill Fields, London. D. The Oldham family stone, 1819, Thorney, Cambridgeshire, England.

sheafs of corn, garlands, hands, lambs, mirrors, Neptune, Time, Death, palms, pineapples, Psyches, pyramids (erect and falling), shells, torches, trees, trumpets, weepers, Faith, the cross, Hope and her anchor, Charity and the heart, the Last Judgment, Resurrection of Christ, Biblical illustrations (sacrifice of Isaac, the Good Samaritan, *Noli me Tangere*, Agony in the Garden, Flight into Egypt).[16] Needless to say the vocabulary of English 18th century carving reflected their closer relationship to the sources of urban styles. New England saw few Biblical illustrations or allegories of Hope, Faith, and Charity until the 19th century, nor did the New England carvers have much use for representations of Neptune, cornucopias, Psyches, or weepers, the darkly garbed ladies so very important at a proper Puritan funeral. Hope was one of the most popular allegorical figures and may be seen with her traditional attribute, the anchor, on a mid-18th century stone, Toft, Cambridgeshire (plate 136A).[17] She is being embraced by a putto, symbolic of the victory of Resurrection and life over death through the agency of love. At times Hope could be transformed into a traditional weeper figure as on the James Gee stone, 1816, Toft, Cambridgeshire (plate 136B).[18] Another variant cut with a portrait cameo, may be seen on a mid-18th century stone (plate 136c), again from Toft.

The standing figure of Hope made its appearance in the rural English churchyard about 1750. Excepting the seated figure on the Clough stone (plate 70A), one of her first 19th century appearances was on the Calvin Warner stone, 1853, Harvard, Massachusetts (plate 136D).

The weeper, a traditional neoclassical figure, appeared in England about the same time as the figure of Hope, but could be used in a variety of combinations. On the French stone of the 1760's (plate 137A), and also on the Oldham family stone, 1819, Thorney, Cambridgeshire (plate 137B), putti appear as weepers. In the background of the French stone the sky is illuminated with shafts of light in the manner of baroque painting of the 16th century. The use of such atmospheric effects in relief sculpture can be traced to the Italian Renaissance.[19]

More conventional weepers may be seen on the Sharman family stone, 1837 (plate 138A), and on a stone cut in the mid-18th century (plate 138B), both in Thorney, Cambridgeshire. Notice that on the Sharman stone a cornucopia and a hooped snake appear flanking the central figure. The hooped snake was used in New England on the Jayne stone, but as far as I know the cornucopia was never used. The traditional figure of the weeper was first brought to America on mourning pictures incorporating this theme and no home was com-

PLATE 136. A. Mid-18th century stone, Toft, Cambridgeshire, England. B. Detail of the James Gee stone, 1816, Toft, Cambridgeshire, England. C. Mid-18th century stone, Toft, Cambridgeshire, England. D. Detail of the Calvin Warner stone, 1853, Harvard, Massachusetts. White marble. 23¾ x 45¾.

A.

B.

PLATE 137. A. Detail of the French family stone, ca. 1760, Bunhill Fields, London. B. Detail of the Oldham family stone, 1819, Thorney, Cambridgeshire, England.

A.

B.

PLATE 138. A. Detail of the Sharman family stone, 1837, Thorney, Cambridgeshire, England. B. Detail of a mid-18th century stone, Thorney, Cambridgeshire, England.

plete without one of these sentimental mementos.

Scenes of the sacrifice of Isaac appear with some regularity during the last quarter of the 18th century and well into the 19th century in England. Some examples may be seen on a stone of 1833 in King's Lynn, All Saints, Norfolk; at Great Casterton, Rutland, 1803; at Gillingham, Kent, 1795; at Margate, Kent, 1797; at Pulborough, Sussex, 1792; at Rusper in 1791; at Wisbach, St. Mary's in 1828; and twice at Soham, Cambridgeshire on the Clark stone of 1810 (plate 140A), and on the Wallis stone of 1820 (plate 139). The designs were almost certainly taken from a cultivated urban example, perhaps even from an engraving of the famous Ghiberti bronze, and transformed in provincial versions heading rapidly toward the vernacular tradition.

No such Biblical allegories made their way to New England. Another theme popular in England was the depiction of the last judgment such as the one of the Vallar stone, 1776, East Dean, West Sussex (plate 140B), but such dramatic presentations did not tempt the mind of the New Englander.

In addition to these and other allegories and narratives, the mid-18th century saw the mild proliferation of the use of the cross, once anathema to the English. Burgess said, "The fear of possible Roman Catholic ascendancy in England left its mark on Georgian symbolism, so that, in an officially Christian country, we find a virtual absence of the Cross as the prime instrument of Salvation, and an anomalous preference for the use of pagan imagery."[20]

"There are about a score of monuments at Weston in which the Cross is prominent, either alone, or in combination with the skull, angel-heads or passion emblems. Others have been given pictorial treatment in delicate relief, showing the Cross with a skull at its foot set in a realistic landscape."[21] The William Sharman stone, 1807, Thorney, Cambridgeshire, is illustrative of the high allegorical style incorporating the use of the cross on an English gravestone of the early 19th century.

Stonecarving in old and New England have thus far exhibited few stylistic similarities. There were, however, some pockets of retrogression. There were areas in England untouched by the rapid diffusion of the English baroque forms and themes. There were areas which had neither a well-established workshop tradition nor the benefit of good models from which to work. Stonecarving in Dover, Cornwall, and Scotland exhibits borrowings often much more remote from the urban high styles than we have previously seen. The Ann Pettefor stone,

PLATE 139. Detail of the Wallis stone, 1820, Soham, Cambridgeshire, England.

A.

B.

PLATE 140. A. Detail of the Jonas and Mary Clark stone, 1810, Soham, Cambridgeshire, England. B. Detail of the Vallar family stone, 1776, East Dean, West Sussex, England.

1774, Southwold, Suffolk (plate 141), is illustrative of a thread of English stonecarving far removed from the normative tradition and resembling the distortions and simplications of much New England carving. The models for the Pettefor stone may have been popular woodcuts rather than more sophisticated engravings. The development of coastal New England stonecarving follows the same pattern and both traditions have much in common stylistically. In both there is a propensity to handle a fluid, graceful style in terms of a hard linear treatment; for want of skill to turn volume into line, depth into façade, and naturalistic detailing into flat ornament.

This then was the direction of the English stonecarving tradition: from the cultivated metropolitan styles to the provincial dilutions and finally to the vernacular versions illustrated by the Pettefor stone of 1774. It appears that both the vernacular English tradition and the New England provincial tradition were united by the common bond of borrowing from printed materials. Indeed, much cultivated English stonecarving also reveals borrowings from printed sources and themes held in common, but the style is at once more knowledgeable and more articulate than either the New England or the English vernacular tradition. For example, the Pettefor stone shows a hooped snake as does the more sophisticated Sharman stone of 1837 (plate 138A), and an identical theme may also be seen on the Jayne stone of 1776 in Marblehead, Massachusetts (plate 6). There must have been a common source which has not yet come to light. Hence it can be assumed that the Pettefor stone, like the New England examples of provincial carving, participated in the cultivated style of English carving via the indirect source of the printed page.

Another theme common to both sides of the Atlantic which had a run of popularity in emblem books and broadsides was the tree being put to the axe. On the Elizabeth Brown stone, 1773, Bunhill Fields, London, Time fells a tree. On the Norton stone of 1751 in Durham, Connecticut (plate 41B), the hand of God is similarly engaged. Time appears felling trees in New England only in the 19th century, but the hand of God wielding the hatchet was used in the Connecticut Valley as early as the middle of the 18th century. The dove which appears on an "atmospheric relief" in Thorney descends in the same manner on the Hayden stone of 1797 in Essex, Connecticut (plate 91E). The sheaves of wheat growing from the skull on an 18th century stone from St. Andrew's, Hampstead, London, appear in variant form on the Jackson stone of 1743 in Plymouth, Massachusetts, as a living tendril

PLATE 141. The Ann Pettefor stone, 1774, Southwold, Suffolk. England.

(plate 8A). The book in the hand of the mourner on a late 18th century stone from Thorney, Cambridgeshire, appears in the hands of the figures on the Cook stone in Kingston, Massachusetts (plate 101). The trumpeting angel on the Flavell stone of 1777 in Bunhill Fields, London, appears often in New England as on the Clark stone in Chelmsford, Massachusetts (plate 31A).

Almost all the themes cited had currency both in the emblem book literature of the period and also in the more popular broadsides. For example, the hooped snake, the skull with the sheaves of wheat bursting forth from it, the hourglass, the heart; and many other themes may be seen in George Wither's emblem book published in London in 1635.

Carvers on both sides of the Atlantic used printed material as sources but the trained carvers did not need to use popular woodcuts and engravings as their only models. It is not yet clear if any English stonecarver directly affected carving in New England. On the one hand checklists of English and New England carvers reveal not a name in common,[22] while on the other, the Sarah Wellington stone, 1707, in Thorney (plate 142), looks too much like the David Forbes marker, 1729, in Windsor, Connecticut (plate 143), to rule out all possible contact at this time. In addition, several New England carvers like John Stevens I, (1646–1746) were born in England, but in the case of Stevens we know that he did not take up the craft until his arrival in Boston during the closing years of the 17th century.[23] It is possible, however, that a number of English rural carvers, like the man who cut the Pettefor stone (plate 141), made the trip and escaped the checklists. Too little is really known of what rural carving was like in England prior to *ca.* 1690 to come to any final conclusions. From the surviving evidence it is not possible to tell whether an even older ornamental style existed before. If indeed there was an older English style it might possibly have influenced ornamental stonecarving in Essex County, Massachusetts, after *ca.* 1668.[24] There still exists in England a small group of stones which does not belong to the cultivated or the provincial traditions of English stonecarvings so far examined.

The Andrew Brownsmith stone, 1698, Cherry Hinton, Cambridgeshire (plate 144), bears a family resemblance to the Webb marker of 1715 and through it to the urbane Baskervile tomb. The Sarah Pimble marker, 1726, Linton, Herefordshire (plate 145), in contrast, is a very rare example of English rural stonecarving conceived almost wholly in terms of abstract geometric shapes. It seems that either one of two things could have happened. The provincial baroque formula might

PLATE 142. The Sarah [Wellington?] stone, 1707, Thorney, Cambridgeshire, England.

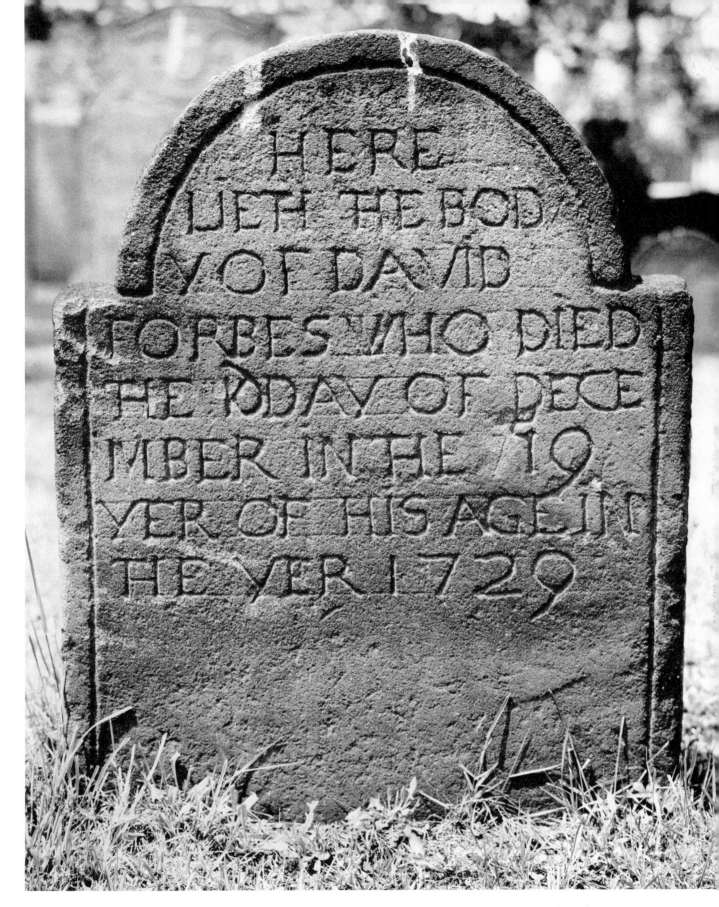

PLATE 143. The David Forbes stone, 1729, Windsor, Connecticut. Red sandstone.

PLATE 144. The Andrew Brownsmith stone, 1698, Cherry Hinton, Cambridgeshire, England.

PLATE 145. The Sarah Pimble stone, 1726, Linton, Herefordshire, England.

have become so flattened that the pure linear quality of the guide lines took over and was developed until the pleasing geometric effects of the Pimble marker were achieved. Were the intermediary steps available, a sequence of abstraction might have been set up between the Brownsmith and the Pimble markers similar to the one which takes place on Gallo-Roman coinage. Alternatively, the Pimble stone might have been the heir to a far older geometric style which was suppressed with the coming of the baroque stones after *ca.* 1690. The Pimble marker might have been cut by a carver who borrowed only the compositional "shell" of the Brownsmith stone but preferred to fill it with older geometric detailing.

Indeed, the Pimble marker may have been representative of a common style which fell into disuse when the baroque became popular. The Mary Greenhill stone, *ca.* 1690–1710, Shorn, Kent (plate 146A), a similarly dated fragment from Chalk, Kent (plate 146B), and an additional four Kentish stones (plate 147) testify to the fact that an abstract, geometric tradition was not totally absent from rural England in the late 17th and early 18th centuries. It is even possible that we are dealing with Anglo-Saxon rural survivals. None of these examples fit into either the burgeoning baroque family or into the slightly earlier Renaissance and late Medieval motifs which now and again surface in English stonecarving.

In spite of the fact that examples of English ornamental stonecarving are rare, the possibility that many such local styles were suppressed after the introduction of the baroque style *ca.* 1690 cannot be ruled out. Indeed, we might ask if these extraordinary stones represent a lost tradition of ornamental carving or simply the surfacings of local eccentricities in more placid stylistic waters. Could these stones be the last remains of a style which was carried across an ocean to flower in New England while withering away at home?

In summary, English stonecarving after *ca.* 1690 was bound up with the diffusion of a cultivated metropolitan style to the provinces. There it was finally reduced to the vernacular tradition which turned volume into line and undulating restless space into flatter, more frontal surfaces. The spread of these cultivated styles through a network of more or less knowledgeable local workshops was the hallmark of the English style. In New England there was neither the professionally trained class of stonecarvers bringing cultivated styles to the hinterland nor the ready availability of high urban stylistic and thematic materials. The connection between the Kentish stones, the Pimble

A.

B.

PLATE 146. A. Detail of the Mary Greenhill stone, ca. 1690/1710, Shorn, Kent, England. B. Detail of a stone fragment, ca. 1690/1710, Chalk, Kent, England.

PLATE 147. Four details of Kentish gravestones, early 18th century.

marker from Linton, and the New England ornamental tradition is a problem which ought to be investigated more fully. The rural carvers of New England seem to have either invented new themes for their needs or borrowed from an unknown English source; possibly the same tradition from which the Pimble stone sprang, if indeed there was such a tradition. The theme most used by rural Puritan carvers was that of the soul effigy in heaven, a device rarely seen in coastal New England and not at all in England to my knowledge.[25]

There is only the most scanty evidence that the six-pointed rosette was brought to New England via 17th century English stonecarving. The rosette was a common enough device on Hellenistic provincial gravestones and sarcophagi and was almost certainly brought to England in this context by the Romans (plate 149). That it survived the collapse of Roman influence is clear from the surfacing of the same motif on a stone font from Landrake, Cornwall, from the last quarter of the 12th century, although in this case it may have as easily been a "Celtic" survival. In any event the six-pointed rosette did survive and somehow surfaced on the James Colley stone, 1692, Frampton-on-Severn, Gloucestershire (plate 148), functioning in much the same manner as it did on Roman gravestones. Were there more of these stones it could be believed that the New England use of these forms owes something to 17th century English precedent. Unhappily this is not the case. According to Frederick Burgess, an authority on English rural stonecarving, this is a unique example. It would seem unlikely then, that a whole tradition in New England was in point of fact based upon a single atypical example in a lonely English churchyard. It would seem far more likely that the Frampton-on-Severn marker was a member of a far larger family of carved rosettes which was transplanted by the New Englander just before it faded out in England. Alternately, it is equally possible that the New England rosettes stemmed from another and as yet unknown source or even that they were re-invented by the New England stonecarvers. Answers to these questions will have to await further investigations.

Stylistically, the differences between England and coastal New England are clear. No matter how provincial English carving became (plate 131), a sense of nascent volume was almost always present while in New England the major movement was away from volume toward line and flatness as befits a tradition drawn from popular woodcuts and engravings. A similar style emerges in England whenever the workshop tradition became too attenuated, as on the Pettefor stone (plate

PLATE 148. The James Colley stone, 1692, Frampton on Severn, Gloucestershire, England.

ROMAN TOMB-STONE
TO L. SEMPRONIUS FLAVINIUS,
A SOLDIER OF THE NINTH LEGION
FOUND OPPOSITE THE CITY

Hübner. p. 52. Nº 184
Arch. Journ XVII

PLATE 149. Romano-British tombstone.

141), and carvers had to make use of popular engravings and woodcuts.

II. ENGRAVINGS, WOODCUTS, AND EMBLEM BOOKS

THAT the stonecarvers of New England participated in the baroque tradition by means of the printed page seems clear. It is also clear that there was no large scale immigration of highly trained carvers to New England,[26] nor were any gravestones imported.[27] Indeed, Mrs. Forbes' checklist shows that the majority of stonecarvers were locally born.

One of the most significant survivals in 18th century New England was the theme of the reclining skeleton seen on the William Sinclear stone, 1753, Spencer, Massachusetts (plate 150A), which was almost certainly taken from an English broadside such as the one printed for George Cockayn in 1691 in London (plate 150B).[28] The Cockayn woodcut was in turn derived from a popular medieval theme in use for centuries (plate 150C).[29]

Borrowing from broadsides was far more popular in New England than copying from the more erudite emblem books, although upon occasion themes were taken from them.[30] It is known that Alciati's emblem book was in the Harvard library in the early 18th century but none of the designs found their way onto gravestones.[31] The emblem books of Francis Quarles proved more popular. The Joseph Tapping stone of 1678, King's chapel, Boston, Massachusetts (plate 151A), was taken from Francis Quarles' famous *Hieroglyphiques of the Life of Man*, printed in London in 1638 (plate 151B).

Along with borrowings from emblem books and broadsides, the New England carver also quoted thematic devices known in England for centuries but as yet the bridge between the cultivated English and the provincial New England tradition has not been discovered. An engraving by Charles Delaram after an original by Nicholas Hilliard shows Queen Elizabeth crowned with stars and surrounded by clouds. On the Hannah Jackson stone, 1763, Plymouth, Massachusetts (plate 113B), a provincial version of the same theme had been cut suggesting the divinity of the soul of Mrs. Jackson. Both quoted a thematic tradition common in English art.

Other borrowings can be traced with more accuracy. The John Watson stone of 1753, Plymouth, Massachusetts (plate 151C), was almost certainly derived from an engraving such as one cut for Reverend Isaac Watts in 1722 and published as the frontispiece to a book in 1727[32] (plate 151D). By 1795 on the Samuel Hall stone, Meriden, Con-

PLATE 150. A. Detail of the William Sinclear stone, 1753, Spencer, Massachusetts. Slate. 19½ x 14. B. Detail of the broadside of George Cockayn, 1691. C. Medieval mosaic from Rome.

A.

B.

C.

D.

PLATE 151. A. Detail of the Joseph Tapping stone. See plate 14. B. Engraving from Francis Quarles' *Hieroglyphiques of the Life of Man*, London, 1638. C. Detail of the John Watson stone, 1753, Plymouth, Massachusetts. Slate. 27¼ x 33. D. Detail of the frontispiece of Isaac Watts' *Horae Lyricae*, London, 1727. Engraving cut in 1722.

necticut (plate 152A), there was enough printed material in America to make the search for likely sources that much easier. This borrowing seems to have been from a sermon printed in Hartford, Connecticut in 1792[33] (plate 152B), on the election of Governor Samuel Huntington. Similar stones appear in Meriden, Wallingford, Southington, Farmington, and Enfield in Connecticut, among other places. Broadsides printed in America were a rich source of thematic material. The row of carved coffins on the Pember stone (plate 153A) may be seen on any one of a number of broadsides such as the one titled "On the Death of Five Young Men who was [sic] Murthered, March 5th 1770" (plate 153B),[34] or on the elegy printed for Mrs. Fessenden in 1770[35] or on another cut for the tragedy at Salem, Massachusetts, in 1773.[36]

In addition to English and American broadsides, engravings, and emblem books, the New England primer was another richly illustrated source for local carvers to draw upon. Primers can be traced back in New England to 1683.[37] All contained an illustration of Adam and Eve flanking the tree of the knowledge of good and evil such as the one shown in plate 153c.[38] An almost identical relief may be found on the Sarah Swan stone, 1767, Bristol, Rhode Island (plate 153D). It is likely that a primer was the source. A running hourglass is shown in the same primer (plate 154A), and another appears on the Thomas Brenton stone, 1772, Newport, Rhode Island (plate 154B). The theme could have been taken from a primer (plate 154A). Time with his hourglass and scythe appears in most primers and a similar standing figure may be seen on the Isabella Tawley stone dated 1737, in Marblehead, Massachusetts (plate 19). A skeleton armed with the dart of death may also be seen in primers, and a similar figure reappears on the Polly Harris stone, 1787, Charlestown, Massachusetts (plate 154D), although the design was a popular one and could have been taken from an English broadside such as the one illustrated in plate 154c. It is even possible that Germanic folklore may have had some influence. (See plates 155A and 155B and footnote 72, chapter II.)

Most borrowed themes can be traced back only to 18th century sources, because earlier broadsides and engravings have not survived. The only American broadside which looks as if it might have been a "source" for 17th century stonecarving in Greater Boston was cut in 1710 for Rebekah Sewall (plate 156). This later date does not rule out the possibility that the format may be much older. Both surviving broadsides and the gravestones of the period framed the inscriptions with bands of mortality emblems topped with a skull or a winged

A.

B.

PLATE 152. A. Detail of the Samuel Hall stone, 1795, Meriden, Connecticut. Red sandstone. 24½ x 33¾. B. Detail of a woodcut in Timothy Stone's *A Sermon Preached Before His Excellency Samuel Huntington Esquire*, Hartford, Connecticut, 1792.

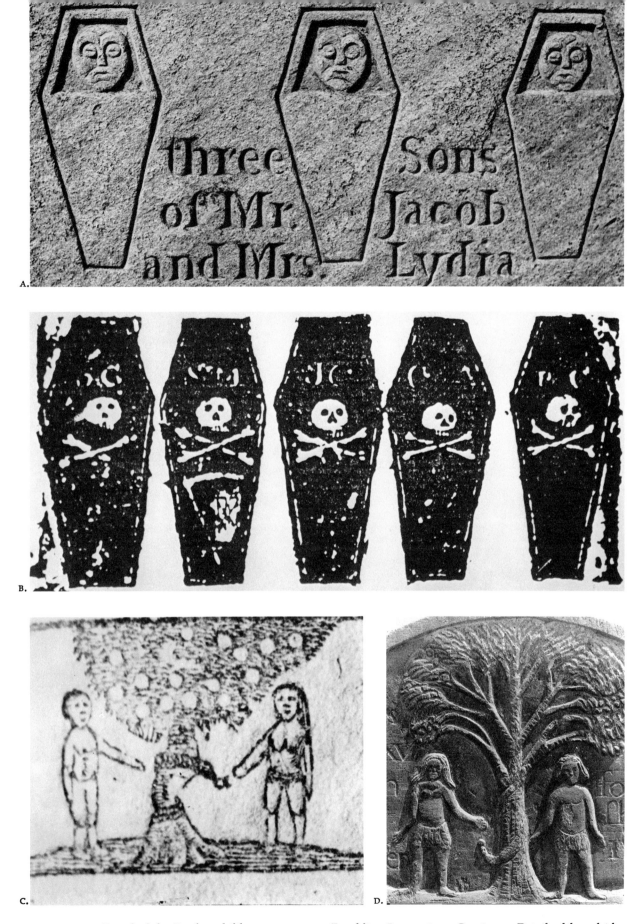

PLATE 153. A. Detail of the Pember children stone, 1773, Franklin, Connecticut. Granite. B. Detail of broadside published March 5, 1770. C. Detail from a New England Primer published in Haverhill, Massachusetts, in 1811. D. Detail of the Sarah Swan stone. See plate 13.

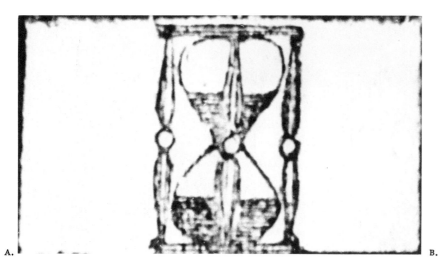

PLATE 154. A. Detail of a New England Primer. See plate 153C. B. Detail of the Thomas Brenton stone, 1772, Newport, Rhode Island. Slate. C. Detail of an 18th century English broadside. D. Detail of the Polly Harris stone, 1787, Charlestown, Massachusetts. Slate. 22¼ x 24¾.

A.

B.

PLATE 155. A. Detail of a European Provincial wood carving. Probably 17th century. B. Detail of the Nicholas Larrance stone, 1710, Charlestown, Massachusetts. Slate. 22¼ x 24¾.

PLATE 156. Broadside cut for Rebekah Sewall, 1710.

death's head. All the emblems found in the Sewall broadside are to be found on New England gravestones. The John Watson stone, 1678, Cambridge, Massachusetts (plate 165A), made use of similar crossed picks, shovels, and bones, the death's head, and the Latin motto *Memento Mori*. The winged hourglass set upon a skull on the Sewall broadside may be seen on the Kendel stone cut about 1678 in Wakefield, Massachusetts (plate 164B). Twin flanking skeletons may be seen in more refined form on the Ruth Carter stone of 1697–1698 in King's Chapel, Boston, Massachusetts (plates 168 and 169), suggesting a common source for both.

It is not known if any stonecarver took an entire design from any one particular broadside, but from the evidence it looks as if devices were picked up from a number of sources and put together by the stonecarvers in relation to their needs of the moment. For example, there is no stone in New England which used all the emblems on the Sewall woodcut, but at one time or another every theme was incorporated into the vocabulary of Greater Boston stonecarving.

In summary, stonecarvers used broadsides, engravings, woodcuts, book plates, and illustrated primers for their borrowings. Consequently their stonecarving reveals a sharp linear, metallic quality more normally associated with the graphic arts than with sculpture and certainly not at all associated with the baroque softness of much English carving. (See plates 157A and 157B.)

III. THE ORIGINS OF THE PROVINCIAL BAROQUE STYLE IN MASSACHUSETTS: 1647–1735

1. Early New England Stone Markers: 1647–1735

MANY of New England's earliest stone markers were roughly cut boulders bearing a simple initial and date. The "E. L." marker, 1647 (the inscription has been recut), Ipswich, Massachusetts (plate 158), is the earliest surviving example of a common type found throughout New England suggesting that the first markers were probably fashioned from stone rather than wood. By the 1650's in and around Boston boulders were dressed on one side to make inscriptions easier to carve. The Samuel Danforth stone, 1653, Roxbury, Massachusetts (plate 159A), is a good example of the type. Notice that the lettering is set within the confines of deeply cut horizontal guide lines. By 1658 on the William Paddy stone, King's Chapel, Boston, Massachusetts (not

A.

B.

PLATE 157. A. Detail from Isaac Watts' *Horae Lyricae*. See plate 151D. B. Detail of the Sarah Hunt Stone, 1799, Rumford, Rhode Island. Slate. Signed by G. Allen, Jr.

PLATE 158. The 'E. L.' stone, Ipswich, Massachusetts, 1647. A re-cut inscription, but probably one of the earliest stones extant in New England. M. U. 13½ x 17.

A.

B.

PLATE 159. A. The Samuel Danforth stone, 1653, Roxbury, Massachusetts. M. U. B. The Sarah [Hammond?] stone, 1674, Watertown, Massachusetts. Slate.

illustrated), the semidressed boulder had turned into a fully dressed gravestone with the traditional tripartite division into a central panel and two flanking slender wings. By this time the heavy horizontal guide lines had been omitted by the most forward-looking carvers. The 1660's saw the introduction of fine slates in the Charlestown area which replaced the older crude granites from which stones had formerly been hewn. Slate is far easier to carve than granite; it is durable and abundant in and around Greater Boston. It remained popular with stonecarvers until late in the 18th century. The Faithful Rowse marker, 1664, Charlestown, Massachusetts (plate 160), is a good example of an early but carefully carved slate gravestone. Note that the deep horizontal guide lines have been omitted. Ten years later in "provincial" towns such as Watertown, carvers still retained guide lines in spite of the fact that they had gone out of fashion in Boston and Charlestown some years before. The Sarah ———— (Hammond?) stone, 1674, Watertown, Massachusetts (plate 159B), is a good example.

Both the Paddy and the Rowse markers reveal a shift from the epigraphical practice of the early 1650's. Sometime between 1653 and 1658 it became a common practice to substitute "suspended periods" between each word for the older colons. The process of elision was carried even further and by *ca.* 1678 most of the more advanced carvers had eliminated all unnecessary punctuation between words.

Meanwhile in Watertown as late as 1675 both horizontal guide lines and "suspended periods" were still being used on the Mehetabel Gearfield stone (plate 161A). By 1677 on the Nathanael Hammond stone in Watertown (plate 161B), the guide lines had finally been omitted but "suspended periods" were still retained. Such epigraphical archaisms are plentiful throughout New England. The cheerfully awry Isaac Morgin stone of 1696, Enfield, Connecticut (plate 162A), is a rather late survival of the colon separation. By the time of the Henry Burt marker of 1735 in nearby Northampton, Massachusetts (plate 162B), the use of the colon had finally been suspended. The need to punctuate was so great, however, that from time to time throughout the 18th century many rural stones were apt to break out in an epidemic of dots. The Moses Wheeler stone of 1724 in Stratford, Connecticut (plate 232D), is a good example.

2. The Charlestown Carver

THE Charles River set apart the work of two stonecarvers who practiced their crafts on either bank in the 1670's and '80's. From the extant

PLATE 160. The Faithful Rowse stone, 1664, Charlestown, Massachusetts. Slate. 20 x 7½.

A.

B.

PLATE 161. A. The Mehetabel Gearfeild stone, 1675, Watertown, Massachusetts. Slate. B. The Nathanael Hammond stone, 1677, Watertown, Massachusetts. Slate.

A.

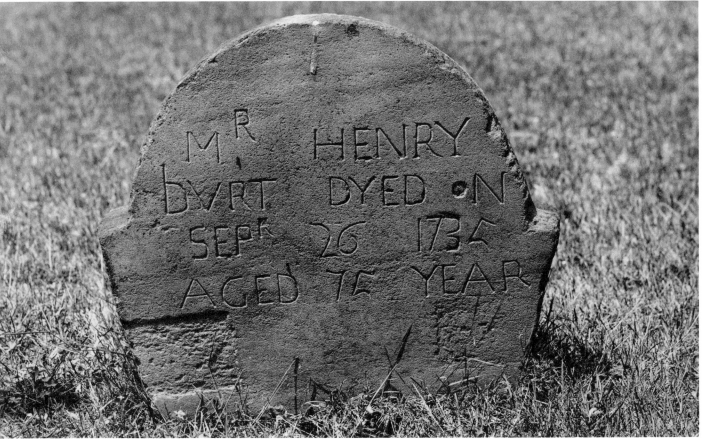

B.

PLATE 162. A. The Isaac Morgin stone, 1696, Enfield, Connecticut. M. U. 26½ x 18¾. B. The Henry Burt stone, 1735, Northampton, Massachusetts. Red sandstone. 22¼ x 19.

evidence it would seem that the earliest carving, stemming from motifs derived from broadsides, developed north of the Charles River possibly as early as 1674 and certainly by 1678. Several years later a far more sophisticated style developed south of the Charles.

The name of the carver whose works are to be seen primarily in Charlestown, Cambridge, Watertown, Malden, Wakefield, Woburn, The Granary, and King's Chapel is not known. For want of a better name we shall call him the Charlestown carver.[39]

The earliest stone attributed to him is the Ann Erinton marker of 1653, Cambridge, Massachusetts (plate 163A). There is, however, some reason to dispute this early date.[40] The epigraphical evidence suggests that all stones cut in the 1650's should bear heavily incised horizontal guide lines as well as the colon separation, but none of these features is visible. Moreover there is a virtual replica of the Erinton stone in Charlestown bearing the later date of 1674 which suggests that the Erinton example was also cut in that year and simply replaced an earlier more simple marker. Finally, no other symbolic designs appear before *ca.* 1676 and the fan-sunburst motif on the Erinton stone appears only in the 1670's and 1680's suggesting once again that a later date would be more correct than an earlier one. The Mary Allin stone, 1678, Malden, Massachusetts (plate 163B), and the Dorcas Brakenbury marker, 1682, Charlestown, Massachusetts (plate 163C), are additional examples of the same motif.

By 1676 on the Thomas Call stone in Malden, Massachusetts (plate 164A), emblems such as the hourglass, the crossed bones, the shovel, the coffin, the pick, begin to appear in a horizontal frieze set upon a thin lintel supported by three carved columns with stepped capitals. This stone may well be the first use of architectural ornament in New England.

A more complex example, attributed to the Charlestown carver, is the Kendel stone which could not have been cut before 1676 nor after 1678 from comparative evidence (plate 164B). In this example a skull was raised up on a pillar and flanked by two winged cherubim (the earliest angelic representations to appear in Greater Boston). The enlarged cranium, the pencil-thin eyebrows, the splayed-out calligraphic nose, the feathering of the wings in horizontal tiers characterize the John Watson stone of 1678, Cambridge, Massachusetts (plate 165A), as well.

"Coined" wings rather than wings in "tiers" were used both on the Joanna Ingles marker, 1678 (plate 165B), and on the Joseph Farnum

A.

B.

C.

PLATE 163. A. Detail of the Ann Erinton stone, dated 1653 but probably cut in 1674, Cambridge, Massachusetts. Slate. 19½ x 18¼. B. Detail of the Mary Allin stone, 1678, Malden, Massachusetts. Slate. C. Detail of the Dorcas Brakenbury stone, 1682, Charlestown, Massachusetts. Slate. 20 x 17.

PLATE 164. A. Detail of the Thomas Call stone, 1676, Malden, Massachusetts. Slate. 21¼ x 15½. B. Detail of the Thomas Kendel stone, ca. 1678, Wakefield, Massachusetts. Slate. 21¾ x 25¼.

A.

B.

C.

PLATE 165. A. Detail of the John Watson Stone, 1678, Cambridge, Massachusetts. Slate. 24½ x 22½. B. Detail of the Joanna Ingles stone, 1678, Copp's Hill, Boston, Massachusetts. Slate. c. Detail of the Joseph Farnum stone, 1678, Copp's Hill, Boston, Massachusetts. Slate.

stone of that same year (plate 165c), Copp's Hill, Boston, Massachusetts. The "coining" of the wings was carried over into the design of the Neal children stone, 1671, The Granary, Boston, Massachusetts (plate 54A). Because of both the "coining" of the wings and the highly developed architectural motifs a date of 1678 for the Neal children stone is far more likely than 1671. Even using 1678 as the most likely date, the marker remains the earliest use of a classical temple façade in New England. The theme does not reappear in such emphatic form until the neoclassical revival of the 19th century. The Call stone of 1676, Malden, Massachusetts (plate 164A), can be seen as a prelude to the ambitious and carefully carved Neal children stone which brought into vogue the use of architectural motifs which later became staples of gravestone design. The stone is almost certainly the work of the Charlestown carver.

Another important stone from his workshop was the Joseph Tapping marker, 1678, King's Chapel, Boston, Massachusetts (plate 55). The central allegory was taken from Francis Quarles' *Hieroglyphiques of the Life of Man* published in London in 1638 (plate 151B). The treatment of the skull is similar to that on the Call and Kendel stones (plates 164A and 164B). Moreover, there is an extended use of architectural motifs found on both the Call and the Neal children stones. Four lightly carved pillars flank two gothic arches with foliated interstices. The latter appear on the Neal children stone in variant form. Just as the Neal children stone was the first New England gravestone cut in the form of a classical temple façade so too the Tapping marker was the first New England appearance of a scroll-topped stone. Variants of the Tapping scroll-topped stone began to appear in the 1690's and then vanished only to reappear once again the Connecticut Valley after about 1750. Moreover, this was the first appearance of an allegory in New England. True allegories of Time and Death appear only a few more times in Greater Boston, although both Time and Death were used separately on many other occasions as emblems rather than allegories.[41] The Gothic arch, which surprisingly made an appearance on the Tapping stone, faded out of the repertory of stonecarving until the Gothic revival of the 19th century.

The sources of the Charlestown carver and his followers were primarily popular broadsides; but on at least one occasion an emblem book was used. The legacy of the Charlestown carver was a well-formulated repertory of mortuary emblems and one allegory combined with architectural devices where heretofore there were only

unornamented stones in Greater Boston. Of perhaps more consequence than the vocabulary of thematic devices which the Charlestown carver left, was the fact that he was the first to make the use of
such visual devices respectable in a community which had formerly
eschewed all visual art of a religious nature.

Working as he did with engravings and broadsides many of his
stones and those of his followers echo the flatness and hardness of
much 17th century graphic art. When a higher class of models was
used, such as on the Tapping and the Neal stones, the Charlestown
carver showed a capacity for carving which might have proved excit-
ing had more polished examples been available.

3. The Carver Who Signed Himself "J. N."

ON the south banks of the Charles River the majority of significant
17th century stones were cut by a carver who initialled some late stones
"J. N." There is no further documentation available at this time. The
signed stones include the Cleverly marker of 1703, Quincy, Massachusetts (plate 166A), the Edward Tompson example of 1705, Marshfield, Massachusetts (plate 166B), and the Ichabod Wiswall marker of
1700 in Duxbury, Massachusetts (plate 166c). Similarly signed stones
are the Martha Hall example of 1701 in Roxbury, Massachusetts, the
Sarah Dolbeare marker in Copp's Hill, 1701, and the Mehitable Hammond stone of 1704 in Newton, Massachusetts.

Stones cut in the manner of "J. N." may be found in Duxbury,
Marshfield, Newton, Copp's Hill, The Granary, Roxbury, Quincy,
Dorchester, and King's Chapel. Few of them crossed north over the
river Charles (Map 6). Unlike the crude emblematic stones most often
cut by the Charlestown carver, "J. N." was using highly sophisticated
engravings rather than rough woodcuts for his models. In addition to
the themes initiated slightly earlier north of the Charles and naturally
picked up to the south of the river, "J. N." introduced several new
devices. He was the first New England carver to use peacocks, as on
the John Cleverly stone, 1703, Quincy, Massachusetts (plate 49A), a
theme later picked up in eastern Connecticut, the gadrooned urn or
goblet (plates 170 and 171), the inhabited zoomorphic scroll (plate
167), and the enigmatic Dagons or Tritons which ornament his most
representative stones (plates 170 and 171). The use of Dagons on Puritan gravestones is puzzling in the light of the fact that they were associated with paganism and the evil doings of Thomas Morton and his
merrymen. Mount Dagon was apparently the third name given to a

A.

B.

C.

PLATE 166. A. Detail of the John Cleverly stone, 1703, Quincy, Massachusetts. Slate. B. Detail of the Edward Tompson stone, 1705, Chelmsford, Massachusetts. Slate. C. Detail of the Ichabod Wiswall stone, 1700, Duxbury, Massachusetts. Slate.

PLATE 167. The Benjamin Hills stone, 1683, The Granary, Boston, Massachusetts. Slate.

town originally called Mount Wollaston. It was at this site that Morton and his rowdy crowd disported themselves in such an extraordinarily lewd manner. It became common knowledge that they danced lasciviously around a Maypole and frisked about with Indian women. Such naughtiness enraged both the Pilgrims and the Puritans and Morton was soon sent packing. Yet pagan Dagons remained to grace the stones of many a proper Boston family in the late 17th century in spite of the Mount Dagon incident some years before. The redoubtable William Bradford humorlessly intoned,

> After this they fell to great licenciousness, and led a dissolute life, powering out them selves into all profanenes. And Morton became lord of misrule, and maintained (as it were) a schoole of Athisme. And after they had gott some good into their hands, and gott much by trading with the Indeans, they spent it as vainly, in quaffing and drinking both wine and strong waters in great exsess, and, as some reported, 10 li. worth in a morning. They allso set up a Maypole, drinking and dancing aboute it many days togeather, inviting the Indean women, for their consorts, dancing and frisking togither, (like so many fairies, or furies rather,) and worse practises. As if they had anew revived and celebrated the feasts of the Roman Goddes Flora, or the beasly practieses of the madd Bacchinalians. Morton likewise (to shew his poetrie) composed sundry rimes and verses, some tending to lasciviousnes, and others to the detraction and scandall of some persons, which he affixed to this idle or idol Maypolle. They chainged allso the name of their place, and in stead of calling it Mounte Wollaston, they call if Meriemounte, as if this joylity would have lasted ever. But this continued not long, for after Morton was sent for England, (as follows to be declared,) shortly after came over that worthy gentlman, Mr. John Indecott, who brought over a patent under the broad seall, for the govermente of the Massachusets, who visiting those parts caused that May-polle to be cutt downe, and rebuked them for their profannes, and admonished them to looke ther should be better walking; so they now, or others, changed the name of their place againe, and called it Mounte-Dagon.[42]

Dagons appear on the Benjamin Hills stone, 1683 (plate 167) and on the Jacob Eliott stone, 1693 (plate 170), both in The Granary, Boston, Massachusetts. Moreover they are to be seen once again on the Michael Martyn stone, 1682 (plate 171A), the William Greenough marker, 1693 (plate 171B), and on the undated Briggs stone (plate 171C), all in Copp's Hill, Boston, Massachusetts. Dagons appeared with foliated or scaly tails and with or without breasts suggesting a male-female distinction in the mind of the carver. An upswept coif was very popular with the lady Dagons (plate 170), while stringier hanks of hair were suitable for the boys (plates 167 and 171A). Needless to say lady Dagons are not Dagons at all but Nereids. In any event it is not clear what pagan water deities were doing on Puritan gravestones. Another iconographic puzzle is the solitary appearance of squirrels inhabiting foliated scrolls on the Hills marker (plate 167).

Several other important stones may be attributed to the hand of "J. N." The Ruth Carter marker 1697–1698, The Granary, Boston, Massachusetts (plate 62A), reveals a variant motif of the one used on the initialled Reverend Edward Tompson marker of 1705 in Marshfield, Massachusetts (plate 62B). Both seem to have been cut by the same man at different times. Moreover the border panels of the Carter stone (plates 168 and 169) reveal a fine pair of standing skeletons which are so refined in pose and gesture that they were almost certainly taken from engravings. The total effect of the relatively sophisticated work of "J. N." was to move carving in Greater Boston a step further away from the crude woodcut tradition which until then had been the prime source of copying. Indeed, the carving techniques themselves of "J. N." are far in advance of the work of the Charlestown carver who executed the clumsy Tapping allegory of 1678. Where the latter was content to cut in two flat planes, "J. N." on the Carter stone attempted to carve in terms of half-rounded forms. The difference can be thought of as the distinction in architectural motifs between the unfluted pilaster and the engaged column, the latter being far more sculptural than the former.

This new spatial effect is surely an advance over what had gone before. The technique was taken over by William Mumford who populated Boston's burial grounds with thousands of dreary stones. A full account of his work may be found in Mrs. Forbes' book.[43]

4. Joseph Lamson: 1658–1722

UNTIL late in the 1690's carving on both sides of the Charles River was simply a matter of attempting to emulate printed material stemming from Europe. That "J. N." was more successful than the Charlestown carver does not diminish the fact that there is never a spark of originality in his borrowed designs. The first carver who actually created what can be called a "localism" or a true provincial variant of the English manner, was Joseph Lamson who may have studied with the Charlestown carver in his youth.[44] Lamson was born in Ipswich, Massachusetts, in 1658 of William and Sarah Lamson. In 1675 or 1676 he sailed off on an expedition of the Connecticut River with Captain Turner of Mystic Side (later Malden).[45] Upon his return he seems to have settled in Charlestown and in 1679 married Elizabeth Mitchell.

PLATE 168. Left detail of the Ruth Carter stone, 1697/98, The Granary, Boston, Massachusetts. Slate. 27 x 28¼.

PLATE 169. Right detail of the Ruth Carter stone, 1697/98, The Granary, Boston, Massachusetts. Slate. 27 x 28¼.

PLATE 170. Detail of the Jacob Eliott stone, 1693, The Granary, Boston, Massachusetts. Slate. 25¾ x 27¾.

A.

B.

C.

PLATE 171. A. Detail of the Michael Martyn stone, 1682, Copp's Hill, Boston, Massachusetts. Slate. B. Detail of the William Greenough stone, 1693, Copp's Hill, Boston, Massachusetts. Slate. C. Detail of the John Briggs stone, date under ground line, probably cut ca. 1690/1710. Slate, Copp's Hill, Boston, Massachusetts.

Among his many accomplishments he was a mariner, a cordwainer, a surveyor, and finally a prolific stonecarver.[46] Probate records mention that he was paid for the Hammond stones of 1711–1713 in Watertown, Massachusetts (plate 172A),[47] the Samuel Fletcher stone of 1705 in Chelmsford, and the Richard Kaets stone of 1712 in Concord,[48] but the latter two are of inferior quality.

In addition to the stones given to Joseph Lamson by probate records, the Lamson family as a whole left a good many signed stones dotted about New England. The Reverend Jonathan Pierpont stone of 1709 in Wakefield (plate 173) bears the initials "N. L." as does the Ephraim Beech stone of 1716 in Stratford, Connecticut (plate 172B), the Mary Rous stone of 1714 in Charlestown,[49] and the Mercy Oliver marker, Cambridge, Massachusetts (plate 174A). The Mary Reed stone of 1712–1713, and the Prudence Turner stone, 1717, both in Marblehead, Massachusetts, bear the initials "C. L." Joseph Lamson had two sons, one Nathaniel, 1692–1755, and the other Caleb, 1697–1767, who both carved stones.[50] Noting, however, that Nathaniel was but sixteen years old when the Pierpont marker was cut in 1709, it seems reasonable to assume that he was merely helping in his father's shop and not yet the master of it. When he took over between *ca.* 1711 and 1716, the carving becomes far more mechanical and less imaginative.

Most of the stones attributed to Lamson are to be seen north of the Charles in Charlestown, Malden, Wakefield, Cambridge, Woburn, Chelmsford, Marblehead, Billerica, Concord, and Lexington. Few of his stones found their way across the Charles into Boston proper or the adjacent burial grounds although his stones traveled as far south as Stratford, Connecticut. His work can also be seen as far north as at least North Andover, Massachusetts.

The most impressive feature of Lamson's work is his inventive carver's mind which did not depend so blindly upon printed sources for material. Indeed, Lamson himself introduced few new themes into New England stonecarving but perfected those already in use and in the process created the first portrait effigies in New England.

The William Dickson stone, 1692, Cambridge, Massachusetts (plates 24 and 25), attributed to Lamson, shows two imps of death cut in large scale on the border panels. Lamson had used the same theme the year before on the John Stone marker of 1691, Watertown, Massachusetts (plates 26A and 26B). Naked imps had been used as early as the 1680's, but they had never been as boldly cut as when Lamson began to experiment with them in 1691.

A.

B.

PLATE 172. A. Detail of the Prudence Hammond stone, 1711, Watertown, Massachusetts. Slate. Given to Joseph Lamson via a probate record. B. Detail of the Ephraim Beech stone, 1716, Stratford, Connecticut. Slate. Cut with the initial 'N. L.,' probably for Nathaniel Lamson, son of Joseph Lamson. 21 x 19.

PLATE 173. The Jonathan Pierpont stone, 1709, Wakefield, Massachusetts. Slate. Signed with the initials 'N. L. probably for Nathaniel Lamson, son of Joseph Lamson. 30 x 27¼.

A.

B.   C.   D.

PLATE 174. A. Detail of the Mercy Oliver stone, Cambridge, Massachusetts. Slate. Signed with the initials 'N. L.,' probably for Nathaniel Lamson, son of Joseph Lamson. B. Details of the Rebekah Row stone, 1680, Charlestown, Massachusetts. Slate. 27¼ x 17. C. Detail of the Walter Hastings stone, 1699, Cambridge, Massachusetts. Slate. 20½ x 18. D. Detail of the Elizabeth Codman stone, 1708, Charlestown, Massachusetts. Slate. 23¼ x 16¾.

Just as the Egyptians disposed the various parts of the body between profile and frontal views to simplify their plastic conception of form, so too Lamson followed the same principles following his native intelligence rather than a series of diagrams or engravings. In the Dickson stone Lamson had rethought some of the most fundamental problems of the plastic arts and had created a blunt, primitive image far removed from the bland borrowing we normally associate with provincial styles. Indeed, the reliance of Lamson on his own native vision of form rather than upon tired-out engravings and woodcuts is an indication of a new interest in invention where there had been previously an uninspiring dependence upon the printed page.

Lamson was also the first to codify the use of soul effigies in foliated and floral border panels, although he was by no means the first to use the motif. Stones such as the Rebekah Row marker, 1680, Charlestown, Massachusetts (plate 174B), may have been cut by Lamson under the influence of the Charlestown carver. By 1699 on the Walter Hastings stone, Cambridge, Massachusetts (plate 174c), Lamson had forged a far more effective abstract style than he demonstrated on the Row marker. In an effort to reconcile the need for seminaturalistic effects with the linear abstraction of the calligrapher, Lamson leaned far more heavily upon his experience as an engraver than on his limited experience as a sculptor. The Peter Tufts stone of 1702–1703, Malden, Massachusetts and the Jonathan Remington stone, 1700, Cambridge, Massachusetts (plates 66 and 67), are representative examples. By 1710 on the Rebekah Bunker stone, Cambridge, Massachusetts (plates 68 and 69), he transformed the "tobacco-leaf collars" into a series of angular forms and suspended under them what look for all the world like breasts.

By the time of the Elizabeth Codman stone of 1708, Charlestown, Massachusetts (plate 174D), Lamson had moved from his abstract phase based upon the glyptic technique of the calligrapher to a more sculptural vision of the features of the human face. The eyes, which now fit into sockets, are cut in the shape of almonds and the nose is no longer a pendant but more of a button. The lips too have become far more naturalistic, now being formed of twin incisions rather than a single slash. The following year he created the first portrait effigies ever cut in New England (plates 175, 176, and 177). From the Dickson stone of 1692 to the Pierpont portrait of 1709 (plate 102), Lamson had in effect relived part of the movement of Western art from abstraction to naturalism. The Tufts and Remington stones show Lamson abstract-

A.

B.

PLATE 175. A. The Captain and Mrs. Pyam Blower stone, 1709, Cambridge, Massachusetts. Slate. 25¾ x 22¾.
B. The John Russell stone, 1709, Copp's Hill, Boston, Massachusetts. Slate.

PLATE 176. Detail of the left panel of the Blower stone. See See plate 175A.

PLATE 177. Detail of the right panel of the Blower stone. See See plate 175A.

ing elements from the optical world and progressing toward a calligraphic view of nature; but by the time of the Codman stone of 1708 he had apparently solved some of his most vexing problems in the difficult changeover from a glyptic engraver's technique to a sculptor's vision of volume and modelling. It is a pity that we do not as yet have any stones which can be attributed to Lamson between 1702 or 1703 and 1708 when the shift from one way of looking at things to another took place.

The three earliest portrait effigies Lamson created in 1709 are the polished Reverend Jonathan Pierpont marker, Wakefield, Massachusetts (plate 102), the Captain and Mrs. Pyam Blower stone, Cambridge, Massachusetts (plates 175A, 176, and 177), and the damaged John Russell stone, Copp's Hill, Boston, Massachusetts (plate 175B). The smoothly finished Pierpont marker is surely one of the finest stones in New England and, in addition, it is initialled "N. L.", probably for Nathaniel Lamson, his son. It is a shame that it still remains outdoors where it is prey to the depredations of nature and the vandalism of man. The Pierpont stone is a masterful blending of the glyptic and the modelled modes of stonecarving which held great promise for the future. The moment had been reached when a schematic pictographic vision of nature had merged with a more modelled optical view forming the experimental basis of an "archaic style." But the very nature of the craft as a popular rather than a cultivated one negated the possibility of building upon what Lamson had discovered. It is the fate of traditions lacking self-consciousness to endlessly redo the past. Lamson's sons, Caleb and Nathaniel, quietly slipped back into formula carving without once having realized what their talented father had accomplished.

IV. THE GROWTH OF THE PROVINCIAL BAROQUE STYLE IN MASSACHUSETTS: 1722–1815

1. William Codner and His Followers

BETWEEN the time of the death of Joseph Lamson in 1722 and the work of William Codner, beginning about 1743, there is an interval which can be called a period of calm after the hurried borrowings and innovations of the forty-eight years between 1674 and 1722. A great number of stones were cut by Caleb and Nathaniel Lamson who simply mass-produced the formulas invented by their father and contributed little to Greater Boston carving. The decline in quality might be traced to the lack of talent on the part of the Lamson sons, to the greater demand for stones which made individual craftsmanship impossible, or to the new prohibitions against the spending of money at funerals which first appeared in 1720–1722 and again in 1741–1742.[51] It is likely that all three were contributing causes.

According to Mrs. Forbes,[52] William Codner, 1709–1769, was a pupil of Nathaniel Emmes, 1690–1750, an undistinguished Boston carver to whom the Nathaniel Newall stone is given via a probated will.[53] William Codner was the son of James, a cooper, who lived on Cross Street in Boston nearby William Mumford and Emmes.[54] The latter was one of the appraisers of the estate of James Codner when he died in 1738.[55] Between 1731 and 1764 Codner was paid by seventy-five estates for gravestones, but according to Mrs. Forbes many were of very low quality except the one made for William Clark,[56] Copp's Hill, Boston, Massachusetts (plate 178A). Codner received £40 for his share of the work while the artist who designed the stone, Thomas Johnson, was paid a good deal more for this and other services.[57] The stone has had an interesting history. It was taken over by Samuel Winslow and is know as the Winslow stone to this day and still stands in Copp's Hill. It was not usual for a stone to be reused but the action of Winslow may have been sanctioned by the fact that the stone bore a secular rather than a religious theme.

Contacts between Codner and Johnson seem to have begun in earnest about 1743 and proved to be illuminating for the former if not for the latter. Johnson undoubtedly steered Codner to themes which had been unavailable to him prior to this time. Indeed, after 1743 there is such a demonstrable improvement in his work that it may be assumed that Codner learned a great deal about stonecarving itself from Johnson. It is possible to see the same hand which carefully carved the fruit swags on the Clark stone at work on the Rebekah Gerrish stone, 1743, King's Chapel, Boston, Massachusetts (plate 16A), and on the Samuel Adams marker, 1728 (plate 16B), in the same burial ground. If the Adams stone can be attributed to Codner it would mean that it was carved in the 1740's rather than in 1728 as the date indicates. Moreover, by virtue of the carving of the swags on the Clark stone, the Jackson stone of 1743 in Plymouth, Massachusetts (plates 8A and B), can also be attributed to him. The richly carved border panel on the Jackson stone may be seen in plate 65B. In 1768 the Reverend Shearjashub Bourne stone in Roxbury, Massachusetts (plate 178B), was cut by Codner and documented by a probated will.[58] From this important

A.

B.

PLATE 178. A. Detail of the Clark arms, 1743, Copp's Hill, Boston, Massachusetts. Slate. B. The Reverend Shear Jashub Bourne stone, 1768, Roxbury, Massachusetts. Slate.

stone a number of Plymouth County portraits can be attributed either to his hand or to his workshop.

The treatment of the eyes on the Bourne marker of 1768 and on the Rawson portrait of 1744, but dated 1715,[59] Mendon, Massachusetts (plate 179), are so similar that they both probably came out of the Codner workshop. If we except the Lamson portrait effigies of 1709, then the Rawson stone of 1744 becomes the first extant attempt at portraiture in New England. It is probable that the pose set within the cameo was borrowed from an engraving. The John Watson stone of 1753, Plymouth, Massachusetts, may have also been cut by Codner (plate 151c). Indeed, if we give the latter stone to Codner it would seem likely that the Patience Watson stone of 1767, Plymouth, Massachusetts (plate 180), stemmed from the same workshop. Both Watson portraits led to a vogue for portraiture in Plymouth which did not run its course until the end of the second decade of the 19th century. The Elizabeth Morton stone (plate 181), and the Hannah Lewis marker (plate 182), both cut in 1790, are obvious borrowings from the Watson stone of 1767. The Captain John Virgin stone, 1814, was the last of the Plymouth portraits executed in the old style. It is significant to note that the carvers of the Morton and the Lewis stones tried to emulate the style of the already provincialized Watson marker of 1767 but thoroughly misunderstood the attempt of the Codner workshop to overcome the limitations of a purely glyptic technique by toying with modelled forms. Both the Morton and the Lewis stones reverted to a wholly flat conception of form dependent upon line rather than volume for its plastic effects. Nothing significant had been passed on to the later carvers.

Portraits in the manner of the Codner workshop continued to be cut throughout the 18th century. The Sarah McKeon stone, 1776, Ipswich, Massachusetts (plate 183A), shows the surfacing of the type in northern Massachusetts.

In sum, Codner revived the allegorical manner of carving momentarily after 1743 and probably carved the first portrait stone in New England for Reverend Rawson in 1744. The rise of the portrait stone is an indication of the slow movement away from religious themes and it is ironic to note that ministers as a class led the way. In their desire to be remembered in the communities they served their stone effigies became tribal totems of a life departed rather than symbolic visions of a life to come. Indeed, the most ostentatious stone in the Ipswich burial ground was the marker cut for Reverend Nathaniel Rogers in 1775

PLATE 179. Detail of Rev. Grindall Rawson stone, dated 1715, cut in 1744, Mendon, Massachusetts.

PLATE 180. Detail of the Patience Watson stone, 1767, Plymouth, Massachusetts. Slate. 33 x 35.

PLATE 181. Detail of the Elizabeth Morton stone, 1790, Plymouth, Massachusetts. Slate. 22 x 27½.

PLATE 182. Detail of the Hannah Lewis stone, 1790, Plymouth, Massachusetts. Slate. 21¾ x 28.

A.

B.

C.

PLATE 183. A. Detail of the Sarah McKeon stone, 1776, Ipswich, Massachusetts. Slate. B. Detail of the Reverend Nathaniel Rogers stone, 1775, Ipswich, Massachusetts. Slate. C. Detail of the Ebenezer Fisk stone, 1775, Lexington, Massachusetts. Slate. 29 x 36¾.

(plate 183b). These enormous icons set a fashion for display which was to alter drastically the egalitarian uniformity of the traditional New England burial ground. Smaller portraits were churned up in the wake of the Rawson and Rogers stones such as the one cut for Ebenezer Fisk in 1775 in Lexington, Massachusetts (plate 183c). The most magisterial of all was the Reverend William Whitwell portrait with its dry Latin inscription and flinty stare, 1781, Marblehead, Massachusetts (plate 184).

2. Daniel Hastings: b. 1749

THE growth of secular themes in stonecarving can be further illustrated in the works of Daniel Hastings who was born in 1749,[60] in Newton, Massachusetts. According to Mrs. Forbes, he cut the Caleb Dana stone in Cambridge, Massachusetts for which there is an extant probate record.[61] It is by virtue of this record that she gives him the Reverend William Whitwell stone of 1781 in Marblehead, Massachusetts, and the Anna Barnard stone of 1774 in the same burial ground (plates 184 and 185). In addition he probably cut the Nathaniel Rogers stone of 1775 in Ipswich, Massachusetts and the Thomas Barret stone of 1779, in Concord, Massachusetts.

Both the Whitwell and the Barnard stones are splendid examples of the provincial baroque style, although neither reveals a particularly religious sentiment. Compared with the Pierpont marker of 1709, the Whitwell portrait is cold, hard, flinty, ruthless, and magisterial where the Pierpont effigy was simple in its expression of childlike piety. Portrait stones by Hastings were very popular although all could not afford the elaborate treatment Reverend Whitwell received. Stones by Hastings, cut from a fine grade dark grey slate, are to be seen throughout Greater Boston in the latter half of the 18th century.

3. George Allen: d. 1774

THUS far no carver of gravestones seems to have been a highly skilled craftsman at first, although all learned the craft and improved with age. George Allen does not fit into this pattern. He might not have been a stonecarver at all but an engraver who was hired to execute several stones. He signed the John Hunt stone of 1716 in Rumford, Rhode Island (plate 70b), and according to Mrs. Forbes lived in Rehoboth.[62] It is clear that he had available models of putti and cut them into the stone with surprising precision. Where he lacked a model (for the winged angel-effigy) he became at once more mechanical and his

PLATE 184. Detail of Rev. William Whitwell stone, 1781, Marblehead, Massachusetts. Slate.

PLATE 185. Detail of the Anna Barnard stone, 1774, Marblehead, Massachusetts. Slate.

skill failed. His work represents the spread of the provincial baroque style outside Boston. The careful foliate ornament and the superior composition of the stone inspired a number of copies in Rumford and Providence and might be said to have set off a minor revival of the provincial baroque style of Allen in those towns. The John Hunt stone of 1751, the Abell Carpenter stone of 1755, both in Rumford, emulate his high style with little success. The repercussions of the Hunt stone of 1716 were felt as late as the early 20th century when the last surviving member of the Tingley family of stonecarvers took over the design for the Hunt stone and used it as a replacement for the Rebekah Tingley marker of 1790.[63]

V. THE PROVINCIAL BAROQUE STYLE IN RHODE ISLAND: 1690–1815

1. The Stevens Family

JOHN STEVENS, I, moved to Newport, Rhode Island, from Boston in 1705, where he had apparently learned the craft of stonecarving from William Mumford.[64] Stevens brought a son, John Stevens, II, with him who was born in 1702. Prior to the arrival of Stevens in Newport most of the gravestones were brought from Boston. After 1750, John Stevens, II, began to export stones from the workshop on Thames Street to eastern Connecticut where they formed the basis of a local style (see Map 5). Between 1728 and 1732 the busy shop turned out at least sixty-two carved gravestones and tombstones.[65] The family left a daybook which was probably kept by John Stevens, II, but there are other hands visible and it must be studied by a trained epigrapher before it will make a great deal of sense.[66]

Both the work of John Stevens, I and II, have little interest except insofar as their work reveals the transition between the earlier Boston derived death's head and what the family called "cherubim."[67] After 1769, another John Stevens, called John Stevens, III, for the sake of clarity (he signed his stones John Stevens, Jr.), began to carve and must certainly be considered one of the unfulfilled talents of American art. Unfortunately he could not seize the opportunities which were laid open to both West and Copley and the precocious promise of his early work remained unrealized. A glance at a few of his signed stones will suffice to demonstrate that he had enormous natural skills. According to information obtained from the Newport Historical Society it is generally believed that he was born in 1760.[68] Many of his signed stones are dated between 1771 and 1773. Attributed stones range in time from 1769 to 1775. That he was carving major works between the ages of nine and fifteen seems highly unlikely. Stevens signed the Mercy Buliod marker of 1771, Newport, Rhode Island (plate 186A), as well as the William Rogers stone of 1772, also in Newport (plate 187A). In 1773 he signed the Esther Halliock stone, Mattituck, Long Island. The Captain Nathaniel Waldron stone, 1769, Newport, Rhode Island (plate 188), can be attributed to him on the grounds of the central portrait being almost identical to the one cut on the signed Rogers stone of 1772. The Phillis Lyndon stone, 1773, Newport, Rhode Island, is attributed to his hand as well as the Jonathan Wyatt stone of 1775, Newport (plate 187B). In view of the overwhelming chronological evidence of the stones themselves it would seem to me that John Stevens, III, was born somewhat before 1760 but certainly after 1750. One of the last stones he signed was that of Isaac Church in 1789, Newport, Rhode Island (plate 186B). By this time his youthful enthusiasm for carving had vanished.

Comparing the Rogers stone of 1772 (plate 187A) and the Wyatt stone of 1775 (plate 187B), one sees that the young man learned a great deal about relief carving in a very short time. The features of the Wyatt portrait are linear except for the passage around the mouth which is not only accurately modelled but foreshortened as well. Indeed, in spite of the signs of the engraver's technique the strokes are bold, the chisel is sure, and the design is clear. The pity is that Stevens was unable to pursue a career in the arts after this propitious beginning.

That Stevens must have used engravings for his models is indicated by the stola-clad female figures on the border panels of the Captain Nathaniel Waldron stone, 1769 (plate 188). Such classicizing motifs could not have been invented. Indeed, the stone is the earliest in New England to bear the unmistakable imprint of the neoclassical style. That Stevens was the first to use neoclassical devices is not surprising in the light of the fact that the family seems to have been very fond of reading and must have had access to a good library. Some of the books they knew are,[69]

> The English Rogue or the Witty Extra-vagant, and three days later on March 7, 1767, Paradise Lost. On March 19th he read, A Genuine History of the Irish Rogues and on the 30th A Discourse addressed to the Sons of Liberty. On April 10th he read, The History of the Heathen Gods and on May 4th, De Laune's Plea for the Non-Conformists.

In all, about twenty-one different books were read between January 1

A.

B.

PLATE 186. A. Detail of the Mercy Buliod stone, 1771, Newport, Rhode Island. Slate. B. Detail of the Isaac Church stone, 1789, Rhode Island. Slate. Signed by John Stevens, Jr.

A.

B.

PLATE 187. A. Detail of the William Rogers stone, 1772, Newport, Rhode Island. Slate. B. Detail of the Jonathan Wyatt stone, 1775, Newport, Rhode Island. Slate.

PLATE 188. Detail of the Nathaniel Waldron stone, 1769, Newport, Rhode Island. Slate.

and June 15, 1767.

The Stevens family used a fine blue-black slate imported from a nearby quarry. A document of June 18th, 1726, reveals that Stevens bought a load of gravestones from a man named Brayton[70] for 3 shillings and a tombstone for 6 shillings. The price indicates that the stones were undressed blanks to be cut, smoothed, and polished in the Thames Street workshop (which is still in operation).

As we already know, the Stevens family shipped a large number of gravestones to eastern Connecticut after *ca.* 1750. The Ursula Mc-Curdy marker, 1781, Norwich, Connecticut (plate 191A), attributed to John Stevens, III, is representative of the type while the Sary Brewster stone of 1773, again in Norwich (plate 191B), is the work of a rural Connecticut craftsman. If we did not know that stones like the McCurdy marker appeared in Connecticut as early as 1750 we might have assumed that the natural movement of style was from the barbarous crudities of the Brewster marker to the painful provincialisms of the McCurdy stone. Such was not the case. As we know, the already provincialized "cherubim" stones, such as the McCurdy marker, were the models from which the carver of the Brewster stone worked. With this fact in mind it is clear that seminaturalistic motifs in the hands of rural craftsmen are swiftly transformed into pure ornament. The progressive ornamentalization of the provincial styles which stemmed originally from Europe will be the theme of a later discussion.

2. John Bull: 1734–1808

JOHN BULL, 1734–1808, the son of Henry Bull and Phebe Coggeshall,[71] married Ruth Cornell of Middletown, Rhode Island, in 1769 and by 1775 had moved there from Newport. He signed several unusual stones which mark him as an important carver. The Charles Bardin stone, 1773, Newport, Rhode Island (plate 104A), bears the only extant representation of God in New England as well as the initials "J. B.", presumably for John Bull. During his early years he was a sailor and must have acquired more visual sophistication than most other members of his later profession. That he would risk such a representation in New England at all tells us a great deal about the changes wrought in God's New Zion in little more than a century. In 1673 such an image would have caused a scandal but one hundred years later it seems to have been accepted with equanimity and has endured into the second half of the 20th century without any signs of mutilation.

The simple undulate border panels used on the Bardin stone are repeated on the Elizabeth and Nathaniel Coggeshall stones, 1773, Newport, Rhode Island (plates 189A and 189B). Considering the fact that Bull was connected to the Coggeshall family on his mother's side and that the border panels of the initialled Bardin stone and those of the Coggeshall stones are identical it is doubly likely that Bull was the carver of the latter.

The Benjamin Wyatt marker, 1767, Newport, Rhode Island (plate 190), is provisionally attributed to him. It is certainly one of the most moving images in all New England. The sorrowing eyes seem to express a universal grief in the mortality of man, a grief only partially tempered by the conception of the immortality of man's soul. Surely this stone reflects the observation of Jonathan Edwards that men who love the beauty of this world are slow to exchange it for the joys of the next. Though many of the carvings proclaim a cheerful message of Resurrection, there are also a considerable number of this more melancholic disposition. The emotional range of New England imagery is wide, yet it does not include the element of religious-sexual ecstasy which is common in much baroque religious art, nor does it encompass the excesses of sentimentality which were to be found abroad in 19th century tomb art. Looking at death with perhaps more primitive directness than was the case with the more practiced tomb artists of Europe, the New England stonecarver could rarely mask his feelings with a series of dissembling clichés carved into stone.[72]

VI. THE PROVINCIAL BAROQUE STYLE IN CONNECTICUT IN THE 18th CENTURY

1. Massachusetts and Rhode Island Prototypes in Connecticut

MAP 5 shows the movement of provincial baroque stones into Connecticut from Newport and Greater Boston. Boston cut stones are to be found in large numbers in Stratford, Connecticut, as early as the beginning of the 18th century (plates 193A and 235A). Rhode Island stones are to be found in eastern Connecticut as early as the 1750's. The McCurdy example (plate 191A), though not distinguished in itself, is a type seen throughout the area and very important for the development of eastern Connecticut carving.

Given such stones as models local carvers could either attempt naturalistic improvements, which would mean some knowledge of the plastic versus the glyptic technique of carving, or descend into pure linear ornament by a process of reduction and simplification. For want

PLATE 189. A. Detail of the Elizabeth Coggeshall stone, 1773, Newport, Rhode Island. Slate. B. Detail of the Nathaniel Coggeshall stone, 1773, Newport, Rhode Island. Slate.

PLATE 190. Detail of the Benjamin Wyatt stone, 1767, Newport, Rhode Island. Slate.

of technique they chose the latter path.

The carver of the Brewster stone, 1773, Norwich, Connecticut (plate 191B), almost certainly used a Rhode Island stone similar to the McCurdy example as a model. Examples of both prototypes and copies may be found in Storrs, Franklin, Mansfield Center, Norwich, Norwichtown, Ledyard, New London, Groton, Pachaug, and Plainfield among other places.

2. Connecticut Variants

As the 18th century progressed Connecticut Valley carvers became more adept at miming the coastal provincial baroque style, although it is not known at this time whether or not they worked exclusively from imported stone prototypes, from printed models, or from both. The Nathanael Sutlief stone, 1760, Durham, Connecticut (plate 192A), is a provincial copy of a shield and acanthus motif used widely in England on such monuments as the Webb stone (plate 129). The Sutlief stone and others like it influenced the development of the Connecticut Valley style of carving by blending together provincial baroque and ornamental elements in a manner unique to the Valley tradition. Another Connecticut Valley example which echoes the baroque tradition is the Reverend Samuel Woodbridge stone, 1746, East Hartford, Connecticut (plate 192B).

VII. THE ORIGINS AND DEVELOPMENT OF THE NEOCLASSICAL STYLE IN NEW ENGLAND: 1769–1815

THE last stylistic wave to wash over the shores of New England in the 18th century was the neoclassic. Although there are a few stones which show the traces of the rococo, it cannot be said to have been a major influence.[73] One of the first stones to appear in Massachusetts with the new devices was the John Hurd stone cut in 1784 in The Granary, Boston (plate 192D). The bent willow, the cinerary urn, and the tomb were all present. Only the traditional stola-clad weepers, so prevalent on English stones, were missing.

The Hurd stone is, however, more baroque in style than neoclassic and illustrates the difficulty the carvers had in adjusting to the new style. The scroll top and the bulbous, oversized cinerary urn were carried over from the earlier style. The classical sentiments of restraint and balance are not to be seen in this bloated representation, although for all intents and purposes the outward motifs were correct and proper.

A.

B.

PLATE 191. A. Detail of the Ursula McCurdy stone, 1781, Norwich, Connecticut. Slate. 24 x 37. B. Detail of the Sary Brewster stone, 1773, Norwich, Connecticut. Slate. 14 x 22.

A.

B.

C.

D.

PLATE 192. A. The Nathanael Sutlief stone, 1760, Durham, Connecticut. Red sandstone. 27 x 54. B. The Reverend
Samuel Woodbridge stone, 1746, East Hartford, Connecticut. Red sandstone. 30¼ x 36. C. The Marcia
Holmes stone, 1800, Kingston, Massachusetts. Slate. 20¼ x 48. D. The John Hurd stone, 1784, The Granary,
Boston, Massachusetts. Slate. 25 x 44¾.

The clash between the old and the new styles was short lived and soon even carvers in far off Palmer Center, Massachusetts, knew how to create pleasing monuments to suit the new taste; the Cargill stone of 1813 (plate 60) is a good example of the type. Where the Hurd stone of 1784 still attempted to achieve a sense of volume to the point of cutting the inscription following the supposed line of the cinerary urn as it curved backward in space, the carving of the Cargill stone of twenty-nine years later is a flat friezelike pattern of architectural forms moving horizontally. By 1800 almost every burial ground in New England save for those sunk in a totally rural atmosphere reflected the forms and themes of the new style. The Marcia Holmes stone of 1800, Kingston, Massachusetts (plate 192c), is an example of the diffusion of the style in Massachusetts in less than twenty years after its inception. There are literally hundreds of these stones in the burial grounds of Kingston and Plymouth.

Many of the early 19th century neoclassical stones in Plymouth County look as if they had been colored; if so, it would be the first evidence of polychrome in New England. The Holmes stone of 1800 reaches extremes in neoclassical sentiment or sentimentality. The epitaph reads,

> Nor pain, nor grief, nor anxious fear
> Invade thy bounds. No moral woes
> Can reach the lovely Sleeper here,
> And Angels watch her soft repose.

Before the introduction of neoclassical motifs into New England the Yankee enthusiastically pictured the flight of the soul to heaven upon his gravestones. Later it was no longer fashionable to portray the naïve joys of Christianity when shiny new neoclassical sentiments had just been imported from England. A mark of culturally provincial people is the degree to which they abandon their own values and become the slaves of one imported fashion after another. That the coastal New Englander always remained closer to European and English models than did his rural cousin is surely true in the field of stonecarving. Indeed, many coastal gravestones are nothing more than pale shadowings of English styles. Rural New England, however, was almost totally free of this eroding influence until the final triumph of the neoclassical style. It was not so much that the sentiments of the neoclassical age were any less correct than those which they had replaced; it was simply that the imagery of Imperial Rome and to a lesser extent of Olympian Greece had little real relevance in rural New England. It is difficult to see how the relatively poor farmers and shopkeepers who frequented their local stonecarver could have truly participated in a style more at home in a salon than in a vegetable patch.

The style forged by the rural New Englander isolated from the high urban motifs of coastal New England had a great deal more virtue than the charming neoclassical pretentions which replaced it. The bumptious aspirations of a newly emerging America are nowhere more appallingly revealed than in the transformation of style from the natural rural idiom of abstraction to a hollow provincialized one. The enthusiastic fervor with which Americans devour every new artistic style was as evident in the late 18th century as it is apparent today. In the Waldron stone (plate 188) American aspirations far outran American abilities.

The lack of co-ordination between the new imagery and the old style is apparent upon the Betsey Russell stone, 1790, Stratford, Connecticut (plate 193A), where the curvilinear provincial baroque style cannot be adjusted to the exigencies of the newer neoclassical imagery which demanded a more severe linear treatment. The result was a stone cut in the old spirit but using the new motifs. Aspiration once again outran performance. Desire and technique were only joined later in the 19th century on stones such as the Oren Alley marker, 1822, Durham, Connecticut (plate 193B), when the flair of the earlier carving had been replaced with the deadly mechanical commercial flatness of the new style.

Other neoclassical motifs began to work their way up the Connecticut Valley as early as 1780 in the form of profile portraits seen in plates 194 through 201. Neoclassical profile portraiture may have originated via engravings such as the one printed in a 1792 Hartford election sermon which served as a prototype for the Samuel Hall stone of 1795 (plates 152A and 152B).

Noble variants of the Connecticut neoclassical profile-portrait style may be seen in the burial grounds of South and East Glastonbury, Connecticut, although strangely enough neither in Glastonbury proper nor in Wethersfield. The Hannah and Dorothy Treat stone, 1799 and 1796, East Glastonbury (plates 194A and 194B), are representative examples, while the William Holmes stone, 1800 (plate 195), is one of the most dramatic. Surely the grandest of all is the Holmes stone of 1795 in East Glastonbury (plate 196), in which four profile portraits appear in an archaic friezelike procession across the top hori-

A.

B.

PLATE 193. A. Detail of the Betsey Russell stone, 1790, Stratford, Connecticut. Slate. 15½ x 24. B. Detail of the Oren Alley stone, 1822, Durham, Connecticut. White marble.

A.

B.

PLATE 194. A. Detail of the Hannah Treat stone, 1799, East Glastonbury, Connecticut. Red sandstone. 20½ x 38.
B. Detail of the Dorothy Treat stone, 1796, East Glastonbury, Connecticut. Red sandstone. 21¾ x 25¾.

zontal band of the stone. It will be noted that the women were differentiated from the men by hairbows, and infants from both by closely cropped hair (plate 195).

Further up the Connecticut Valley in Farmington another carver was at work as early as 1777 but his stones lack the dignity and resolve of the East and South Glastonbury markers. The Noah Andruss stone, 1777 (plate 197), and the Daniel Grindley marker, 1781 (plate 198), are representative of his work. If these examples are not back dated, and there is no reason to believe that they are, they are the earliest neoclassical profile portraits to appear in the Connecticut Valley.

Another carver working in the Meriden-Wallingford-Southington area produced a large number of stones between *ca.* 1781 and 1795 which were variants of the Farmington portraits. The Reverend John Wightman stone, 1781, Southington, Connecticut (plate 199A), the Abel Yale stone, 1784 (plate 199B), the Deacon John Hough marker, 1788 (plate 200A), and the Samuel Hall stone, 1795 (plate 200B), the latter three in Meriden, Connecticut, are examples. Crude copies of the Meriden-Wallingford-Southington portraits appear in and around Enfield, Connecticut, in the 1790's.

Far more interesting than these attempts to emulate stones such as the Hough-Hall examples (plates 200A and 200B), are several late 18th century Meriden carvings which seem to be looking for a way to transform the neoclassical profile formula into the abstract idiom of rural art. Just as the provincial artist's mind will begin to simplify the complex spatial undulations of baroque modelling by making a series of systematic reductions (such as the ones which took place between the Baskervile and Webb monuments, plates 126 and 129), so the carver of the Lucretia Hough stone, 1797 (plate 201A), and the Mary Simpson marker, 1799 (plate 201B), both in Meriden, attempted to reduce the Hall-Hough formula (plates 200A and 200B) by eliminating all excessive detail and thus all linear ornamentation. What was really taking place was not a movement from a provincial adaptation of a high metropolitan formula to the depths of barbarism, but a far more complex visual process masked by the technical crudeness of the execution. Indeed, the Amasa Brainard stone, 1798, East Haddam, Connecticut (plate 202), an obvious product of the radical abstractionism of the rural Connecticut ornamental style (stemming in part from motifs derived from neoclassical profile portraits), is certainly what the carver of the Hough-Simpson stones would have liked to have achieved but

PLATE 195. Detail of the William Holmes stone, 1800, East Glastonbury, Connecticut. Red sandstone. 16 x 22½.

PLATE 196. The Holmes children stone, 1795, East Glastonbury, Connecticut. Red sandstone, 48 x 45.

PLATE 197. Detail of the Noah Andruss stone, 1777, Farmington, Connecticut. Red sandstone. 26 x 40.

PLATE 198. Detail of the Daniel Gridley stone, 1781, Farmington, Connecticut. Red sandstone. 24 x 46.

A.

B.

PLATE 199. A. Detail of the Reverend John Wightman stone, 1781, Southington, Connecticut. Red sandstone. 23¾ x 39½. B. Detail of the Abel Yale stone, 1784, Meriden, Connecticut. Red sandstone. 24½ x 40¾.

A.

B.

PLATE 200. A. Detail of the Deacon John Hough stone, 1788, Meriden, Connecticut. Red sandstone. 24½ x 42¾.
B. Detail of the Samuel Hall stone, 1795, Meriden, Connecticut. Red sandstone. 24½ x 33¾.

A.

B.

PLATE 201. A. Detail of the Lucretia Hough stone, 1797, Meriden, Connecticut. Red sandstone. 23 x 43½. B. Detail of the Mary Simpson stone, 1799, Meriden, Connecticut. Red sandstone. 26 x 48¼.

PLATE 202. Detail of the Amasa Brainard stone, 1798, East Haddam, Connecticut. Red sandstone. 41 x 22½.

could not. In this splendid rural carving the outward conventions of a borrowed European style have been totally transformed into the rustic idiom of abstract geometric carving. It is astonishing to note that the sleek functional simplicity of the Brainard portrait is a presentiment of modern art and not far removed from the more sophisticated Brancusi portraits of Madam Pogany. Looking at New England rural stone-carving in the light of what has been learned about art in the last hundred years it is no longer possible to maintain that art always seeks a more perfect naturalism and any movement away from mimesis is a return to barbarism. It seems to me that this is looking at art in a mirror borrowed from the Greeks and the Romans. By freeing ourselves from this classicizing prejudice and antiquarian fixation it is possible to see the Brainard stone as an attempt to transform an alien imagery into the more familiar idiom of pictographic abstraction. But in dealing with these problems it must always be remembered that we are dealing with a form of popular art which did not have enough time to become a cultivated form of expression before it was cast aside in the triumph of the neoclassical style in rural New England. The question is not one of artistic expectations fulfilled but of aesthetic directions formulated. As we shall see in the next sections, I believe that there can be no question that a rural vision of form was emerging. Whether or not it was a particularly "American" vision is altogether another question. The curtain was rung down on this act of creation, however, when stones such as the Elizabeth Watson marker, 1798, Plymouth, Massachusetts (plate 203), which are nothing more than sterile secondhand copies of English neoclassical prototypes, took the public's fancy.

VIII. THE ORIGINS AND DEVELOPMENT OF THE ORNAMENTAL STYLES IN NEW ENGLAND: 1668–1815

1. The Ornamental Style in Plymouth County, Massachusetts: 1728–1770

A. THE SOULE FAMILY

The earliest stones in Plymouth County were imported from Greater Boston in the late 17th century. Types such as the Lieutenant William Hescy marker, 1689, Wakefield, Massachusetts (plates 204A and 204C), were commonly exported far and wide (see Map 5). One of the earliest locally cut stones was the John Holmes marker, 1728, Middleboro Center, Massachusetts (plates 204B and 204D). The latter is in reality nothing more than an ornamental façade sheathing an essen-

PLATE 203. The Elizabeth Watson stone, 1798, Plymouth, Massachusetts. Slate. 24 at base x 34.

A.

B.

C.

D.

PLATE 204. A. Detail of the William Hescy stone, 1689, Wakefield, Massachusetts. Slate. 27½ x 22. B. Detail of the John Holmes stone, 1728, Middleboro Center, Massachusetts. Slate. 18½ x 19. C. Detail of the left border panel of plate 204A. D. Detail of the right border panel of plate 204B.

tially provincial baroque stone. Just as the carver of the Brewster marker (plate 191B) turned the "naturalistic" effects of the McCurdy marker (plate 191A) into flat abstract ornament, so too the carver of the Holmes stone transformed the provincial formulas of the Hescy stone into a flatter more antispatial design which was well on its way toward abstraction.

By the time the Gershem Holmes stone of 1739, Plymouth, Massachusetts (plate 205A), the movement toward an ornamental effect had become even more pronounced. The formation of the skull followed pleasing flat geometric patterns while the feathering of the wings was reduced to nothing more than crossing undulate and curved lines spread out at both tips as if hinting of weight and substance. On the Washbun stone of 1743 in Kingston, Massachusetts (plate 205B), cut four years later, the splayed-out wing tips, so obviously a part of both the Holmes stones, had vanished suggesting that we are witnessing a process of serial abstraction. It was no longer necessary to suggest that the effigy had corporeal substance because it now existed in terms of itself and not in terms of the seen optical world. Moreover, the bald profile effigy suspended just over the mouth of the skull on the Holmes stone of 1739 had been replaced by the earlier heart palmette motif used on the 1728 Holmes marker.

By the time of the Mary Holmes stone of 1749, Kingston, Massachusetts (plate 205C), a critical period of transition had been reached and the imagery retreated into itself as if in confusion. The iconography had been changing from a death's head into what I take to be a soul effigy. At this point the carver was not sure which way to turn and so relied upon massive whirls and a diminution of the face to achieve his purposes. In this period of transition, ornament engulfs image. The resolution came on stones such as the Sarah Hall marker of 1756, Kingston, Massachusetts (plate 205D), where the imagery appeared once again in positive form, but now transformed into a soul effigy. Many of the older characteristics of the death's head had been carried over into the new imagery such as the feathered background, the cleft in the cranium, and the splayed-out calligraphic nose. The heart palmette mouth had become a T-cross and the eyes had begun to be formed with the aid of a compass.

A local Plymouth County style, which had started out as nothing more than a linear treatment of a provincial baroque formula, had become completely transformed stylistically and iconographically in a period of less than twenty-eight years.

PLATE 205. A. Detail of the Gershem Holmes stone, 1739, Plymouth, Massachusetts. Slate. 15½ x 19¾. B. Detail of the Wilborah Washbun stone, 1743, Kingston, Massachusetts. Slate. 18½ x 23½. C. Detail of the Mary Holmes stone, 1749, Kingston, Massachusetts. Slate. 19½ x 23½. D. Detail of the Sarah Hall stone, 1756, Kingston, Massachusetts. Slate. 18¾ x 24.

The men who carved these stones may have been members of the Soule family of Plympton, Massachusetts. Ebenezer Soule was born in Plympton in 1710 or 1711 and died in 1792.[74] The attribution is based upon the probated will for the estate of John May which paid Soule £5.3.5, for four pairs of gravestones in May of 1772.[75] The Sarah May stone (daughter of John May) 1761, Plymouth, Massachusetts (plate 206B), still stands and was almost certainly carved by the Soule family. The Deborah Samson stone, 1769, Kingston, Massachusetts (plate 206A), is a far more carefully cut variant of the same motif. Ebenezer, Sr., had a son Ebenezer who was born in Plympton in 1737 and died in 1811. According to Mrs. Forbes, members of the Soule family did a great deal of moving about (see Map 4).[76] Ebenezer Soule died in Hinsdale, New Hampshire, in 1792,[77] but it is not known when or why he left Plympton. Stones cut in the manner of the May and Samson examples are rarely seen in Plymouth County after *ca.* 1770 and it might be that members of the family began their migrations into rural New England at this time. Other stonecarving members of the family were Beza and Coomer Soule, both of whom worked for a time in Worcester Country, Massachusetts.[78] Beza died in Deerfield, Massachusetts, in 1855. Since almost all the members of the Soule family left Plympton to carve elsewhere it is remarkable to note that they failed to bring with them the elements of the Soule style which distinguished their work in Plymouth County for thirty years. The problem of what the Soule family carved after *ca.* 1770 remains a vexing one, but prior to their migrations they left their marks in Marshfield, Duxbury, Kingston, Plymouth, Plympton, North Carver, Middleboro Center, and Halifax, among other places (see Map 8).

The Eleazar Churchill stone, 1754, Plymouth, Massachusetts (plate 207), is attributed to their workshop and is far different from the John Watson stone of that same year in Plymouth which is attributed to the Codner workshop (plate 151C). The bold design of the former is composed of a series of circular motifs bearing more the calligrapher's than the sculptor's mark, suggesting that the Soules were more concerned with designed abstractions than with optical miming. By 1754 then, the ornamental style of carving in Plymouth had reached a point of formal sophistication far in advance of the gropings of the provincial baroque style which never amounted to anything more than pale shadowings of more robust English models. Indeed, it seems that by the time of the Josiah Cotton stone of 1756, Plymouth, Massachusetts (plate 208), a dilution of the abstract motifs is evidenced. There

A.

B.

PLATE 206. A. Detail of the Deborah Samson stone, 1769, Kingston, Massachusetts. Slate. 24 x 27¼. B. Detail of the Sarah May stone, 1761, Plymouth, Massachusetts. Slate.

PLATE 207. Detail of the Eleazar Churchill stone, 1754, Plymouth, Massachusetts. Slate. 22 x 26½.

is a softening of the treatment of the hair from the bold coil-volutes of the 1754 Churchill stone to the timid but more comforting hairdo on the Cotton stone while feathered wings enigmatically sprout from the ears. In the transformation much of the primitive power of the earlier imagery had been lost.

In summary, the Soule family began with a simple linear façade over a provincial baroque base and proceeded to understand it in terms of the New England propensity for turning volume into line and for eliciting the maximum surface effects for the minimum of incised lines.

2. The Ornamental Style in Essex County, Massachusetts: Phase I: 1668–1730

A. THE HAVERHILL CARVERS I, II, AND III

The John White marker of 1668 in Haverhill, Massachusetts, is the oldest ornamented stone in New England[79] (plates 209 and 210). The design of the White stone, unlike that of the Holmes stone of 1728 (plates 204B and 204D), was not taken from an exported Boston prototype. Indeed, there were no ornamented stones in greater Boston before *ca.* 1674–1676, some six to eight years after the White marker was cut. The question is whether or not we can accept the date of the latter as authentic? Based upon comparative evidence the answer is yes. The unornamented stones which have come down to us from Greater Boston in the early 1650's all bear the heavy horizontal guide lines and the colon separation. By 1658 on the William Paddy marker in King's Chapel the former had been eliminated and the latter transformed into "floating periods." By the 1670's the progressive carvers had dropped the latter as an archaism. To be sure, the earlier colon separation does surface from time to time as on the Morgin stone of 1696 in rural Enfield, Connecticut (plate 162A), but such cases are rare and there is usually something which distinguished them from the more authentic early stones; in the case of the Morgin stone it is the omission of the heavy horizontal guide lines. The White marker of 1668 has both the inscribed horizontal guide lines and the colon separation suggesting that the date stands as authentic until someone proves otherwise.[80]

Many themes which were to become part of the vocabulary of the ornamental rural New England style of carving are to be seen on the White marker. This is the first appearance of the coil-volute on the border panels, the web rosettes and a winged effigy under the central lunette which we have reason to believe may be a soul effigy. The foot-stone (plate 210) has borders of heart palmettes which surfaced in the

PLATE 208. Detail of the Josiah Cotton stone, 1756, Plymouth, Massachusetts. Slate. 23¼ x 24.

PLATE 209. The John White stone, 1668, Haverhill, Massachusetts. Schist. 13¾ x 15½.

PLATE 210. The John White footstone. See plate 209.

18th century in Plymouth County in variant form. Moreover at the base of each vertical border panel there seem to be abstract trees or shrubs. Hovering just under a weather-worn soul effigy, the form of an abstract hourglass can be seen. Similar stones cut until *ca.* 1699 will be attributed to the Haverhill carver I. Like motifs appear in Haverhill, North Andover, Rowley, and Ipswich before the 18th century but in the latter case they very well may be the work of an independent workshop armed with the same motifs.

The Timothy Swan stone, 1692, North Andover, Massachusetts (plate 211A), is very close to the John White stone of 1668 and is attributed to the Haverhill carver I. By the time of the Sary Michel stone of 1705 in Haverhill (plate 211C), another hand is at work, although the connection with the earlier stones is clear. The Ebenezer Ayer stone, 1699, Haverhill, Massachusetts (plate 211B), seems to fall into the same category. For the sake of convenience these stones should be attributed to the Haverhill carver II.

As early as 1674 on the Thomas Hart stone (plate 214A), a similar style emerged in Ipswich, Massachusetts but was accompanied by twin abstract birds touching beaks just above the central soul effigy. Because this variant design more properly belongs to Ipswich than to Haverhill these carvings should be attributed to the Ipswich carver I. The Sarya Wilcom stone, 1705, Rowley, Massachusetts (plate 211D), is almost certainly an 18th century variant of the Ipswich style.

After the appearance of the Michel marker in Haverhill (plate 211C), there is a sharp break in the chronological sequence of stones until the appearance of the Ruth Peaslee marker of 1723 (plate 212A), which shows a soul effigy hovering above a tendril-vine motif while web rosettes loom large on either side. This may be the first appearance in Haverhill of the double outlined soul effigy (notice the caplike band over the head). The use of double outlined faces may be seen in more mature form on the Samuel Green stone, 1759, Lexington, Massachusetts (plate 218).

It was not the practice to double outline the soul effigy *per se* in Ipswich, but as on the Alice Hart stone of 1682 (plate 214B), the outlines were consequences of the banded chain ornament surrounding the effigy. Another feature of the Peaslee stone which was to endure until the 1770's was the teardrop rather than the oval-shaped head which had been characteristic of the Haverhill style up until that time. Stones such as the Peaslee example and the Elizabeth Clark marker, 1728, Haverhill, Massachusetts (plate 212B), can be attributed to the

PLATE 211. A. Detail of the Timothy Swan stone, 1692, North Andover, Massachusetts. Schist. B. Detail of the Ebenezer Ayer stone, 1699, Haverhill, Massachusetts. Schist. 23½ x 19. C. Detail of the Sary Michel stone, 1705, Haverhill, Massachusetts. Schist. 15¼ x 14. D. Detail of the Sarya Wilcom stone, 1705, Rowley, Massachusetts. Schist. 21¼ x 21¼.

A.

B.

PLATE 212. A. Detail of the Ruth Peaslee stone, 1723, Haverhill, Massachusetts. Schist. 24½ x 24. B. Detail of the Elizabeth Clark stone, 1728, Haverhill, Massachusetts. Schist. 23½ x 20.

Haverhill carver III. According to Mrs. Forbes[81] a stonecarver named Robert Mulican lived just across the river in Bradford, Massachusetts, between 1688 and 1765. Mulican may very well turn out to be the Haverhill carver III. One of the strongest examples of the Haverhill manner of carving is the Nathaniel Peaslee stone, 1730, (plate 213), which owes nothing to the provincialisms flowing into coastal New England from Boston.

Stones cut in the manner of the Haverhill carvers may be seen in Portsmouth, New Hampshire, Merrimac, North Andover, Georgetown, Rowley, Ipswich, Boxford, and Danvers, Massachusetts.

B. THE IPSWICH CARVERS I AND II AND IA AND IB

The lack of dated stones between 1668 and 1699 in Haverhill is certainly an irreparable loss; the fact that similar stones appear in Ipswich as early as 1674 and continued to be carved into the 1720's is something of a consolation. The Thomas Hart stone, 1674, Ipswich, Massachusetts (plate 214A), is similar to the White and Swan markers save for the addition of banded bird ornaments. The use of "ornimorphic" motifs distinguishes Ipswich stones from those carved in nearby Haverhill. The Alice Hart stone, 1682, Ipswich, Massachusetts (plate 214B), is a slightly later example of the same motif. Both examples can be attributed to the Ipswich carver I. The Hazel Wood stone, 1714, Rowley, Massachusetts (plate 214C), seems to me to be a product of the same workshop and is attributed to the Ipswich carver II.[82] A variant of the Wood marker is the John Ropper stone, 1709, Ipswich, Massachusetts (plate 214D).

In addition to the use of "ornimorphic" motifs in and around Ipswich, local carvers created a series of primitive stones ranging in date from 1689 until 1721 which substituted curly hair for the banded chain ornament which had heretofore framed the central soul effigies. The Mary Hart stone, 1689, Ipswich, Massachusetts (plate 215A), is an early example of the type while the John Bridgham stone, 1721, (plate 215C), Ipswich, Massachusetts, is one of the last. For the sake of convenience let us attribute these stones to the Ipswich carvers IA and IB. Stones attributed to the latter surfaced in Rowley, Massachusetts, during the third decade of the 18th century. The Thomas Hart stone (plate 215B), and the Mary Burpe marker (plate 215D), both cut in 1721, are typical examples. The Hart-Burpe stones formed a link between the earlier Ipswich style and later Rowley variants which I believe to have been locally carved.

PLATE 213. Detail of the Nathaniel Peaslee stone, 1730, Haverhill, Massachusetts. Schist. 25¼ x 26.

A.

B.

C.

D.

PLATE 214. A. Detail of the Thomas Hart stone, 1674, Ipswich, Massachusetts. Schist. 17½ x 19. B. Detail of the Alice Hart stone, 1682, Ipswich, Massachusetts. Schist. 20½ x 22. C. Detail of the Hazel Wood stone, 1714, Rowley, Massachusetts. Schist. D. Detail of the John Ropper stone, 1709, Ipswich, Massachusetts. Schist. 23½ x 23½.

A.

B.

C.

D.

PLATE 215. A. Detail of the Mary Hart stone, 1689, Ipswich, Massachusetts. Schist. 20¼ x 22. B. Detail of the
Thomas Hart stone, 1721, Rowley, Massachusetts. Schist. 17¼ x 16¼. C. Detail of the John Bridgham stone,
1721, Ipswich, Massachusetts. Schist. 17¾ x 19. D. Detail of the Mary Burpe stone, 1721, Rowley, Massachusetts. Schist. 21¼ x 19.

The first phase of the development of the Essex County ornamental style drew to a close about 1730 and was marked by extended use of banded chain ornament, which often turned "ornimorphic"; emphasis on the geometric family of rosettes; a strictly linear conception of abstract form; and by the adoption of a variant curly headed effigy in the place of the older less florid one. Stones cut in this manner seemed to stem from centers in Ipswich, Haverhill, and Rowley. The style endured until at least the 1730's.

3. The Ornamental Style in Essex County, Massachusetts: Phase II: 1730–1750

A. THE ROWLEY CARVER AND HIS INFLUENCE

With the placing of the Thomas Hart and the Mary Burpe stones in Rowley as early as 1721 (plates 215B and 215D), the models upon which a local style could be erected were already present. Certainly by the time of the Mary Pickard marker, 1743, Rowley, Massachusetts (plate 216D), a style unique to Rowley had emerged. The Mary Plats stone, 1726, Rowley, Massachusetts (plate 216A), may be an early example of the work of the Rowley carver, although it is still possible to associate the former with the work of the Ipswich carver IB. I tend, however, to think that the Plats stone was locally carved because the small close-set eyes were characteristic of later Rowley rather than earlier Ipswich carving. By the time of the Thomas Hale stone, 1730, Rowley, Massachusetts (plate 216B), the motif of wavy hair seen on the Plats stone had been replaced by large six-pointed rosettes which suggest an influence from Haverhill. Later still on the Humphrey Hobson stone, 1742, Rowley, Massachusetts (plate 216C), the eyes had become thin slits and the effigy freed from a contiguous connection with ancillary forms, this connection being one of the major characteristics of the first phase of the development of the Essex County ornamental style. On the Pickard stone of 1743 (plate 216D), the effigy was once and for all freed from its chains of bondage and allowed to float freely against a plain background. The trend was to continue into the third phase of the style and is evident on the extraordinary Samuel Green marker, 1759, Lexington, Massachusetts (plate 218).

According to Mrs. Forbes a carver named Robert Leighton lived in Rowley and carved the Moses Bradstreet stone of 1738.[83] If the latter proves to be similar to the stones illustrated in plate 216 then it can be assumed that Leighton was the Rowley carver.

The use of banded double outlines which held the effigies in a

A.

B.

C.

D.

PLATE 216. A. Detail of the Mary Plats stone, 1726, Rowley, Massachusetts. Schist. 21 x 22. B. Detail of the Thomas Hale stone, 1730, Rowley, Massachusetts. Schist. 26¾ x 26½. c. Detail of the Humphrey Hobson stone, 1742, Rowley, Massachusetts. Schist. 30¼ x 30. D. Detail of the Mary Pickard stone, 1743, Rowley, Massachusetts. Schist. 24¾ x 24.

schematic grid was nothing more than a New England rural variant of the Northern *Horror Vacui*, a term which describes the propensity of "Barbarian" artists to cover every inch of surface with abstract designs. By the time the curly headed variants of the Ipswich carvers IA and IB were introduced in the late 1680's, the fascination with chain ornament was already beginning to subside. The Rowley variants make it even more clear that by the 1730's there was no longer a formal need for the use of contiguous forms and the effigies were set loose to hover against an unornamented background plane.

The first phase of the Essex County ornamental style was characterized by the use of banded double outlines, chain and "ornimorphic" ornament and, in the last years, by the curly-headed variant. This phase drew to a close in the 1730's in Haverhill and ten years earlier in Ipswich. Phase two began to develop in Rowley as early as perhaps 1726 and prospered there until the late 1740's. It may be characterized by the freeing of the central effigy from the networks of banded and undulate ornament which had formerly encased it. Similar stones are to be seen as far west as Harvard, Massachusetts, where they apparently became the models for the development of Phase III of the Essex County ornamental style which commenced after *ca.* 1736 in Middlesex County.

4. The Spread of the Essex County Ornamental Style to Middlesex and Worcester Counties: Phases II and III: 1736–1772

A. THE WORSTER FAMILY

Stones attributed to the Rowley carver appear in Harvard, Massachusetts, by 1736—e.g., the Hazadiah Priest stone (plate 217A, Map 7). Before 1736 there were no such stones in the burial ground. The Priest marker was cut in July of 1736 and by December of that same year a variant had been cut on the Silas Rand stone (plate 217B). Notice how the facial contour has changed into a teardrop shape and how the schematic features have become enlarged suggesting another hand and a further movement of the style. By 1739 on the Hannah Clark stone (plate 217C), the incisions have become deeper and the carving more sure of itself. The eyes, which were simple slits on the Rand stone, are beginning to open up. The style went through a series of adjustments until the Samuel Green variant of 1759 (plate 218).

Stones cut in this manner form Phase III of the Essex County ornamental style and were sent out from Harvard as far as Brookfield, Massachusetts, in the west and Watertown in the east (Map 7). According

A.

B.

C.

PLATE 217. A. Detail of the Hazadiah Priest stone, 1736, Harvard, Massachusetts. Schist. 25 x 28. B. Detail of the Silas Rand stone, 1736, Harvard, Massachusetts. Schist. 20 x 21. C. Detail of the Hannah Clark stone, 1739, Harvard, Massachusetts. Slate. 19¾ x 21½.

to Mrs. Forbes these stones were all cut by Moses and Jonathan Worster, a father and son who lived in Harvard.[84] Jonathan, the father, was born in Bradford, Massachusetts (near Haverhill where the Essex County ornamental style originated), in 1707. He died in Harvard in 1754. In 1756 the executor of the estate of Josiah Burge of Westford, Massachusetts, went to Harvard and paid the widow Worster £3.14.0 for gravestones.[85] It is upon this probate record that Phase III of the Essex County ornamental style can be attributed to the Worster family.

Examples cut after 1754 would have been executed by Moses Worster who was born in 1739. It appears that Moses carved the stone for his father (plate 219), as well as the Green example of 1759. The latter is a more successful example and remains a high point of the Essex County ornamental style Phase III. An image of power and force had been created with limited means out of the hard dark slates of the Pin Hill quarries (Map 2)[86] and is illustrative of how far rural carving could go without the obtrusive influence of 17th and 18th century European styles.

Stones cut in this manner were placed throughout central Massachusetts (Map 7) until 1772 when Moses Worster finally succumbed to the attraction of the coastal provincial style. He ruined whatever sense of abstraction he had had in his fingertips by attempting to emulate a watered-down naturalism which was foreign to his own native vision of form. The Rebekah Worster stone, 1772 (plate 220), is illustrative of the collapse of rural carving into an insipid imitation of a low copy of a European model. Rebekah Worster was the wife of Jonathan and the mother of Moses.

With the cutting of the Rebekah Worster stone of 1772 the thread of a stylistic development which began in Haverhill, Massachusetts, in 1668 was broken. Rural forms could no longer remain isolated from the impact of coastal provincialisms and the collapse of the Worster family style is a foretaste of the total collapse of rural imagery with the rapid diffusion of neoclassical imagery after 1800.

5. The Spread of the Essex County Ornamental Style to Eastern Connecticut: Phase I: 1722–1730

A. JOSHUA HEMPSTEAD: 1678–1758

Joshua Hempstead first mentions the carving of gravestones on Monday, June 11, 1722.[87] On Thursday, August 12, 1725, Hempstead penned the following note in his diary: "I markt. a pr of Gr. Stones for Sister Patience Hodsell."[88] The stone may be seen in plate 222A.

PLATE 218. Detail of the Samuel Green stone, 1759, Lexington, Massachusetts. Slate. 27¾ x 33¾.

PLATE 219. The Jonathan Worster stone, 1754, Harvard, Massachusetts. Slate. 30¾ x 39.

PLATE 220. The Rebekah Worster stone, 1772, Harvard, Massachusetts. Slate. 21¾ x 31½.

Joshua Hempstead was born on September 1, 1678, in New London, Connecticut, and died there in 1758.[89] Hempstead was, among other occupations, a farmer, a surveyor, a house and ship carpenter, an attorney, a sailor, a judge of probate, a merchant, and a stonecarver.[90] In the course of the diary Hempstead mentions numerous stones that he cut, all in the style of the Hodsell marker, but never once mentions where he got the designs or what if anything, they may have meant to him. What we know of his borrowings and whom he influenced has to be reconstructed. The diary gives us no clues.

Between 1720 and 1730 a number of grey schists carved in the manner of the Hodsell stone begin to appear in the New London area although we had formerly associated them with Essex County in Massachusetts (Map 7). The Hanah Johnson stone of 1717 in Rowley (plate 221A), is representative of the style which formed the models for Hempstead to copy and bring to Connecticut. The Joanna ——— fragment, it will be noted, is a copy of the Rowley stone of 1717 (plate 221B) and represents the diffusion of the Essex County ornamental style Phase I into Eastern Connecticut after 1720. The Ann Eams stone, 1732, New London, Connecticut (plate 221C), and the Hodsell stone (plate 222A) are variants on the same theme.

Two variants were used by Hempstead between 1722 and about 1732: effigies suspended in banded outlines, and others which turn into birds touching beaks just above the central soul effigies. Plates 221B and 221C show the latter variants and plates 222A, 222B, and 222C the former. It seems that the abstract birds appeared later than the abstract banded double outlines. For example, the Ann Mason stone, 1724, Windham, Connecticut, the Patience Hodsell stone of 1725 (plate 222A), and the John Arnold stone of 1725 (plate 222C), are all without "ornimorphic" devices, and are all dated 1725 or before. The first bird ornament to appear in eastern Connecticut was on the William Hall stone, 1727, in Mansfield Center, Connecticut (plate 222D). It can thus be assumed that designs from Essex County, Massachusetts, were imported to eastern Connecticut between 1722 and 1727 without bird motifs, but after that date they were introduced. We will remember that the first extant appearance of banded bird motifs was on the Thomas Hart stone of 1674 in Ipswich, Massachusetts.

Between 1722 and 1730 stones of both types were placed in a number of burial grounds in eastern Connecticut by Hempstead and formed the basis of the development of the Connecticut ornamental style. Hempstead-carved stones in Phase I of the eastern Connecticut

A.

B.

C.

PLATE 221. A. Detail of the Hanah Johnson stone, 1717, Rowley, Massachusetts. Schist. 23¼ x 21. B. Detail of the Joanna——stone, cut ca. 1720/1730, Norwichtown, Connecticut. Granite. 14¾ x 9½. C. Detail of the Ann Eams stone, 1732, New London, Connecticut. Slate/schist. 20 x 19¾.

A.

B.

C.

D.

PLATE 222. A. Detail of the Patience Hodsell stone, 1725, New London, Connecticut. Schist. 16½ x 13½. B. Detail of the Joshua Abell stone, 1725, Norwichtown, Connecticut. Schist. 20 x 20. C. Detail of the John Arnold stone, 1725, New London, Connecticut. Schist. 23 x 25. D. Detail of the William Hall stone, 1727, Mansfield Center, Connecticut. Schist. 19¼ x 19¼.

ornamental style have been found in New London, Stonington, Ledyard, Montville, Norwichtown, Pachaug, Plainfield, Franklin, Windham, Lebanon, and Mansfield Center (Map 7).

6. The Development of the Ornamental Style in Eastern Connecticut: Phase II: 1725–1750

A. THE COLLINS MASTER

Stones sent up the Thames River and then overland to Mansfield Center, Connecticut (Map 7), formed the background for the development of Phase II of the eastern Connecticut ornamental style. After 1725 variants on the original Hempstead theme begin to be cut inland around Lebanon and Columbia and were shipped out to Tolland, Coventry, Mansfield Center, Hebron, Colchester, Franklin, Norwichtown, Windham, Canterbury, Plainfield, Pachaug, and Ledyard (Map 7).

In this second phase of eastern Connecticut ornamental carving there is a decided movement away from a blind reliance upon the formulas Joshua Hempstead brought with him from Essex County in Massachusetts. The second phase, created by the Collins master and Benjamin Collins of Columbia (who died in 1759) can be called a local or regional variant on the Essex County style, whereas the stones of Hempstead were simply outright borrowings.

A 1725 fragment (plate 223A), the Deacon Thomas Leffingwell marker, 1733, (plate 223B), and the Bingham stone (plate 223C), are all in Norwichtown, Connecticut and attributed to the Collins master. The Collins master borrowed the double outlined soul effigy from Joshua Hempstead but added feathered wings and altered the details of the face by connecting the eyebrows and the nose and suspending almond-shaped double-outlined eyes under the brows. That feathered wings were added at all suggests an influence from an outside source, possibly from early examples of Connecticut Valley carving or from imported provincial baroque stones from Boston.

As a variant to the winged soul effigies the Collins master carved a series of curly headed effigies illustrated by the Exercise Conant marker, 1722, Mansfield Center, Connecticut (plate 224B), and the more carefully carved Thomas Cushman stone, 1727, Lebanon, Connecticut (plate 225A). The features of the more traditional Joseph Rennals stone, 1728–1729, Norwichtown, Connecticut (plate 224A), are similar to those on both the Conant and the Cushman markers suggesting that the same hand was at work.

A.

B.

C.

PLATE 223. A. Detail of a stone cut ca. 1725, Norwichtown, Connecticut. Schist. B. Detail of the Deacon Thomas Leffingwell stone, 1733, Norwichtown, Connecticut. Granite. 25½ x 26½. C. Detail of the Thomas Bingham stone, 1729/30, Norwichtown, Connecticut. 26½ x 26.

After *ca.* 1730, it becomes more difficult to distinguish between the work of the Collins master and Benjamin Collins. The Christopher Huntington stone, 1735, Norwichtown, Connecticut (plate 225B), and the Joshua Huntington stone, 1745, Norwichtown, Connecticut (plate 226), are both alike and different. The latter was signed by Benjamin Collins. Either Benjamin Collins learned about carving from the Collins master or he might himself have been the Collins master.

B. BENJAMIN COLLINS: D. 1759

Benjamin Collins was known to have been in Columbia, Connecticut, as early as 1722.[91] The earliest dated and signed stones are in Pachaug, Connecticut, bearing a 1726 date,[92] but they are so eroded they are no longer useful for purposes of attribution. During the 1730's he signed several other examples in Danielson and Columbia, Connecticut, which are in an equally poor state of preservation[93] but resemble his signed work after 1745 suggesting the possibility that the few signed stones of the 1720's and 1730's may have been back dated. The earliest clear example of the Benjamin Collins style is the 1745 Joshua Huntington stone (plate 226), Norwichtown, Connecticut, where the shift from stones attributed to the Collins master is apparent. The effigy on the Joshua Huntington stone, in contrast to that on the Christopher Huntington marker, has widened eyebrows, more closely set eyes, a bulbous nose, and a downturned mouth, all attributes of the Collins style in the 1740's and 1750's.

In 1746 Benjamin Collins signed the Samuel Post stone, Norwichtown, Connecticut (plate 227A); similar but unsigned examples may be found in Tolland, Coventry, Columbia, Hebron, Colchester, New London, Danielson, Ledyard, Norwichtown, Pachaug, Franklin, Plainfield, Scotland, Canterbury, Windham, and Mansfield Center (see Map 7). In 1750 Collins signed the Humphrey Davenport marker, Coventry, Connecticut (plate 227B), a stone decidedly more organic in ornament than geometric. The foliate motifs may have been derived from prints, wood or metalwork of the period, either English or colonial.

The shift in Collins' work from strict geometric organization to an emphasis on foliate ornament marks the end of Phase I of the development of the eastern Connecticut ornamental style, and the beginnings of Phase II. The latter may be seen primarily in the work of Zerubbabel Collins (the son of Benjamin Collins) between *ca.* 1759 and 1778. Phase III was reached after *ca.* 1780 when Zerubbabel was already living in Vermont and had evolved the style which was eventually to

A.

B.

PLATE 224. A. Detail of the Joseph Rennals stone, 1728/29, Norwichtown, Connecticut. Granite. 29½ x 23. B. Detail of the Exercise Conant stone, 1722, Mansfield Center, Connecticut. Granite.

A.

B.

PLATE 225. A. Detail of the Thomas Cushman stone, 1727, Lebanon, Connecticut. M. U. 23¼ x 27½. B. Detail of the Christopher Huntington stone, 1735, Norwichtown, Connecticut. Granite. 47½ x 36½.

PLATE 226. The Joshua Huntington stone, 1745, Norwichtown, Connecticut. Granite. 34¾ x 44½.

A.

B.

PLATE 227. A. Detail of the Samuel Post stone, 1746, Norwichtown, Connecticut. Granite. 26¼ x 30½. Signed by Benjamin Collins. B. Detail of the Humphrey Davenport stone, 1750, Coventry, Connecticut. M. U. 33¼ x 21. Signed by Benjamin Collins.

lead to stones such as the Rufus Collins marker, 1790, Columbia, Connecticut (plate 229).

7. The Development of the Eastern Connecticut Ornamental Style: Phase III: 1750–1797

A. ZERUBBABEL COLLINS: 1733–1797

Zerubbabel Collins was born in Columbia, Connecticut, in 1733 and died in Shaftsbury, Vermont, in 1797. In 1786 Zerubbabel Collins was paid £7.10.0 for the James Breckinridge stone in Bennington, Vermont.[94] It is similar to the Rufus Collins stone of 1790 in Columbia, Connecticut (plate 229). Prior to the time that Zerubbabel sold his farm and moved to Vermont in 1778,[95] he carved and placed stones throughout eastern Connecticut after *ca.* 1759. The marker he executed for his father in 1759, Columbia, Connecticut (plate 228A), is an early example of work attributed to his hand and was cut in sunken relief in a manner similar to the technique his father used on the signed Humphrey Davenport stone of 1750 in Coventry, Connecticut (plate 227B). By 1769 on the Elizabeth Clark stone, Columbia, Connecticut (plate 228B), he had reversed the figure and ground relationship established earlier on the Collins stone of 1759 (plate 228A), and in addition he had begun to manipulate what must be called a rural form of modelling. The Samuel Guild stone, 1771 (plate 228c), Columbia, Connecticut, is a later variant with the wings formulated in a manner which was to last until the 1790's. The highly ornamental style of Zerubbabel Collins was forged in eastern Connecticut but brought to fruition in Vermont. Later examples of his work may be seen as far south as Columbia, Connecticut, and as far north as Poultney, Vermont.

With the absorption of organic foliate motifs into the vocabulary of Connecticut carving after 1750, Zerubbabel had the option of becoming progressively more naturalistic in the manner of provincial coastal carving, or adopting the new motifs to the older geometric vision of hieratic form. That Collins did not choose to move in the manner of coastal provincial carving is an indication of the fascination that the ornamental style had for the rural carvers at the expense of the coastal style; the latter style remaining always closer to a true miming of nature, however humble its achievements compared to those of European art. The Rufus Collins marker, 1790, Columbia, Connecticut (plate 229), is one of the high points of the development of rural carving and may be considered Phase III of the development of the eastern Connecticut ornamental style (in spite of the fact that these stones

A.

B.

C.

PLATE 228. A. Detail of the Benjamin Collins stone, 1759, Columbia, Connecticut. Granite. 26¼ x 31½. B. Detail of the Elizabeth Clark stone, 1769, Columbia, Connecticut. Granite. C. Detail of the Samuel Guild stone, 1771, Columbia, Connecticut. Granite. 29 x 46½.

were by this time being carved in southern Vermont). In terms of its refined ornamentalism, the Collins stone is comparable in technique if not in iconography, to much Mesopotamian stonecarving.

The influences upon Zerubbabel Collins are not altogether clear. Certainly the Humphrey Davenport stone (plate 227B), must be considered one of them, but there were others as well. For example, the Lydia Phelps stone, 1757, Hebron, Connecticut (plate 230A), bears a remarkable resemblance to the Ann Dewey marker, 1768, Columbia, Connecticut (plate 230B), attributed to Zerubbabel Collins. The Phelps stone was cut some eleven years before and was placed in nearby Hebron where Zerubbabel might have become familiar with it and other examples of Phase III of the Connecticut Valley ornamental style.

8. The Origins and Development of the Connecticut Valley Ornamental Style: Phases I, II, and III: 1644–1815

SOME of the earliest surviving stone markers in New England are to be found in Windsor, Connecticut. It seems that by the time of the Ephraim Huit tombstone of 1644 (plate 231A), a stonecarving tradition had already been established. By 1657 a gravestone had been cut for Joseph Drake. The John Bissell stone of 1677 (plate 231B), with its molded frame and recessed inscription, is an example of the type which was to endure well into the 18th century (see the David Forbes marker, 1729, Windsor, Connecticut (plate 143), and may very well have been brought from England (see the Sarah ———— [Wellington?] stone, 1707, Thorney, Cambridgeshire, plate 142). During the course of the early years of the 18th century the heavy moldings were dropped but the main features of the early Windsor stones were retained. The Sarah Chester marker, 1698, Wethersfield, Connecticut (plate 231C), the Elizabeth Chedsey stone, 1687, New Haven, Connecticut (plate 232A), the Thomas Morten marker, 1708, South Windsor, Connecticut (plate 232B), the Mary Coit stone, 1713, New London, Connecticut (plate 232C), and the Moses Wheeler gravestone, 1724, Stratford, Connecticut (plate 232D), are all variants of the Windsor type. It was not, however, until the second decade of the 18th century that symbolic motifs made any significant inroads upon the Connecticut plain style. The Abigail Johnson marker, 1724, New Haven, Connecticut (plate 233A), the James Hickox stone, 1725, Durham, Connecticut (plate 233B), the Marcy Halle stone, 1719, Glastonbury, Connecticut (plate 233C), and the Hannah Goodrich gravestone, 1721, Glastonbury, Connecticut (plate 233D), show some of the first symbolic motifs to appear on

PLATE 229. The Rufus Collins stone, 1790, Columbia, Connecticut. White marble. 20¾ x 27.

A.

B.

PLATE 230. A. Detail of the Lydia Phelps stone, 1757, Hebron, Connecticut. Red sandstone. 29 x 50¼. B. Detail of the Ann Dewey stone, 1768, Columbia, Connecticut. Red sandstone. 24¼ x 35½.

A.

B.

C.

PLATE 231. A. Tombstone of Ephraim Huit, 1644, Windsor, Connecticut. Red sandstone. B. The John Bissell stone, 1677, Windsor, Connecticut. Red sandstone. C. The Sarah Chester stone, 1698, Wethersfield, Connecticut. Red sandstone. 18¾ x 26¾.

A.

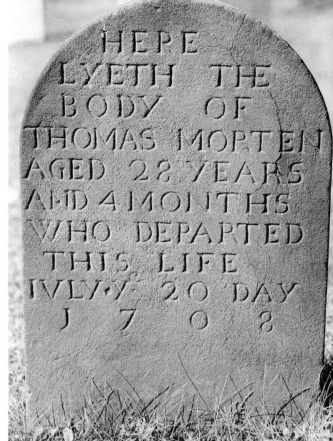

B.

C.

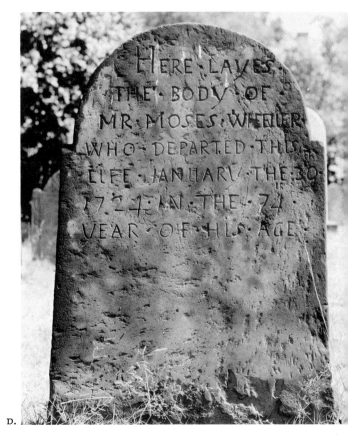

D.

PLATE 232. A. The Elizabeth Chedsey stone, 1687, New Haven, Connecticut. Red sandstone. B. The Thomas Morten stone, 1708, South Windsor, Connecticut. Red sandstone. 20 x 29½. C. The Mary Coit stone, 1713, New London, Connecticut. M. U. D. The Moses Wheeler stone, 1724, Stratford, Connecticut. 27 x 44.

locally carved Connecticut Valley gravestones. Whirl rosettes appear on the border panels of the Johnson and Hickox stones,[96] while a crude frieze of mortality symbols appears on the Halle stone and what I take to be trees of life on the Goodrich marker. None of these motifs were to surpass the popularity of the winged death's head in the Connecticut Valley in the late 1720's and 1730's.

The Nathaniel Bissell stone, 1714, South Windsor, Connecticut (plate 234A), marks one of the earliest appearances of a skull flanked by scythes and picks in the Valley. The theme may very well have been derived from either a printed broadside or from an imported Boston stone. By 1725 on the Steven Hickox stone, Durham, Connecticut (plate 234B), the death's head had been winged and continuous foliate ornament had made its appearance upon the border panels in emulation of the floral and foliate border panels which were so popular in Greater Boston and in Rhode Island. The Hickox stone is in reality nothing more than a rural adaptation of a provincial design and marks the first phase of Connecticut Valley ornamental carving. In sharp contrast to the foliate border panels on the Hickox stone, Connecticut carvers sometimes varied the design by cutting the borders with continuous geometric coils such as those seen on the Lieutenant Joseph Smith stone, 1725, Durham, Connecticut (plate 234C). The use of the continuous coil motif may have been borrowed from either Joshua Hempstead or the Collins master who were both working in eastern Connecticut at this time. With both organic and geometric border panels available most local carvers chose the former and by the 1730's stones such as the Lieutenant David Bissell marker, 1733, South Windsor, Connecticut (plate 234D), dotted the burial grounds of the Connecticut Valley. Not all were carved by the same hand. The local "accent" differs from town to town, but there can be no question that such stones gained the ascendancy and reflect Phase I of the Connecticut Valley ornamental style.

Convincing aspects of Connecticut borrowings from greater Boston stonecarving may be seen by comparing the Boston-cut Joseph Grimes slate, 1716, Stratford, Connecticut (plate 235A), with the Keziah Stiles monument, 1727, North Haven, Connecticut (plate 235B). Stones such as the Grimes marker surfaced in Stratford, Connecticut, among other places, as early as the first decade of the 18th century and were undoubtedly the models for stones such as the Stiles example. Moreover such stones as the Reverend Edward Tompson slate, 1705, Marshfield, Massachusetts (plate 235C), reveal a ga-

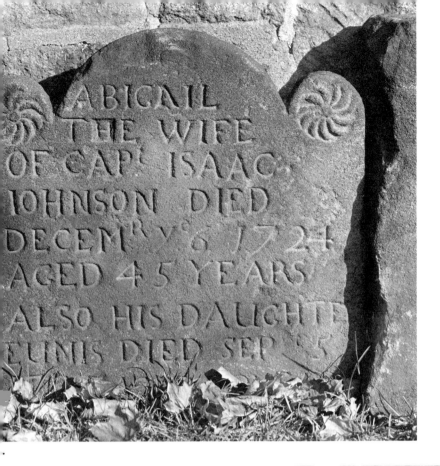

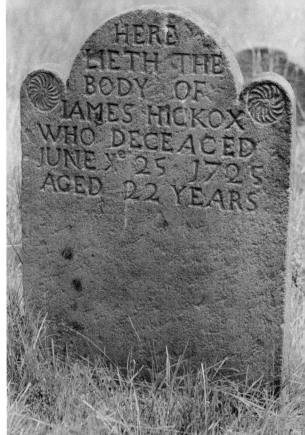

B.

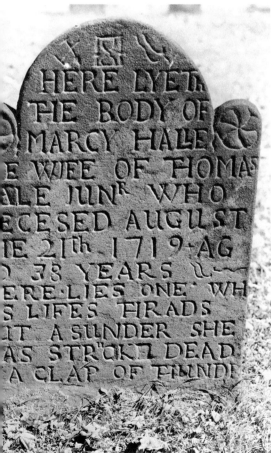

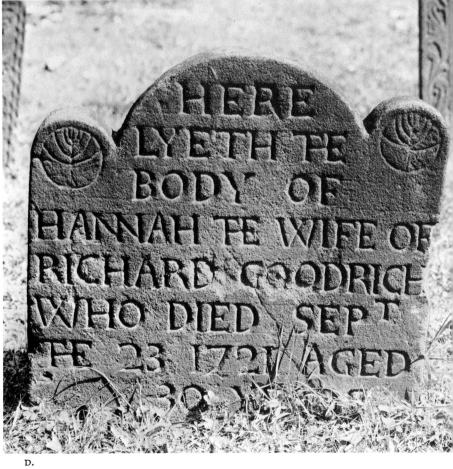

D.

PLATE 233. A. The Abigail Johnson stone, 1724, New Haven, Connecticut. Red sandstone. B. The James Hickox stone, 1725, Durham, Connecticut. Red sandstone. 19 x 28. C. The Marcy Halle stone, 1719, Glastonbury, Connecticut. Red sandstone. D. The Hannah Goodrich stone, 1721, Glastonbury, Connecticut. Red sandstone. 21¼ x 19½.

A.

B.

C.

D.

PLATE 234. A. The Nathaniel Bissell stone, 1714, South Windsor, Connecticut. Red sandstone. 20½ x 29. B. The Stephen Hickox stone, 1725, Durham, Connecticut. Red sandstone. C. The Lieutenant Joseph Smith stone, 1725, South Windsor, Connecticut. Red sandstone. D. The David Bissell stone, 1733, South Windsor, Connecticut. Red sandstone. 23¾ x 26.

drooned flowering urn later quoted on the Calup Tood [Todd?] marker, 1731, North Haven, Connecticut (plate 235D), suggesting the possibility that if such stones were sent from Greater Boston to Marshfield other examples may very well have made their way to Connecticut.

During the 1740's and 1750's the second phase of Connecticut Valley carving commenced with the slow transformation of the death's head into what I take to be angel heads and/or soul effigies depending upon the particular case. Both iconographic themes and ornamental motifs underwent vast changes in these critical years. Part of the development can be sensed by the slow change which engulfs and transforms the death's head between the Joseph Hickox stone, 1725, Durham, Connecticut (plate 236A), and the William Wolcott marker, 1749, South Windsor, Connecticut (plate 236D). Notice that the serrated row of teeth symbolizing grim death has slowly been eliminated from the serial representations with only minor moments of retrogression and ambiguity such as is suggested by the curious Sarah Skiner stone, 1753, South Windsor, Connecticut (plate 236c), where it is not clear whether a symbol of death or life is being represented. Archaic carry-overs even occur on the Reverend Isaac Chalker and the Deacon Daniel House stones cut well into the 1760's (plates 3c and 3D), where it is clear that soul effigies rather than death's heads were by that time being represented. Further amplifications of the new imagery occur between the time of the Phebe Strickland marker, 1750, South Windsor, Connecticut, and the Reverend Isaac Chalker stone, 1765, East Glastonbury, Connecticut (plates 3A and 3D). Stones in the latter series may be thought of as a substyle of Phase III of the Connecticut Valley ornamental style. The same sequence of events can be traced through the Ebenezer Gill stone, 1751, Portland, Connecticut (plate 237A), the Katherine Rosseter marker, 1756, Durham, Connecticut (plate 237B), and the Abigail Camp example, 1769, Durham, Connecticut (plate 237C). While the Gill stone of 1751 can still be thought of as bearing the marks of the older death's head theme, it is apparent that by the time of the Rosseter and Camp stones the imagery had been radically transformed stylistically and iconographically. The latter two examples are representative of the transitional period between Phase II and Phase III of the Connecticut Valley ornamental style.

Phase III of the Connecticut Valley style was in part brought about by the influence of provincial baroque stonecarving upon Connecticut carvers between 1740 and 1760. By this time local talent had become far more adept at miming the coastal styles as the Reverend Samuel

A.

B.

C.

D.

PLATE 235. A. The Joseph Grimes stone, 1716, Stratford, Connecticut. Slate. Signed 'C. L.,' probably for Caleb Lamson, son of Joseph Lamson. B. The Kezia Stiles stone, 1727, North Haven, Connecticut. Red sandstone. 22 x 22½. C. The Reverend Edward Tompson stone, 1705, Marshfield, Massachusetts. Slate. D. The Calup Tood [Todd?] stone, 1731, North Haven, Connecticut. Red sandstone. 20½ x 22½.

A.

B.

C.

D.

PLATE 236. A. Detail of the Joseph Hickox stone, 1725, Durham, Connecticut. Red sandstone. 19 x 28. B. Detail of the Jacob Strong stone, 1749, South Windsor, Connecticut. Red sandstone. 29½ x 32½. C. Detail of the Sarah Skiner stone, 1753, South Windsor, Connecticut. Red sandstone. 20¼ x 31. D. Detail of the William Wolcott stone, 1749, South Windsor, Connecticut. Red sandstone. 31½ x 40½.

A.

B.

C.

PLATE 237. A. Detail of the Ebenezer Gill stone, 1751, Portland, Connecticut. Red sandstone. 30 x 41½. B. Detail of the Katherine Rosseter stone, 1756, Durham, Connecticut. C. Detail of the Abigail Camp stone, 1769, Durham, Connecticut. Red sandstone. 21½ x 38.

Woodbridge marker, 1746, East Hartford, Connecticut (plate 192B), and the Captain Nathanael Sutlief stone, 1760, Durham, Connecticut (plate 192A), demonstrate. Both are adaptations of the baroque motifs to the materials and potentialities of Connecticut carving. These provincial baroque stylistic forays into rural Connecticut immeasurably enriched Connecticut Valley carving throughout the last half of the 18th century. But the rural vision of form was by now so deeply impressed upon the carvers of the Valley that they rarely emulated borrowed styles after the middle of the 18th century but radically transformed them to suit their own needs.

The Joseph Atwater stone, 1769, Cheshire, Connecticut (plate 238A), the Reverend Joseph Tibbals marker, 1774, Durham, Connecticut (plate 238B), the Joel Parmele stone, 1788, Durham, Connecticut (plate 239A), and the Sarah Johnson monument, 1790, Durham, Connecticut (plate 239B), are representative examples of Phase III of the Connecticut Valley ornamental style. Possibly the earliest dated stone in the Connecticut Valley florid style is the Anne Williams marker, 1750, Wethersfield, Connecticut (plate 243). Slightly later but still in the 1750's is the important Lydia Phelps monument, 1757, Hebron, Connecticut (plate 230A). Remembering that Phase III of the Connecticut Valley ornamental style (plates 240, 241, 242, and 243) is marked by florid carving and the extended use of scroll motifs, they are very close indeed to the late work of Zerubbabel Collins (plates 229 and 244), and similar in spirit to stones cut by the Manning family (plate 246c) suggesting that the florid Connecticut Valley style deeply influenced carving throughout Connecticut after 1750 and, as we shall subsequently see, carving in western Massachusetts as well. The style had many local accents but there can be no doubt that there was a mother tongue. It is still not clear where in Connecticut it developed. Hopefully, subsequent investigations will enlighten us on this matter.

9. *Connecticut and Western Massachusetts Ornamental Carving: Phase III: 1750–1815*

A. THE MANNING FAMILY

Josiah Manning, one of the most important carvers in eastern Connecticut, was born in Hopkinton, Massachusetts, in 1725 and died in Connecticut in 1806.[97] In the 1730's his father bought a farm near what is now Scotland, Connecticut, and sometime after 1748 Josiah settled down near the town of Franklin on the Windham road. Gravestones attributed to his hand begin to appear in great numbers after about

A.

B.

PLATE 238. A. Detail of the Joseph Atwater stone, 1769, Cheshire, Connecticut. Red sandstone. 18½ x 43½.
B. Detail of Rev. Joseph Tibbals stone, 1774, Durham, Connecticut. Red sandstone. 30¼ x 52.

A.

B.

PLATE 239. A. Detail of the Joel Parmele stone, 1788, Durham, Connecticut. Red sandstone. 31¾ x 56¾. B. Detail of the Sarah Johnson stone, 1790, Durham, Connecticut. Red sandstone. 34¼ x 67.

A.

B.

PLATE 240. A. Detail of the Ashbel Woodbridge stone, 1758, Glastonbury, Connecticut. Red sandstone. 30½ x 59¼. B. Detail of the Ann Garnsey stone, 1787, Durham, Connecticut. Red sandstone. 26¼ x 50¼.

PLATE 241. Detail of the Joseph Atwater stone. See plate 238A.

PLATE 242. The Sarah Johnson stone, 1790, Durham, Connecticut. Red sandstone. 34¼ x 67.

PLATE 243. The Anne Williams stone, 1750, Wethersfield, Connecticut. Red sandstone. 22¼ x 41.

IN MEMORY OF
Mrs. Lydia Bennitt, the wife
of Mr. Henchman Bennitt:
who died March 31ſt 1791, in
the 46th year of her age.

All you that read with little care,
Who walk away and leave me here;
Should not forget that you muſt die,
And be Intomb'd as well as I.

Pr. 7. Dollars.

PLATE 244. The Lydia Bennitt stone, 1791, Columbia, Connecticut. White marble. 20¼ x 31½.

1760. The earliest signed example is the Jane Tyler marker of 1741, Brooklyn, Connecticut; but the style is by then so advanced and the stone so lonely in the 1740's that it can be thought of as a back-dated example. The Manning children stone, 1750, Norwichtown, Connecticut, attributed to Josiah Manning, (plate 245A), may be another example of back-dating since similar motifs do not appear until some ten years later.

The Abigail Manning stone, 1770, Scotland, Connecticut (plate 245B), was signed by Rockwell Manning who put his own age at thirteen years when he carved the stone. According to Dr. Caulfield, Abigail was the mother of Josiah and the grandmother of Rockwell.[98] The date given as Rockwell's birth is 1760, but if this is true then he could not have carved his grandmother's stone in 1770 because he would have been ten, not thirteen, years of age. Perhaps the marker was erected in 1773 and simply back dated or perhaps Rockwell was born three years earlier in 1757. That Rockwell borrowed motifs from his father is evidenced by the Chloe Stoughton marker, 1769, Norwichtown, Connecticut (plate 245C).

In addition to this thin attenuated style which can be attributed to the Manning family, they also executed a number of stones in a manner similar to both the florid Connecticut Valley style after 1750 and to the later work of Zerubbabel Collins. The Ebenezer Backus stone, 1768, Norwichtown, Connecticut, is initialled "J. M." presumably standing for Josiah Manning (plate 246A). Similarly the John Hurlbutt stone, 1788, East Hartford, Connecticut (plate 246B), was signed by Rockwell Manning. The Huckens Storrs marker, 1788, Mansfield Center, Connecticut (plate 246C), is another example. Stones by the Mannings are distributed throughout eastern Connecticut in numbers so vast that we can assume that theirs was a very large and busy workshop.

B. JOHN WALDEN: D. 1807

During the last decade of the 18th century and into the first few years of the 19th century, a carver named John Walden, who lived in Windham, began to compete with the Mannings and seemed to have had a great deal of success. The signed Disire Maples stone, 1798, Norwich, Connecticut (plate 247A), and the Anna Webb marker, 1805, Scotland, Connecticut (plate 247B), attributed to him, are typical examples along with the signed Trumbull children stone, 1794, Norwichtown, Connecticut (plate 248A), and the Gamaliel Ripley marker, 1799, Scotland, Connecticut (plate 248B). His style was similar to that of the

A.

B.

C.

PLATE 245. A. Detail of the Manning children stone, 1750, Norwichtown, Connecticut. Granite. 28¼ x 49. B. Detail of the Abigail Manning stone, 1770, Scotland, Connecticut. Granite. Signed by Rockwell Manning. 25¾ x 50. C. Detail of the Chloe Stoughton stone, 1769, Norwichtown, Connecticut. Granite. 29 x 43.

A.

B.

C.

PLATE 246. A. Detail of the Ebenezer Backus stone, 1768, Norwichtown, Connecticut. Red sandstone. 31 x 48. B. Detail of the John Hurlbut stone, 1778, East Hartford, Connecticut. Granite. 25¾ x 51½. Signed by Rockwell Manning. C. Detail of the Huckens Storrs stone, 1788, Mansfield Center, Connecticut. Granite. 29½ x 50½.

Mannings' but far less florid, indicating that at one time or another he might have apprenticed with them. Moreover on the Maples and Webb examples it will be noticed that he retained the banded double facial outlines as the Mannings had done on the stones illustrated in plate 245. This is undoubtedly a carry-over from the work of Joshua Hempstead, which as we will remember was modelled upon Essex County stonecarving prior to 1730 where double outlined motifs first gained prominence in the last half of the 17th century. In eastern Connecticut it was promulgated by both the Collins master and Benjamin Collins but did not achieve any popularity among the carvers of the Connecticut Valley.

It is equally significant to note that both Walden and the Mannings abandoned this archaic characteristic when they began to carve in greater relief as shown in plates 246 and 248. One of the earliest stones to bear Walden's signature is the Esther Palmer marker, 1754, Scotland, Connecticut (plate 249A), which is not only very early but obviously quite similar to the Manning style. Just as the signed Tyler marker of 1741 was almost surely back dated there is reason to believe that the Palmer stone may have been cut at a later date. Further investigations of the Manning-Walden style will undoubtedly clarify the chronology of many of these early examples.

C. THE SIKES FAMILY

Both the florid Connecticut Valley style and the work of the Mannings and John Walden seemed to have influenced a family of carvers named Sikes who worked in western Massachusetts during the last thirty years of the 18th and well into the second decade of the 19th century. Their stones populate Hampshire and Hampton Counties in Massachusetts (see Map 8) and may be seen as far south as Mansfield Center, Connecticut, as far north as at least New Salem, Massachusetts, as far west as at least Northampton, Massachusetts, and as far east as Leicester, Massachusetts. The Joshua Dickinson stone, 1793, Belchertown, Massachusetts (plate 251A), is signed "C. Sikes Sculptr.", while the Hannah Dwight marker, 1792, Belchertown (plate 251B), is initialled "E.S." One of the earliest stones attributed to the Sikes family is the Joseph Bigelow marker, 1774, Spencer, Massachusetts (plate 249B), although it is possible that this is another case of backdating. A far more reliable early example attributed to their workshop is the Solomon Cummings stone, 1779, Palmer Center, Massachusetts (plate 250A). Notice in particular the extended use of the double out-

A.

B.

PLATE 247. A. Detail of the Disire Maples stone, 1798, Norwich, Connecticut. Granite. 21¾ x 33. Signed by John Walden of Windham, Connecticut. B. Detail of the Anna Webb stone, 1805, Scotland, Connecticut. Granite. 30¾ x 60.

A.

B.

PLATE 248. A. Detail of the Trumbull children stone, 1794, Norwichtown, Connecticut. Granite. 37¾ x 26½. Signed by John Walden of Windham, Connecticut. B. Detail of the Gamaliel Ripley stone, 1799, Scotland, Connecticut. Granite. 27¼ x 36½.

A.

B.

PLATE 249. A. Detail of the Esther Palmer stone, 1754, Scotland, Connecticut. 22¾ x 40½. Signed by John Walden. B. Detail of the Joseph Bigelow stone, 1774, Spencer, Massachusetts. Granite. 25½ x 34.

line and the propensity toward geometric abstraction indicating a possible connection with the work of both the Collins master and Benjamin Collins as well as with the work of the Worster family of Harvard. The Pliny Dwight stone, 1783, Belchertown, Massachusetts (plate 250B), attributed to the Sikes family, bears unmistakable marks of the more naturalistic foliated style which surfaced in Connecticut after 1750 and so indicates a strong Connecticut influence. Both foliate organic forms and geometric abstraction characteristic of Phase II of the eastern Connecticut ornamental style and Phase III of the Essex County ornamental style remained dominant characteristics in their work while being suppressed in Connecticut in favor of the more florid late Connecticut style. The William Kentfield marker, 1777, Belchertown, Massachusetts (plate 252A), and the Theodotia Bard slate, 1790, Belchertown, Massachusetts (plate 252B), are representative examples. Moreover the extended use of double outlines on the Artamas Lamb marker, 1791, Spencer, Massachusetts (plate 253A), and on the Joel Crawford stone, 1811, Hadley, Massachusetts (plate 253B), suggests the possibility that the Sikes' were among the last carvers in New England to retain the purity of the older style when elsewhere in New England the neoclassical style was on the ascendancy. Notice in particular the omission of the mouth in both examples, a rather widespread practice in rural New England which at one time must have had iconographic significance.

IX. SUMMARY

BETWEEN about 1650 and 1815 New England stonecarving consisted of a coastal Provincial tradition (see Map 5), informed by succeeding waves of borrowing from baroque to neoclassical; and a rural inland ornamental tradition which, until the last quarter of the 18th century, was relatively free from late "Europeanisms." While the rural carvers were freely inventive, those along the coast were bound by conventions established in Europe years before.

By 1772 the demise of the rural style was prefigured when Moses Worster insisted upon transforming his heretofore powerful abstract style (see plate 218) into the idiom of the provincial baroque which, by the time it reached Harvard, had suffered immeasurable impoverishment at the hands of one minor craftsman after another (see plate 220). It was not, however, the provincial baroque style stemming from Greater Boston which finally mastered the older rural ornamental tra-

A.

B.

PLATE 250. A. Detail of the Solomon Cummings stone, 1779, Palmer Center, Massachusetts. B. Detail of the Pliny Dwight stone, 1783, Belchertown, Massachusetts. Granite. 21½ x 28½.

A.

B.

PLATE 251. A. Detail of the Joshua Dickinson stone, 1793, Belchertown, Massachusetts. White marble. 25¾ x 40. Signed by the Sikes family. B. Detail of the Hannah Dwight stone, 1792, Belchertown, Massachusetts. Granite. 26½ x 47. Signed 'E. S.'

PLATE 252. A. Detail of the William Kentfield stone, 1777, Belchertown, Massachusetts. Granite. 17 x 23½.
B. Detail of the Theodotia Bard stone, 1790, Belchertown, Massachusetts. M. U. 26½ x 47. Signed 'E. S.'

A.

B.

PLATE 253. A. Detail of the Artamas Lamb stone, 1791, Spencer, Massachusetts. Granite. 17½ x 30. B. Detail of the Joel Crawford stone, 1811, Hadley, Massachusetts. Granite. 17¼ x 21¼.

dition of stonecarving; that dubious distinction was left to the neo-classical carvers who sent their stones and pattern books far and wide with so much success that by 1815 the older imagery had everywhere been eliminated.

The beginnings of neoclassicism might have been instructive for the struggling coastal woodworkers and builders whose livelihoods depended upon catering to those who demanded that Arcadian Greece and Imperial Rome be transplanted to a raw America, but it proved to be the death of the vernacular idiom of carving. Indeed, the true principles of neoclassical taste were so foreign to mercantile America that the gifted John Vanderlyn would have been far better off had he never ended his training in Europe for a dubious career in the New World; and Horatio Greenough would have been spared the embarrassment of having to explain that his toga-clad Washington in stone was a simple quotation from the rhetoric of high neoclassical taste if he had never attempted to give America an art worthy of her ideals. The tardiness of America in accepting the true principles of neoclassicism while enthusiastically embracing its more superficial and sentimental aspects is a not very puzzling phenomenon in the history of American culture.

The new imagery swept through rural New England like a great tidal wave replacing the older native vision of form with a new standard of provincial taste which was to be further confused by the Gothic Revival of the 1820's and 1830's. What had heretofore been a rural idiom of seeing and making forms vanished as the frontiers of provincial taste moved further inland and finally engulfed all New England. It remained for the Yankee to turn his ingenuity to the more practical crafts of shipbuilding, machinemaking, gunsmithing, and clockmaking in all of whose forms we can still sense the fundamental New England propensity for sleek, smooth, functional simplicity. Stonecarving had turned "highbrow" but as yet technology was in the hands of the craftsmen. Soon it too would become industrialized.

Had the vernacular idiom of rural carving remained isolated from European styles for another century; had Puritanism retained its 17th century vigor in rural New England for another century, a unique form of sculpture might have emerged from the crude beginnings in stonecarving. It would have indeed been interesting to have had the opportunity to watch the vernacular tradition become cultivated in its own terms.

It was the destiny of rural stonecarving to remain only a whispered promise of what might have been. It was a rural tradition of seeing never fated to transcend its vernacular beginnings because the Middle Ages, whose child it was, vanished along with the Puritans from the face of New England.

Conclusions

I. PURITANISM AND PURITAN ART

It has long been assumed that the American Puritans had no religious art. We now know that the notion has no substance in fact. In little more than 165 years of hurried creation and rapid innovation the Puritans carved an art of great simplicity and power. It was an art which substituted emblems of death, symbols of the Resurrection, and iconic soul representations for the narrative and allegorical cycles we normally associate with high religious art. The imagery endured and prospered until 1815 when it finally succumbed to the neoclassical style.

The older imagery steadily deepened in meaning throughout the 18th century and in 1800 one of its most profound moments was reached on the Lucinda Day stone, Chester, Vermont (plate 108), which pictures a soul being carried toward heaven in the belly of an eagle. The symbol was created long after such primitive religious notions were thought to have collapsed with the rise of the mercantile classes.

It seems as if the visual and the documentary evidence speak in different tongues. By 1800 there was supposed to be nothing left of the old piety. The visual evidence tells a different story. It tells a story not of the decline of piety but of a deepening symbolism. It tells a story of coastal New Englanders fleeing from religion while embracing a burgeoning capitalism; and a rural people rooted to the soil and expressing their age-old hopes and fears in the face of death through the medium of symbols. The old ways obviously lingered longest in the rural backwaters. I see no reason to believe that just because the merchant princes of coastal New England lost their piety in a zeal for business, Lucinda Day and her friends in Chester, Vermont, lost theirs as well.

The fact that the coastal and the rural styles differ radically from one another seems to indicate that a different set of values operated in the two zones throughout the 18th century. This notion in turn gives rise to the impression that we may be dealing with two distinct religious cultures which, as we would naturally suspect, reveal themselves in different forms.

These are the conclusions we are forced to review if we take the evidence of the symbols seriously. How these conclusions will affect the further interpretation of the 18th century piety I have no way of knowing. I would guess, however, that the carved stones which sparkle with the coming of the sun are deep expressions of popular piety and religion and that the burden of proof to the contrary lies with those who have relied upon documentary evidence alone.

In a world on the threshold of the 19th century, stonecarving and its symbolism were something old in Western civilization rather than something new. Symbols like the apotheosis of the soul of Lucinda Day in Chester, Vermont, were as outdated as the antiquity from which they sprang. For the "cultivated" sensibilities of the 19th century it was simply too naïve to carve a soul in the belly of an eagle, even if it were an antique symbol; it was also too naïve to depict souls flashing heavenward as solar orbs on vapor trails, even if such notions were good Orphic ones. The growing popularity of neoclassical imagery made it clear that nobody wanted to retain the old sentiments and New England quietly mantled itself in white marble cinerary urns, arching willows, and noble tombs.

II. THE VERNACULAR AND THE CULTIVATED TRADITIONS IN ART

VERNACULAR art bears many similarities to vernacular language; both are diffused over a wide cultural area in a given period of time and both are the possessions of no one class but the property of all. Everyone in New England spoke a common tongue and at death everyone had a carved stone marker. Until rather late in the 18th century there was relatively little distinction between stones carved for men with heavy purses and those executed for families of lesser means. The cultivated tradition in both art and literature grows out of vernacular forms and is more properly a means of expression suited to urban areas where a professional class of artists or poets can leisurely develop their crafts.

Naturally there are areas where the cultivated and vernacular traditions are difficult to distinguish, but both are distinct at the extremes. For example, Greek folk lore is a product of vernacular experience but the works of Homer are the products of an already cultivated tradition. The eagle on the Lucinda Day stone is a vernacular expression of the more highly cultivated apotheosis of Emperor Titus on the Arch of Titus in Rome.

The cultivated tradition is by its nature self-conscious. The Medieval architect Villard D'Honnecourt was perfectly aware of what was happening in his profession and kept copious records of what he saw and what he learned. Had the New England stonecarver revealed the same craft consciousness, the moment of the transformation from a vernacular to a more cultivated tradition would have arrived. Such was not the case. Joshua Hempstead of New London left us an enormous diary concerning his life and times but never once mentioned from where he borrowed his designs nor what they meant to him. The few surviving sketches in the John Stevens daybook show no indications that they were part of a learning process rather than idle doodles. That there was an evolution of style in rural New England is now beyond question; but it was one which took place unconsciously rather than on the level where style is cultivated for its own sake.

Until 1815 there is no evidence that a movement was underway to turn stonecarving into anything more than what it was—a vernacular manner of symbolizing the passage of souls from time to eternity.

III. AMERICAN ART AND NEW ENGLAND STONECARVING

Those who thirst after a truly American image, an image unsullied by the watered-down provincialisms which are so much a part of all colonial experience, will be quick to call the vernacular tradition of the rural stonecarver both "archaic" and truly American. But before we attempt to elevate the rural style to the glamorous heights of an archaic art form, we must ask ourselves several questions. Before we call these often bizzare carvings particularly American, we had better be quite sure that they appear nowhere else.

Can we imagine, for example, both an archaic and a provincial baroque style flourishing side by side when we know that the term "archaic" simply means earlier in time? Surely few will maintain that the Green stone of 1759 (plate 218) was cut before the Tapping allegory of 1676 (plate 14). Undoubtedly the problem of whether or not the rural style should be called "archaic" will be argued for some time to come unless all pledge to use our terms with the utmost fidelity.

The freedom of the rural forms from late Europeanisms stands apart from the historical problems about the use of terms. Compared to the cultivated forms of European art in the 18th century it is difficult to imagine that Mrs. Forbes had not discovered the first truly American form of sculpture when she stepped into her first New England burial ground long before the turn of the 20th century. Ostensibly such an assumption has much to recommend it. These stones were indeed made in New England by native craftsmen. But purely American strains are not so easily isolated. For example, the Roger Huntington stone of 1785 in Lebanon, Connecticut (plate 254B), bears a striking resemblance to a Romano-British stone fragment cut some 1000 years earlier and now in the British Museum (plate 254A). It seems that the "Celts" were carving in a manner we wish to call purely American long before the Puritans set foot on the rocky shores of Massachusetts. Or again, the Robert Cleave stone, 1730, Portland, Connecticut (plate 107), looks very much like Yugoslavian stela save for the delightful beelike wings on the former. What is common to both traditions cannot be isolated out as particularly American.

Finally, what is "American" about the ornamental style of carving on the Pimble and the Greenhill markers (plates 145 and 146A)? Both are rare examples of English stonecarving. The dilemma of what constitutes an Americanism in style will have to wait until these questions are answered. I suspect that we will find the New England rural stonecarver participating in a universal pattern of form making present in all early art and distinguished only by the eccentricities of individual hands.

I believe that the whole question of what constitutes an Americanism in style might have to be formulated in much broader historical terms. Instead of asking what is American about the Samuel Green stone, what is English about the Pimble marker, what is Yugoslavian about their stela, and what is "Celtic" about the fragment in the British Museum, we should ask ourselves what all of these forms have in common. Is there anything in common to all people who attempt to create forms without a background of workshop experience or easily available cultivated models, as in true folk art? I believe there is. I believe

PLATE 254. A. Detail of a Romano-British stone fragment found in Somerset and now in the collection of the British Museum. B. Detail of the Roger Huntington stone, 1785, Lebanon, Connecticut. M. U. 17¼ x 27.

that the emergence of archetypal themes and forms such as the rosette and its variants, the lozenge, the undulate band, the palmette, and the double outline, in cultures as diverse in time and space as Mesopotamia at the dawn of history and New England in the 18th century, indicates that there is much to learn about the life of forms in early art. Just because two forms seem to look alike there is no reason to believe that there is an historical connection between them; but there is every reason to believe that the forms themselves are being conceived of in the same way.

New England rural stonecarving was a half-finished experiment in form making. Its place in American art must therefore, be described as one of quiet isolation. Nothing of the older tradition remained after 1815 but the silence of a forgotten epoch in our visual history.

Rural stonecarving was marked by a concern for line, a propensity toward geometric effects, and an interest in stylized clarity rather than with a vision of form as modelled volumes; a vision which always seems to be the harbinger of a nascent naturalism. The distance between English and New England stonecarving is nowhere more apparent than when we compare the Sarah Yale stone, 1800, Meriden, Connecticut (plate 256B), and an English stone from about 1770 in Bunhill Fields, London (plate 256A). Where the Meriden stone is pervaded by a rural sense of hieratic stillness, the English example is animated by moving pools of shadow and flickering highlights which give it a sense of modelled volume and substance totally lacking in the Yale marker. The linear purity, the economy of line, and the naïveté of the Yale marker reveal a way of seeing which is common to all forms of early art. The local accents might differ from culture to culture but the basic language remains the same. When the craft of the stonecarver became simply another provincialized form of expression, the "plain style" was suppressed but surfaced again in the forms spawned by the craft-oriented technological revolution of the 19th century.

During the 19th century the same concern for simplicity may be seen on the exterior of the old church in North Branford, Connecticut (plate 255B). Compared to a similar stone example in Stamford, England (plate 255A), the New England variant is rigidly severe while the Stamford example is far more picturesque. With its deeply incised capitals, rich stonework, and ponderous textures it depends for its effect upon a painterly treatment rather than upon a perfect clarity of proportion and linear precision which are hallmarks of the New England rural style.

A.

B.

PLATE 255. A. Detail of a church in the medieval manner in Stamford, England. B. Detail of an early 19th century church in North Branford, Connecticut.

A.

B.

PLATE 256. A. Detail of a stone from the 1770's, Bunhill Fields, London, England. B. Detail of the Sarah Yale stone, 1800, Meriden, Connecticut. Red sandstone.

Modern art has been a series of continuing attempts to reconcile the old tradition of the fine arts with the new image of industrial technology dominated by the chaste but frightening functionalism of the machine. It is ironic to note that what has emerged is far more like the art of the New England stonecarver than the "high" style to which he finally succumbed. We see in rural stonecarving the same preference for simplicity rather than complexity, for line rather than painterly effects, design rather than color, planes rather than rounded volumes, and perhaps most important of all, the substitution of abstraction for naturalism.

In spite of the fact that rural stonecarving was in many ways a truly "primitive" form of expression it did have moments of glorious attainment and revealed for the first time an American propensity for pure line and abstraction which have become a fundamental part of modern aesthetics.

Lamentably this rough promise of sculptural achievement never reached fulfillment. Our monument to New England stonecarving might bear the same epitaph as do many of the stones themselves.

"How many roses perish in their bloom
How many suns, alas, go down at noon."

Notes

INTRODUCTION AND CHAPTER I

1. J. Truslow Adams, *Founding of New England* (1921) Chapter VI.
Adams claimed that four out of five people in Massachusetts had no sympathy for Puritanism but immigrated merely to enjoy the better economic life in New England. Just why a man in search of his fortune would come north when a great deal more profit could be made in the Indies in the south Adams failed to make clear. Adams, moreover, arrived at his now disputed thesis in a questionable manner. It seems that John G. Palfrey, working without the aid of accurate census records, claimed that in 1670 only one man out of five had a vote in Massachusetts. With several turns which I find difficult to follow, Adams used these same figures to "prove" that four out of five New Englanders were somehow not Puritans. According to Adams those who were disenfranchised were precisely those who were not church members. Just what voter registration has to do with Puritan piety will have to be left to the imagination of the reader. Today we do know that many Puritans exempted themselves from all public service by refusing to become freemen. (See the Acts of the General Court in 1647.) Many others were actually men of deep piety but would not become full members of the Church because they were never sure that their souls were in a state of grace. To make spiritual insecurity tantamount to an admission of impiety is surely a bizarre interpretation of the literature. Much more work still needs to be done on the all-important subject of election statistics and what they mean before we can make such claims with impunity. Surely the cautious historian will not allow such wild claims to establish the economic basis for the immigration, although the economic factor cannot be wholly ruled out so long as men need to eat and provide shelter for their families. Economic determinism, so popular in the 1930's, is no longer quite so fashionable and I see nothing in these arguments nor in the way they were documented to make suspect the authenticity of Puritan religion. A detailed discussion and bibliography of this problem may be found in Samuel Eliot Morison's *Builders of the Bay Colony* (Boston, 1930) Appendix.

2. Ralph Barton Perry, *Puritanism and Democracy* (New York, 1944) pp. 627–641.

Perry saw a direct relationship between the radical individualism of Puritan theology and the rise of Democracy. Perry believed that the latter was a product of the former having once transformed theological speculations into more secular ones. It seems to me that Perry is really writing about historical parallels without a bridge, so to speak. Perry is convincing in setting up the parallels; less so in connecting them with an avenue of fact. Given Governor Winthrop's deep rooted fear of democracy, a fear which was undoubtedly shared by many of the leading families of New England, it is very difficult to see how the radical individualism of Puritan theology actually leads to the establishment of democratic institutions. Perry, however, sketched in only one side of the picture. If he was attempting to rebuild the broken reputations of the Puritan fathers then Thomas Jefferson Wertenbaker was set to chastise them even more. See his *The Puritan Oligarchy* (New York, 1947). Wertenbaker has little good to say about the Puritans. He saw no connection at all between radical Protestantism and the rise of Democracy, but was very bold in citing repressive laws which indicated to the author the mechanism of a thoroughly reprehensible Calvinist Colony. The citations roll on like giant waves crashing in upon the shore and they are indeed impressive. Wertenbaker did not, however, make a distinction between the cold law of the books and the humanity of the application. Had Wertenbaker taken the trouble to look beyond the actual statutes to the records of the everyday workings of the courts he would have found that in many cases the strictest punishments were reserved for chronic offenders. It would seem to me that the value of a law lies in the mercy of its application rather than in the dry legalisms of its official phrasing. While the Puritans were by no means more civilized than their cousins across the seas, I see no reason to believe that they were far worse. In point of fact, the Puritans chose to follow the Mosaic code rather than English Common Law concerning the death penalty and in a stroke of the pen narrowed down the capital crimes by a considerable margin. I see this as an indication of Puritan enlightenment. In his section on Puritan art, Wertenbaker missed the point once again, as this book hopes to make clear.

3. Schneider and Parrington had little sympathy for Puritan religion. The former began his book, *The Puritan Mind* (Ann Arbor reprint, 1959), by doubting that the Puritan experiment in Christian living could be made to work and ended his essay by speaking of ungodly Puritans. Certainly their experiment did not work, but their failure tells us little about what the complicated Puritans were really like. To call the Puritans ungodly is another matter altogether. Professor Schneider seems to mean that mere do-gooding is no replacement for the sweet grace of redemption, and none could argue with him. But two points must be made at this juncture. First off, Schneider is using documentary evidence for his interpretation which pertains more to coastal New England in the late 17th and 18th centuries than to rural New England which retained the older ways longer. Hence what might have been true of Boston about 1725 was by no means what was true of rural New England at the same time. Secondly, even if the New England experience was of a piece and there was no real difference between coastal and rural New England, it would still seem to me that Christian ethics have always played a major role in the affairs of the church, and the flowering of ethical thought is by no means a certain indication of a collapse of piety. Simply because zeal often overrides common sense in the affairs of the religious heart is no proof that piety no longer exists. To blame the Puritans for compulsively wanting to do good says very little about the quality of their piety. The Puritans came to New England, it would seem to me,

for the purpose of building a New Zion in the wilderness and this alone is an indication of the seriousness of the experiment. Parrington in his *The Colonial Mind* (New York, 1927) is not so much appalled by Puritan do-gooding as he is fascinated by economic determinism to the exclusion of almost all else. Parrington saw Puritanism as a challenge to the institutionalized English way of life by an emergent middle class bent on individual expression. Puritanism, according to Parrington, was concerned with the discovery of a new system of social organization in harmony with the rights of the individual. I tend to view these events through the other end of the telescope. I see these momentous events as consequences of religious belief rather than their causes. Parrington wrote, "Unless one keeps in mind the social forces that found it convenient to array themselves in Puritan garb, the clear meaning of it will be lost in the fogs of Biblical disputation . . ." It seems that Parrington wants us to believe that Puritan religion was wholly inauthentic and nothing more than a tissue of rationalizations for base economic and social motives. The same picture could be painted of every great spiritual movement if we prefer to look in from the outside. The historian of the 1960's is no longer so obliged and it is my hope that I can interpret the Puritan experience with the grain rather than against it and at the same time retain some degree of objectivity. It seems to me that Puritanism was at base a religious movement which had its hangers-on, doubters, fools, and martyrs, and which certainly had vast economic significance, but the latter flowed from the former and not the reverse. In point of fact I simply do not believe that Puritanism was a way of organizing middle-class society. For better or for worse it was a massive attempt to storm the gates of St. Peter with Everyman for himself.

4. Puritanism was an English way of thinking. Its roots were in the second phase of the English Reformation. The reign of Elizabeth, 1558–1603, is a convenient way to date it. The thirty-nine Articles defined the position of Church and the Book of Common prayer guided its common practice. Still, during the time of Elizabeth there were those who demanded a more complete reform. By the time of James I, after 1604, things had come to a head. Those who pressed for reform were called "Puritans" because they wanted to purify the established Church even further. Many of the intellectual leaders clustered together at Emmanuel College at Cambridge. Among the most important personalities were William Whitaker, William Perkins, Laurence Chaderton, and William Ames. The latter was to have a profound influence on New England Covenant theology. These men followed the reformed attitudes of Zwingli. The question of just how Calvinistic or how Reformed these men were had better be left in the hands of students of English theology. But it is sure that by the time New England was settled, her ministers read more Ames, Perkins, and Preston than Calvin (although they were of course familiar with his work). Because of doctrinal disputes concerning the ordering of the visible church, Puritanism in a larger sense soon fragmented into Congregationalism, Presbyterianism, Episcopalianism, and Baptism on the "right" and Quakerism on the radical "left." Apart from disputes over polity, and except for the radical "left" there was a surprising degree of conformity in New England Puritanism. What the Cambridge Puritans had started in England the New England Puritans transplanted to the new world. Only in New England did the Puritans have a chance fully to reform their Churches.

5. The Puritan believed in being in this world but not of it. As we would expect, this was naturally a very difficult path to follow and many fell from grace along the way. It did not seem to the Puritan, however, that it was any answer to

flee from the world when the world's business had to be done and so he approached life in a way which would have been inexplicable in medieval times.

6. Those who feel that men cannot be in the world but not of it are taking a doctrinal position which is quite beyond anything I would wish to say. Max Weber in his classic *The Protestant Ethic* found that such a position was too difficult to maintain and that later Puritanism often descended into mere rationalizations for commercial ventures and profit taking. Weber was right. The temptations of the flesh were indeed great, but the Puritans were not the first to falter nor will they be the last. Indeed, there is sufficient evidence to support the assumption that from *ca.* 1680 onwards Puritanism as we think of it was fast vanishing as the delicate balance between the demands of the countinghouse and the meetinghouse was becoming more and more difficult to juggle. This does not mean, however, that everyone lost their piety after 1680. Nothing in fact could be further from the truth. Weber merely saw a theocentric culture settled along the Atlantic seaboard shift from concerns of religion to more secular ones as the 18th century progressed. Because some of the rich merchants lost their old zeal in the great seaports of New England does not make Puritanism itself hypocritical. What it does mean is that many flew from orthodoxy while still giving it lip service. But while mercantile concerns were replacing older God-centered values along the coastal belt, what was happening inland? It is deceptive to speak of New England in terms of a total environment when many of the documents cited are culled not from a geographic cross-section but from the larger centers of commerce and speculation where events were moving rapidly and which might in fact eventually prove to be the atypical examples. I would like to know what thoughts were crossing the minds of the people in Durham, Connecticut, in 1750 and of what moment commerce was in the lives of the farmers in Vermont in 1790. I would like to know what the people of Auburn, Massachusetts, were thinking in 1780 and what was going on in Windsor, Connecticut, in 1680. Once we are able to gauge the temperature of piety in those rural hamlets and towns we will be better able to say who lost their piety and where. Until that time it seems to me that we must insist on a far more strict and limited evaluation of the documents which speak only for the educated classes primarily in coastal New England.

7. Perry Miller, whose works on New England culture have added a deeper dimension to our understanding of the complicated motives of Puritanism in New England, has devoted a great deal of his time to studying the beliefs of those who originally settled here. His *Errand Into the Wilderness* (Cambridge, 1956) attempts to see through the problem of why the Great Migration of 1630 took place. While not refusing to take into account the economic motives, Miller saw a larger sense of mission emerging. Using Winthrop's famous "A Model of Christian Charity" as a basic text, Miller finds that they came here to establish their own form of religious polity.

8. In spite of what some historians have written, in the ten years I have been working in Puritan studies, I have come across no documents which refute the position of Miller outlined in note 7.

9. Edmund S. Morgan, *The Puritan Dilemma* (Boston, 1958).

10. Elizabeth came to the throne in 1558. In making an alliance between the Church that her father seized and the State, she did not move the English Reformation as far as many would have liked to have seen it. Those who wanted the Church to move more quickly and with fewer compromises were derisively called "Puritans." Namely, they wanted to purify the Church. When we speak of New England

Puritans we mean a group of nonseparating Congregationalists who in fact did separate from the mother Church in England. When we speak of the Plymouth Colony we mean the separating Congregationalists because they had already cut their ties with England. The distinctions between denomination multiply but the major sects had in common a desire for autonomy in affairs of polity, a Protestant theology, and a common English background. The term "Puritan" stands for something larger and more vague than simply New England Congregationalism while at the same time it can be said to characterize that movement. William Haller, in his *The Rise of Puritanism*, has a good chapter on the backgrounds.

11. Men of great piety need not totally concern themselves with matters of the spirit to the exclusion of all else no matter what the romantics might wish to believe. For example, when good judge Sewall fined a man for being drunk, religious symbols were probably far from his mind, but when he came to bury his daughter they were of supreme importance (see plate 156). The description of Puritanism contained in this book attempts to do justice only to Puritan symbol making and has little to say or to contribute about their more secular, commercial, or political affairs.

12. Sydney E. Ahlstrom, "Theology in America: A Historical Survey," in *The Shaping of American Religion*, ed. James Ward Smith and A. Leland Jamison, (Princeton, New Jersey, 1961) pp. 232–321.

13. *The Autobiography of Thomas Shepard*, ed. Allyn B. Forbes, *Publications of the Colonial Society of Massachusetts*, XXVII (1932), pp. 321–400.

14. *The Poems of Edward Taylor*, ed. Donald Stanford (New Haven, 1960).

15. Perry Miller, *The New England Mind: The 17th Century* (Cambridge, 1954) Chapter I, pp. 3–35.

16. Henri Focillon, ed., *Art Populaire* (Paris, 1931).

17. The diary of Joshua Hempstead, the New London stonecarver, and the daybooks of the Stevens family of Newport offer no explanations of their work or what it might have meant either to them or to their public. For a more detailed commentary see the Bibliographical Notes. No Puritan minister ever to my knowledge mentioned the stone icons in the burial grounds directly, although many of them preached iconoclastic sermons from the pulpit.

18. The religious symbols man has created have in the last one hundred years been studied by historians of both art and religion, anthropologists, and archaeologists. More recently philosophers have become concerned and there is reason to believe that the next hundred years will see a great deal more work done of a co-ordinated nature than has even been contemplated in the past.

19. Carl G. Jung, *Symbols of Transformation* (New York, 1956) p. 232.

20. Carl G. Jung, *Psychological Types*, p. 602 ff.

21. *Ibid.*

22. *Ibid.*

23. Erwin Panofsky, *Tomb Sculpture* (New York, 1964).

24. Cf. Jolande Jacobi, *Complex/Archetype/Symbol* (New York, 1959) p. 95.

25. F. Creuzer, *Symbolik und Mythologie der Alten Völker* (Leipzig, 1810–1823); Goblet d'Alviella, *La Migration des Symboles* (Paris, 1892).

26. See plate 93A.

27. Creuzer, *op. cit.*, pp. 63, 64.

28. Oskar Doering, *Christliche Symbole* (Freiburg, 1933) p. 1.

29. J. J. Bachofen, "Versuch über die Gräbersymbolik der Alten," in *Mutterecht un Urreligion* (Kröner edn., 1954) p. 52.

30. George Hegel, *Philosophy of Mind*, tr. Wallace, p. 76.

31. H. Hoffding, *The Philosophy of Religion*, p. 77.

32. Ernst Cassirer, *The Philosophy of Symbolic Forms* (New Haven, Connecticut, 1953) Vol. 1.

33. *Ibid.*, p. 78.

34. *Ibid.*, pp. 78–80.

35. Susanne Langer, *Philosophy in a New Key* (Cambridge, Massachusetts, 1957).

36. William Marshall Urban, *Language and Reality* (London, 1951).

37. *Ibid.*, p. 407.

38. *Ibid.*, p. 408.

39. H. Flanders Dunbar, *Symbolism in Medieval Thought* (New Haven, 1929).

40. Urban, *op. cit.*, pp. 415–416.

41. Rudolf Otto, *The Idea of the Holy* (New York, 1958) tr. John W. Harvey, p. 5.

42. Urban, *op. cit.*, pp. 582–585.

43. *Ibid.*, p. 584.

44. Otto, *op. cit.*, Chapter II.

45. *Ibid.*, Chapter IV.

46. *Ibid.*, Chapter IX.

47. Otto was apparently influenced by Oswald Siren's *Chinese Sculpture* (London, 1925) Vol. I, p. 20.

48. Paul Tillich, "The Religious Symbol" in *Symbolism in Religion and Literature*, ed. Rollo May (New York, 1960) pp. 75–98.

49. The best review of current knowledge on the symbolism of the shell in antiquity is given in Edwin R. Goodenough's *Jewish Symbols in the Greco-Roman Period* (New York, 1958) Vol. VIII, pp. 95–106.

50. Erwin R. Goodenough, *Jewish Symbols in the Greco-Roman Period* (New York, 1954) Vol. IV, Chapter 2.

51. Erwin R. Goodenough, *Jewish Symbols in the Greco-Roman Period* (New York, 1964) Vol. X, p. 209.

52. *The Poems of Edward Taylor*, *op. cit.*, p. 55. Edward Taylor was born *ca.* 1642 in or near the town of Sketchley, Leicestershire, England. Between his birth and 1668, when he entered Harvard with advanced standing, little is known of his life, although he did teach school at Bagworth, Leicestershire, but refused to take the oath required by the Act of Uniformity of 1662. In 1671, he took a post as minister at Westfield, Massachusetts, where he died at the age of 87 in 1729. His poetry was devotional and written for his own satisfaction. It was never published during his lifetime.

53. See Chapter III, Section VIII: "2. The Ornamental Style in Essex County, Massachusetts: Phase I: 1668-1730," p. 358.

54. *Edward Taylor's Christographia*, ed. Norman S. Grabo (New Haven, 1962) p. 35.

55. See Chapter I, Section II, "Puritan Symbolism in Religion until 1800" for an expanded discussion of this point, p. 33.

56. The Quakers would have little to do with the arid deserts of Puritan thought. The Puritans believed that Revelation through the person of the Holy Ghost came via Scripture alone, and therefore through reason and words, while the Quakers held that only the Holy Ghost was necessary. In this sense they attempted to revise the Puritan use of religious symbols by shortcutting the process of prepa-

ration for sainthood, the rational contemplation of the Scriptures aided by Spirit and replaced reason with the immediacy of the heart. The Quakers believed that ". . . the Testimony of the Spirit is that alone, by which a true knowledge of God hath been, is, and can be, only revealed; . . . Moreover, these Divine, Inward Revelations, which we make absolutely necessary for the Building up of the Scriptures, or right and sound Reason." Robert Barclay, *An Apology for the True Christian Divinity* . . . (Dublin, 1737), p. 18.

This inward Revelation came through the heart of love and not the mind, although in truth Revelation could not controvert either reason or Scripture. Barclay wrote, ". . . we do distinguish betwixt the certain knowledge of God, and the uncertain; betwixt the Spiritual Knowledge and the literal; the saving heart-knowledge, and the soaring head-Knowledge." (p. 20.)

The difference between the Puritan and the Quaker resolves itself into the distinction between the immediate and mediate about which Hegel in later times was to write. The injection of subjective immediacy into the Quaker movement led to abuses, but there can be no denying the fact that the kernel of subjectivity lies somewhere close to the surface in mystical religions and that the Quakers thought it unwise to attempt to suppress it no matter how difficult the application might become in practice. The Puritans, on the other hand, were always afraid that things would get out of hand if subjectivity were not severely circumscribed in the affairs of religion.

The Puritans believed that their formula was better because it kept a safety valve on the subjective dimensions of piety without snuffing out true enthusiasm. But to think of God through the mediate filters of reason and Scripture alone was a rocky road for the multitudes to traverse when all around them there were signs that religion could be much, much more than the quest for grey verbal phantoms seen fleetingly through a text.

57. See Chapter I, Section II, "Puritan Symbolism in Religion until 1800" for an expanded discussion of this point, p. 33 ff.

58. John Duns Scotus (1265–1308) studied at Oxford and later became a professor of philosophy. In 1307 he went to Paris where he defended the doctrine of the Immaculate Conception against the Dominican Thomists. Scotus discussed the problem of attribution in his Oxford Commentary. A summary of his arguments can be found in Frederick Copleston's (S. J.) *A History of Philosophy* (London, 1959), Vol. II, pp. 502 ff.

59. See note 56.

60. See Chapter II: Iconography, Section III, 2. Mutilated Symbols, p. 234.

61. The fundamental difference between Greek reason and Christian Revelation, no matter how speculative the latter might become, is the insistence that reason alone is a faulty medium for the experiencing of Christian truth without the dispensation of grace which operates outside the context of human effort and strife. Or better yet, in the words of Tertullian, "What indeed has Athens to do with Jerusalem . . ." Augustine in his *Confessions* made the same point when he noted that the safest way to truth is not the path which starts with reason and then goes on to faith, but the one which begins in faith and moves inexorably from revelation to reason. According to Christian dogma, this is the core issue never understood by Greek speculation. The best short discussion of the issues is Etienne Gilson's *Reason and Revelation in the Middle Ages* (New York, 1952).

62. Samuel Willard, *A Complete Body of Divinity* (Boston, Massachusetts, 1726). Willard, 1640-1707, was the pastor of the South Church in Boston and

the Vice President of Harvard College. His posthumously published *A Compleat Body of Divinity* was brought out in 1726 by B. Green and S. Kneeland in Boston and was the largest and longest book published in North America up until that time, running some 914 pages in length. In it Willard attempted a systematic exposition of Puritan theology rather than a series of illuminating sermons. For that reason he ranks as one of New England's foremost thinkers although his major work has never been reprinted. The lack of significant scholarship in this area is one of the most baffling lacuna in New England historiography.

63. One of the major contributions of the work of Etienne Gilson has been in getting general acceptance for the idea that the Middle Ages spoke in many "philosophical accents" and not in the language of Thomastic scholasticism alone. See his *L'Espirit de la Philosophie Medievale* (Paris, 1948) and his *Christian Philosophy in the Middle Ages* (New York, 1955).

64. To attempt to simplify the complicated thought of St. Thomas would be to court danger, and I by no means have a sure understanding of the Thomistic system of predication. However, these same arguments loom so large in every consideration of religious symbolism that I have attempted to set down some of the basic aspects of the theory. According to Acquinas both agnosticism and anthropomorphism were to be avoided at all costs because of their obvious dangers for the pious; anthropomorphism because terms are not attributed to God *univoce* and agnosticism because terms cannot be used *aequivoce*. To use a term *univoce* means that a word has the same meaning when applied to two different things. In the case of God, for example, the term "goodness" means the same as it would when applied to a man. According to Aquinas the problem with such thinking was that in order to postulate the transcendence of God in the first place man has already assumed that His "goodness" was not by *genera* like ours. To use a term like God's "goodness" *aequivoce* would, on the other hand, mean that men were using the same word but giving it two distinct levels of meaning which had nothing in common. To use the predicate "goodness" in this context would naturally mean that God's "goodness" was entirely different from man's "goodness."

Such a position would lead to unintelligibility and from unintelligibility to agnosticism according to Aquinas. Thomas believed that he could avoid both pitfalls by demonstrating that the correct posture was to view terms between man and God in relation to proportionality. It seems that when a term is predicated "proportionally" of two different things, the "ratio" between them gives them the necessary resemblance. Indeed, there is even a difference between "proportion" and "proportionality." In these deep metaphysical waters I have found two books helpful. (1) L. B. Geiger, *La Participation* (Paris, 1953) for a longer exposition and (2) Frederick Copleston, *A History of Philosophy* (London, 1959) Vol. II, pp. 347 ff. It must also be added that Thomas himself was not very helpful. Analogical predication is based upon resemblance. Between the numbers 8 and 4 there is a resemblance of proportion, while between the proportions of 6 to 3 and of 4 to 2 there is a resemblance of proportionality, or the resemblance of two proportions to one another.

65. Willard, *op. cit.*, p. 41.
66. *Ibid.*, p. 40.
67. *Ibid.*
68. *Ibid.*, p. 37.
69. *Ibid.*, p. 42.
70. *Ibid.*

71. It seems to me that there is really very little *explicit* formal philosophy in the Scriptures, although as in all things there are philosophical principles *implicit* in these writings which have formed the ground upon which the edifice of the Judeo-Christian belief has been built. During the Roman period Christian apologists in order to defend their faith had to argue in the vocabulary of the educated, which at that time was the language of Greek speculation, thus a religion which began in mystery and was written down with enthusiasm was cast into the brilliant form of Greek speculation in much the same way that Philo attempted to Hellenize Judaism.

72. *Edward Taylor's Christographia, op. cit.*

73. Willard, *op. cit.*, p. 43.

74. *Ibid.*, p. 44.

75. *Ibid.*

76. *Ibid.*, p. 46.

77. On page 43, Willard cautioned, "1. BEWARE *of diving too deep into the Mysteries of the Divinity.* Quaint curiosity here is but a distraction: faithful ignorance is better than temerarious knowledge. Know for certain that when your Understanding hath fluttered as high as the wings of Reason can carry it, you will find such riddles in the Deity, as you will never be able to unfold."

78. Willard, *op. cit.*, p. 50.

79. *Ibid.*

80. *Ibid.*

81. *Ibid.*, p. 51.

82. *Ibid.*

83. *Ibid.*, p. 42.

84. See plates 209-220.

85. Willard, *op. cit.*, p. 54.

86. See plates 28A, 58B, 62B, 102, 105B,173, 178B, 179, 183B, 184, 192B, 199A, 231A, and 238B.

87. Johannes Agricola (1494–1566) was a German Protestant reformer. He studied at Wittenberg, knew Luther, and subsequently became his colleague. They fought over the question of Antinomianism, and Agricola left for Berlin in 1540.

88. Edmund S. Morgan, *The Puritan Dilemma* (Boston, 1958) Chapter 10.

89. Charles Francis Adams, *Antinomianism in the Massachusetts Bay Colony* (Boston, Massachusetts, 1894).

90. Ann Hutchinson and her husband William disembarked at Boston on September 18, 1634. In religious matters she was a follower of John Cotton. Cotton preached that man could do little to effect his own estate, an old Calvinist dogma, and believed that human effort counted for little where eternity was concerned. Mrs. Hutchinson had a brilliant analytical mind and a deep theological bent and she soon found herself heading one of the many discussion groups so popular in Massachusetts where religious questions were debated at some length. In attempting to avoid the dangers of Arminianism she plunged directly into the Antinomian heresy. Because human will had nothing to do with God's free gift of sweet grace through the efforts of the Holy Ghost, human action was consequently directed by the latter during the process known by the term "Justification." The mere fact that a man acted in a "Sanctified" manner was, to Mrs. Hutchinson, no indication that he was "Justified." It became a fashionable game for Mrs. Hutchinson and her loyal following to begin to distinguish those who were merely "Sanctified" from those who were truly "Justified" in the Boston community. By 1636 her teachings

alarmed Governor Winthrop.

91. Wheelwright was Ann's brother-in-law. Throughout the history of New England polity and theology, family and doctrinal disputes seem inexorably linked together and it is not strange that opposing factions grouped themselves along blood lines.

92. Adams, *op. cit.*

93. Jacobus Arminius (1560–1609) was born at Oudewater in South Holland. He studied theology at the University of Leiden. He was ordained in 1588 after many years of studying all over northern Europe. Arminius was the founder of the anti-Calvinistic Reformed movement in Protestantism, having gotten himself involved in the dispute between Coornhert and those who held the infralapsarian position. (Divine predetermination did not precede, but succeeded, the Fall.) Coornhert, on the other hand, held a position of conditional predestination. Apparently all of this wore out the gentle Arminius. In the meanwhile, however, he was moving slowly toward the position of proclaiming the free will of man. After his death Simon Episcopius clarified the ideas more carefully. The most important point was that where the actions of God Himself were concerned His will is absolute, but when it comes to man His decrees are conditional only. The act of salvation is made relative to the acts of the persons themselves while the conditions of God are in harmony with the freedom of man.

94. The term "Religious Affections" as Edwards used it is often difficult to understand. According to Edwards they were the true substance of religion. To get at the problem he distinguished between the understanding, the will, and the affections. The understanding is capable of perception and speculation, and the others are the way in which the soul not so much views things but considers them. It is an inclination or an orientation of attraction or repulsion which Edwards was to call "heart." But by no means do heart-felt affections mean simply emotions. Perhaps it would be even clearer if we said that these inclinations of the soul were the very ground of generated emotion and reason itself, but in substance neither one of them. The will, of course, is the bare understanding now accompanied by the inclination. In other words, in matters where the interpretation of experience becomes involved there are really no neutral observers because outside the system the distinction between understanding and will becomes melted away. The affections, or inclinations, work through the mind for Edwards because they are based upon the apprehension of an idea which the soul or self is attempting to judge. Up until this time love has not been mentioned. According to Edwards love was the root of all affections and a particular affection in itself. The relationship between man and God or between a man and his religion is essentially one of love. This is the essence of true religion.

95. In spite of the notoriety this sermon has attained in the popular mind it was by no means representative of Edwards' thoughts.

96. The consequences of the revivals of the 18th century in New England are traced out in C. C. Goen's book, *Revivalism and Separatism in New England, 1740–1800* (New Haven, 1962).

97. Still the best guide to Edwards' life is Perry Miller's *Jonathan Edwards* (New York, 1949) in spite of the fact that Miller saw Edwards in terms of Locke's phenomenalism to an extent which to me seems extreme.

98. Solomon Stoddard (1643–1729), virtual "Pope" of the Connecticut Valley, was one of the most vital figures in New England history. Not only did he admit all to Communion, in contrast to the Boston-oriented churches, he also associated

the Congregational Churches in the valley in his Saybrook Platform which was officially adopted by the State of Connecticut in 1705. These churches became what Perry Miller calls, for want of a better term, "semi-Presbyterian" which justly describes yet another Puritan controversy. The Great Awakening was nothing new except in intensity and geographic scope. Years before, Stoddard was attempting to inject more passion into Puritan rhetoric than had been the custom of the "Harvard Whisperers." According to Stoddard the word was a hammer and one had to use it with great vigor.

99. Jonathan Edwards, *A Treatise Concerning Religious Affections* (New Haven, 1959) ed. John E. Smith.

100. *Ibid.*, pp. 1–82.

101. *Ibid.*

102. Miller, *op. cit.*

103. Edwards, *op. cit.*, pp. 48, 49.

104. *Ibid.*, p. 95.

105. *Ibid.*, p. 96.

106. *Ibid.*, p. 98.

107. James Davenport was minister of Southold, Long Island, then culturally a part of New England rather than New York. He was also a graduate of Yale. In the summer of 1741 he felt called to preach the Gospel in Connecticut. To say the least he was an emotional orator. In *The Gentle Puritan: A Life of Ezra Stiles, 1727–1795* (New Haven, 1962), Professor Edmund S. Morgan has a brief introduction to the Great Awakening. I am unable to resist quoting his description of Davenport at work.

"Before long the skies above New London and Lyme and other Connecticut towns were rent with shrieks and groans and holy laughter, as Davenport made his way up and down the coast, singing hymns in the streets as he came, gathering a flock behind him like the Pied Piper.

"When Davenport preached, he seemed to count his success by the outcries of agony or joy in his audience. He was most impressive at night, when one could see him on the platform his face lit by flickering, smoking candles, waving his arms, stamping his feet, screaming with rage or joy, the audience swaying before him, as now one person and then another fell to the floor and rolled or jerked in helpless spasms, or leapt for joy and embraced his companions, while a chorus of animal sounds rose up on all sides."

Tennant, according to Morgan, was another "roaring bull." Some of the sources concerning the Awakening are contained in the shorter account by Joseph Tracy called "The Great Awakening" (Boston, 1842).

108. Edwards, *op. cit.*, p. 98.

109. Miller, *op. cit.*, pp. 230–233.

110. Morgan, *op. cit.*, p. 315.

111. Lawrence Stone, *Sculpture in Britain: The Middle Ages* (Baltimore, Maryland, 1955) p. 1.

112. It is unfortunate that Goodenough's idea of mysticism as realized eschatology has never seen the light of publication and never will. Nevertheless he had devoted many lectures to an exposition of this idea and I have attempted to apply its meaning to the New England symbols.

113. Quoted from Evelyn Underhill's *Mysticism* (New York, 1958), p. 85.

114. *Ibid.*, p. 167.

115. Suger entered the Abbey of St. Denis *ca.* 1091 and in 1106 became secre-

tary of the Abbot. In 1118 he was sent by Louis VI to the court of Pope Gelesius II and on his return was appointed Abbot and later Regent of France during the second crusade. He was also instrumental in developing the Gothic style of architecture in France.

116. Erwin Panofsky, *Abbot Suger* (Princeton, New Jersey, 1946) pp. 47–49.

117. John Weever, *Ancient Funerall Monuments* (London, 1631), "To the Reader," page unnumbered.

118. *Ibid.*, Chapter I, Fol. 1.

119. *Ibid.*, pp. 5, 6.

120. *Ibid.*, p. 6.

121. *Ibid.*

122. *Ibid.*, p. 8.

123. *Ibid.*

124. *Ibid.*

125. *Ibid.*

126. *Ibid.*

127. Having just concluded a paragraph about the burial places of the Archbishops of Canterbury, Weever wrote that Cuthbert was the eleventh archbishop of that province and we can probably assume that he was citing Cuthbert of Hereford who died in 758, rather than Cuthbert of Lindesfarne who died in 687.

128. Frederick Burgess, *English Churchyard Memorials* (London, 1963) pp. 49–59.

129. For example, the burial ground in Cambridge is next to a church in Harvard Square and for all intents and purposes it looks as if they were in some way related. Such is not the case. The city of Cambridge has the authority over the old burial ground and is charged with its upkeep. It is one of the best kept up of the old 17th century burial grounds in Massachusetts.

130. Weever, *op. cit.*, p. 8.

131. *Ibid.*, p. 10.

132. *Ibid.*

133. The New Englander brought over a memory of two types of stones with him, the upright gravestone, which was almost always engraved with a religious emblem, and the flat tombstones, which were more likely to have either no symbol at all or if ornament was required it was normally a coat of arms. The tablestones became quite popular in Rhode Island in the 18th century and Newport has many fine examples. The custom is also evident in the Connecticut Valley where some of the earliest burials of important people were marked with tombstones. In and around Massachusetts they were not quite so important being replaced by family crypts which were unusual in other parts of New England. Being far more expensive than the lighter and smaller gravestone they were often the only visible marks of social distinction marring the mostly egalitarian rituals of death in New England. For whom and why many of these stones were cut would make a fascinating story which ought to be brought into the light.

134. Weever, *op. cit.*, p. 10.

135. Burgess, *op. cit.*, pp.117–119, 209.

136. "The superstitious notion that souls were detained in purgatory for a longer or shorter period, according to the number of masses offered for them, naturally excited a strong desire to be buried where an interest in those services was most likely to be effectually secured. Burial in the church was therefore first in request, as placing the tomb of the deceased immediately and constantly before the

officiating priests. As a church became filled with tombs, or the fees for burial in it became exorbitant, the adjacent ground was next sought in the hope of gaining the attention of the priests and worshippers as they assembled for public devotion." From W. H. Kelke, *The Churchyard Manual* (1851) cited by Frederick Burgess.

137. Burgess, *op. cit.*, pp. 20, 21.

138. *Ibid.*

139. *Ibid.*

140. Weever, *op. cit.*, p. 11.

141. *Ibid.*

142. *Ibid.*

143. *Ibid.*

144. See Chapter I, Section VII, "Burial Rituals in New England," pp. 58-64.

145. Stones for children were often smaller in scale and less heavily carved. Other than that they were similar.

146. The trappings of horses at funerals were often emblematic but none are extant. We know of them only through descriptions.

147. See plates 150A and B, 154C, and 156.

148. *The Diary of Samuel Sewall, Collections of the Massachusetts Historical Society*, Fifth Series, Vol. V–VII (Cambridge, Massachusetts, 1878) Vol. I, p. 470.

149. *Ibid.*, Vol. III, p. 246.

150. *The Acts and Resolves Public and Private of the Massachusetts Bay* (Boston, Massachusetts, 1902) Vol. X, Appendix V, p. 200.

151. *The Diary of Samuel Sewall*, Vol. III, p. 400.

152. *John Stevens, His Book, 1705* (Newport Historical Society, undated). A photographic reproduction of an original daybook of a local New England stone-carver.

153. *Letters and Papers of J. S. Copley and Peter Pelham, 1739–1776*, Massachusetts Historical Society (Boston, Massachusetts, 1914), p. 51.

154. *The Acts and Resolves Public and Private of the Massachusetts Bay*, pp. 229, 336, 1086.

155. *The Diary of Samuel Sewall*, Vol. I, p. 470.

156. See plates 164–166.

157. *The Diary of Samuel Sewall*, Vol. III, p. 249.

158. *Ibid.*, Vol. II, p. 307.

159. *Ibid.*, Vol. I, p. 482.

160. The Garvan Collection at the Yale University Art Gallery has a number of mourning rings which bear a definite relationship to the carved stones, painted trappings, and printed broadsides of the time.

161. *The Diary of Samuel Sewall*, Vol. II, p.20.

162. See note 151.

163. *Ibid.*, Vol. III, p. 79.

164. *The American Puritans* ed. Perry Miller (New York, 1956), p. 274.

165. Thomas Hooker, *The Soules Benefit from Union with Christ* (London, 1638) pp. 5, 6.

166. Jonathan Edwards, *Images or Shadows of Divine Things* ed. Perry Miller (New Haven, 1948) p. 44.

167. Wilson and Bagwell, *A Compleat Christian Dictionary* (London, 1665) p. 485.

168. Chapter II, Section III, 2. Mutilated Symbols.

1. See the archives of the Society of Antiquaries, London.

2. Frederick Burgess, *English Churchyard Memorials* (London, 1963) p. 197.

3. Joseph Wilpert, *Roma Setterranea, die Malereien der Katakomben Rome* (Freiburg, 1903).

It has been said that much catacomb art was indirect because Christianity as a still hidden sect had to disguise its symbols in the current pagan vocabulary. Hence Christ became the good shepherd as well as the classical calf bearer. Another view has it that the indirection of much early Christian art is an indication of deeply rooted syncretism. In spite of the fact that the Puritans did not have to hide their symbols at all, except possibly from themselves, they were still indirect, rarely evidencing a specific Christian content.

4, 5. Cult symbols pertain directly to religious rituals. The only ones found in New England are the Communion services on a limited number of stones in Connecticut which are discussed under the heading "The Divine Fluid: Wine." The use of the cross was widespread in New England although it never appeared as a major symbol but always hovered around the periphery of the stone suggesting that there were those in New England who would have objected to a more florid display of the cross.

6. God the Father appears on the Charles Bardin stone, 1773, Newport, Rhode Island (plate 104A).

7. While early Christian iconography did depict images of the soul in bliss in the form of antique *Orans* figures, I have seen no case where the transition of the soul from death to life has been pictured in a state of symbolic dissolution suspended between the attributes of life and death.

8. The term "symbols of transformation" has no connection with the Bollingen translation of Volume V. of C. G. Jung's *Collected Works* titled *Symbols of Transformation* (New York, 1956), nor is there any connection with Jung's *Wandlungen und Symbole der Libide* published in 1912 in the *Jahrbuch für psychoanalytische und psycholathologische Forschungen* (Leipzig) III–IV.

9. See section headed "The Divine Fluid: Wine," for a further explanation of vine symbolism as well as Erwin R. Goodenough's *Jewish Symbols in the Greco-Roman Period* (New York, 1956) Vol. V. Part VIII.

10. *The Poems of Edward Taylor*, ed. Donald Stanford (New Haven, 1960); p. 55.

11. See the Index of New England Stonecarving, owned and collected by the author, described in the Bibliographical Note.

12. *The Poems of Edward Taylor, op. cit.*, p. 287.

13. Thomas Foxcroft, *A Lamentation and Complaint at the Righteous Man's Funeral* (Boston, 1722) pp. 16–18.

14. See the title page of Francis Quarles' *Hieroglyphiques of the Life of Man* (London, 1638).

15. See plates 70, 73, 74, 75, 76, 77, 78, 79, 80, 93B.

16. See plate 1D.

17. See plate 2D. The Wolcott stone is a common type to be found throughout the Connecticut Valley in the 1740's and 1750's.

18. See Chapter II, Section II, "16. The Divine Fluid: Wine" for a further explanation of the symbolism in this stone, pp. 168-180.

19. For a brief encounter with shell symbolism see Goodenough, *op. cit.*, Vol. VII, Chapter X, Part C, p. 95 ff.

20. See note 18.

21. See Chapter III, Section II, "Engravings, Woodcuts, and Emblem Books," p. 274.

22. Jonathan Edwards, *Images or Shadows of Divine Things*, ed. Perry Miller (New Haven, 1948), p. 43.

23. The James Hickox stone, 1796, Durham, Connecticut, 29" x 28", redstone, attributed to Thomas Johnson of Durham, is one of many stones in Durham in the Connecticut Valley style.

24. Samuel Willard, *A Compleat Body of Divinity* (Boston, 1726) p. 234.

25. The Sarah McKeon stone, 1776, Ipswich, Massachusetts, attributed to a follower of William Codner (plate 183A).

26. Willard, *op. cit.*, p. 233.

27. Foxcroft, *op. cit.*, pp. 16–18.

28. The Jedediah Hull stone, redstone, 1783, Cheshire, Connecticut. Photograph in the Index of New England Stonecarving, see note 11.

29. On the Deacon John E. Goodwin stone, 1793, East Hartford, Connecticut. Photograph in the Index of New England Stonecarving.

30. The Eliakim Hayden stone, Essex, Connecticut (plate 91E).

31. The Anthony Levi stone, 1799, Providence, Rhode Island, Slate. See the Index of New England Stonecarving.

32. See plate 61A.

33. Francis Quarles, *op. cit.*

34. Samuel S. Chew, *The Pilgrimage of Life* (New Haven, 1962) pp. 12–34. In Daniel Meisner, *Sciographia Cosmics* (Nuremberg, 1637), Death cuts down the hopes of youth with the scythe of time, while in the "Kitto" Bible in the Huntington Library (engraved by Hieronimus Wierex), Death triumphs over lusts of the flesh by appearing with a sickle in one hand and a winged hourglass in another.

35. The Marcy Brown stone, Providence, Rhode Island, Slate, 23¾" x 25". Photograph in the Index of New England Stonecarving.

36. Thomas Wilson, *A Compleat Christian Dictionary* (London, 1655).

37. *The Poems of Edward Taylor*, *op. cit.*, p.286.

38. Willard, *op. cit.*, p. 233.

39. Edwards, *op. cit.*, p. 137.

40. The Elah Camp stone, redstone, 31¼" x 54¾". Photograph in the Index of New England Stonecarving, see Note 11.

41. See plate 64H and 64I for details and Index of New England Stonecarving for complete stone.

42. Willard, *op. cit.*, p. 524.

43. Foxcroft, *op. cit.*, p.24.

44. Cited in John Warner Barber, *Massachusetts Historical Collections* (Worcester, Massachusetts, 1839) p. 94.

45. For the best short introduction to tree symbolism with bibliography see Goodenough, *op. cit.*, Vol. VII, Chapter III.

46. See plate 196.

47. *The Poems of Edward Taylor*, *op. cit.*, p. 47.

48. The John Brooks stone, red sandstone, 24½" x 42+". See the Index of New England Stonecarving for photograph.

49. The John Rogers stone, 21" x 35+". Photograph in Index of New England Stonecarving.

50. John Calvin, *Institutes of the Christian Religion* (Edinburgh, 1845) p. 560.

51. Wilson, *op. cit.*, section on trees.

52. The hand of God appearing from a cloud and offering the palm of victory was quite common in early Christian times but less so in the Renaissance and Baroque periods, although it still surfaced in emblem book literature from time to time. Nevertheless, the New Englander quotes the original source with such precision that it is difficult to believe that it was derived from emblem book usage where it is always seen in more complicated form.

53. Wilson, *op. cit.*, p. 113.

54. *The Diary of Samuel Sewall, Collection of the Massachusetts Historical Society*, Vol. I, p. 158.

55. Wilson, *op. cit.*

56. Only some of the New England crosses I have found have been published here in plates 45 and 46 in the hopes that those historians who have examined merely the literary evidence about the proverbial New England aversion to the cross will have their eyes opened. It would be interesting to know just what the religious affiliations were of those who had crosses cut on their stones. This has yet to be researched.

57. Peacocks flanking a gadrooned cinerary urn of the type used in New England may be seen on the sarcophagus of Archbishop Giovanni, Church of S. Apollinare in Classe, Ravenna.

58. St. Augustine, *The City of God*, 21.7.

59. Edwards, *op. cit.*, p. 92.

60. Willard, *op. cit.*, p. 233.

61. Barber, *op. cit.*, p. 100.

62. See E. Baldwin Smith, *Architectural Symbolism of Imperial Rome and the Middle Ages* (Princeton, New Jersey, 1956).

63. Karl Baus, *Der Kranz in Antike und Christentum: Eine religiongeschichtliche Untersuchung mit besonderer Berücksichtigung Tertullians*, 1940 (Theophaneia: Beiträge zur Religions — und Kirchengeschichte des Aletrtums, 11).

64. See the famous sarcophagus from S. Maria Antiqua on the Forum in Rome. In this example Jonah appears beneath the *cucurbita* (or gourd plant).

65. Edwards, *op. cit.*, p. 93.

66. *The Poems of Edward Taylor, op. cit.*, p. 354.

67. Wilson, *op. cit.*, p. 1090.

68. Thomas Hooker, *The Soules Benefit from Union with Christ* (London, 1638) pp. 5, 6.

69. *The Poems of Edward Taylor, op. cit.*, pp. 230, 256.

70. European emblem books in which the symbol of the heart appears are legion. Among those which had a vogue in England are George Wither's *A Collection of Emblemes Ancient and Moderne* (London, 1635), the Catholic *Patheneia Sacra* by "H. A." (London, 1633), and Francis Quarles' *Hieroglyphiques of the Life of Man* (London, 1638). The abstract symbol of the heart was popularized by the Jesuits during the Counter Reformation and appears in both Catholic and Reformed texts.

71. *The Poems of Edward Taylor, op. cit.*, p. 17.

72. Wine symbolism is often very difficult to interpret and I find stones such as the Lyman example particularly puzzling (plate 82). It may be that we will have to look for explanations in folk lore rather than in the literary productions stemming from the literary elite. Indeed, the relationships between the Nicholas Larrance stone, 1710, Charlestown, Massachusetts (plate 155B), and a wooden stave,

of European pine and still bearing an import sticker, need to be fully worked out. In the European example (plate 155A), an angel is blowing life into an oak leaf, while in the Larrance stone a broad-leafed acanthus gourd is being thus filled. It has yet to be established that there is any historical connection between the two works, or even that the 18th century New Englanders knew of these old folk stories. I have published these examples side by side to suggest that the study of folk lore and symbolism might prove to be particularly useful. I have no explanations to offer.

73. Willard, *op. cit.*, p. 429.

74. *The Poems of Edward Taylor, op. cit.*, p. 212.

75. *Ibid.*, p. 108.

76. Benjamin Keach, *Tropologia: A Key to Open Scripture Metaphores* (London, 1681).

77. Edwards, *op. cit.* According to Perry Miller, Edwards' "Images" were nothing less than preparatory notes for a modern treatment of Philonic Type theory. If so, then the use of verbal and visual metaphor in New England via Edwards' "Images" and the stone icons of popular religion struggled together to introduce metaphor and both were doomed to failure. It would be interesting to study the failure of both programs in influencing religion and symbolism in the 19th century.

78. See photograph in the Index of New England Stonecarving.

79. Edwards, *op. cit.*, p. 59.

80. For information on the history of this idea see Arthur O. Lovejoy, *The Great Chain of Being* (Cambridge, Massachusetts, 1957).

81. St. Thomas Aquinas, *Summa Contra Gentiles*, tr. Pegis (New York, 1945) Book II, Chapter 45.

82. Edwards, *op. cit.*, p.44.

83. Aquinas, *op. cit.*, Book III, Chapter 78.

84. For information on canopy symbolism see E. Baldwin Smith, *op. cit.*

85. Willard, *op. cit.*, p. 532.

86. See photograph in the Index of New England Stonecarving.

87. Taylor, *op. cit.*, p. 177.

88. *Ibid.*, p. 305.

89. Foxcroft, *op. cit.*, pp. 21, 24.

90. Cotton Mather, *The Soul Upon the Wing* (Boston, 1733) p. 10.

91. *Ibid.*, p. 18.

92. New England sermons are filled with references to the soul as a bird escaping the net of the fowler. Indeed, the imagery was so widespread that there can be little doubt that many of the birds represented on New England gravestones stood for the soul in bliss.

93. See note 40.

94. The Abigail Barber stone, 1797, marble, 20¼" x 36+". See photograph in Index of New England Stonecarving.

95. Increase Mather, *Angelographia* (Boston, 1696).

96. *Ibid.*, p. 7.

97. *Ibid.*, p. 9.

98. *Ibid.*, pp. 109, 3, 25.

99. *Ibid.*, p. 28.

100. *Ibid.*, p. 40.

101. *Ibid.*, pp. 88, 89.

102. *Ibid.*, pp. 90, 91.

103. Frederick Burgess, *op. cit.*, p. 64, fig. 1.

104. Sibylle von Cles-Reden, *The Realm of the Great Goddess* (Englewood, New Jersey, 1962), pp. 75–98.

105. See Chapter II, Section II, "13. Architectural Symbolism."

106. While the symbol is clear to our eyes, there is as yet little literary evidence cut into the stones themselves in the form of epitaphs to suggest that the New Englander actually thought of architectural symbolism in the manner heretofore described. The best I can say is that given the sensitivity of the New Englander to visual symbolism it is more likely than not that he knew the meaning of stones such as the Dwight example.

107. Burgess, *op. cit.*, pp. 116, 117.

108. Cles-Reden, *op. cit.*, p.12.

109. *Ibid.*, pp. 70–98.

110. *Ibid.*, plates 82 and 91.

111. New England imagery in the 17th century was primarily concerned with emblems of death. When the soul image did appear envined or garlanded in border panels it was always doubled on both sides of the stone and cut in small scale hence avoiding possible recognition. By the 18th century in rural New England the use of the single soul effigy had become widespread and dominated the central passages of the stone. It was these later icons which were often mutilated, not the earlier emblems of death.

112. See Chapter III on sources.

CHAPTER III

1. Frederick Burgess, *English Churchyard Memorials* (London, 1963) p. 99.

2. *Ibid.*, pp. 107–110.

3. Churchyard memorials were cut primarily for the "gentry" and the English professional classes. Church monuments were primarily the preserve of the aristocratic classes. The best books on the latter are K. A. Esdaile's *English Church Monuments: 1550–1840* (London, 1946) and Frederick H. Crossley's *English Church Monuments: A.D. 1150–1550* (London, 1921).

4. Burgess, *op. cit.*, p. 112.

5. *Ibid.*, p. 114.

6. *Ibid.*, pp. 116–117.

7. *Ibid.*, p. 117.

8. The churchyard at Redlesham, Suffolk, has a square post with a molded top and is engraved with a death's head and darts. See Burgess, *op. cit.*, p. 117.

9. Burgess, *op. cit.*, p. 118.

10. *Ibid.*

11. *Ibid.*

12. See the David Forbes stone, 1729 (plate 143).

13. Harry Batsford and Charles Fry, *The Cathedrals of England* (London, 1960) p. 118.

14 *Ibid.*, p. 124.

15. Burgess, *op. cit.*, p. 168.

16. *Ibid.*, pp. 173–199.

17. English Portland stone has eroded badly and many inscriptions are no longer legible. From comparative evidence it is likely that this stone was cut in the middle of the 18th century.

18. Burgess, *op. cit.*, pp. 184–187.

19. See H. W. Janson's *The Sculpture of Donatello* (Princeton, New Jersey, 1963) pp. 23–32.

20. Burgess, *op. cit.*, p. 187.

21. *Ibid.*, p. 188.

22. Harriette Merrifield Forbes, *Gravestones of Early New England* (Boston, Massachusetts, 1927) pp. 90–97.

23. Esther Fisher Benson, "The History of the John Stevens Shop," *Bulletin of the Newport Historical Society* (Newport, Rhode Island, 1963) No. 112. It is not clear if any documents are available to substantiate this story.

24. See plates 145, 146, 147, and 148.

25. See Chapter II, Section III, "Modalities of Meaning," p. 232.

26. Forbes, *op. cit.*, pp. 5–7.

27. *Ibid.*, p. 127.

28. A photograph of this important broadside was kindly given to me by Dr. Robert Farris Thompson, Jr.

29. No further information concerning this photograph is available. It came into my hands marked only "Medieval Mosaic, Italy" through Mrs. Joy Davenport Weinberg.

30. See plates 151A and 151B.

31. Samuel Eliot Morison, *The Founding of Harvard College* (Cambridge, Massachusetts, 1935) p. 266.

32. Isaac Watts, *Horae Lyricae: Poems* (London, 1727). See frontispiece printed by John Clark in 1722.

33. Timothy Stone, *A Sermon Preached Before His Excellency Samuel Huntington Esq. L.L.D. Governor* (Hartford, Connecticut, 1792). See ornamental woodcut on opening page of same.

34. Title: "On the Death of Five Young Men Who was Murthered, March 5 1770." Courtesy of Dr. Robert Farris Thompson, Jr.

35. Title: "A Few Thoughts Compos'd on the Sudden & Awful Death of Mrs. Fessenden, May 30, 1770." Collections of the Massachusetts Historical Society. A reproduction of this broadside may be seen in Ola Elizabeth Winslow's *American Broadside Verse* (New Haven, Connecticut, 1930) p. 47.

36. Title: "A Funeral Elegy, Occasioned By The Tragedy, At Salem, June 17, 1773." Collections of the Boston Public Library.

37. Charles F. Heartman, *The New England Primer* (New York, 1934) p. XIV.

38. *The New England Primer* (Haverhill, Massachusetts, 1811). Collection of the author.

39. Thus far the identity of the Charlestown carver is still unknown. There is, however, a record relating to the burial of Reverend Zachariah Symmes and from it Mrs. Forbes suggested that the man whom I am calling the Charlestown carver actually worked out of Boston proper and should thus be called the stone carver of Boston. (See Forbes p. 21). If Mrs. Forbes is right then the work of the carver in question should be more evident to the south than to the north of the Charles, but excepting several important examples, just the reverse is true. I prefer to believe that the carver in question worked in Charlestown and that the Symmes document refers to someone else.

40. Mrs. Forbes saw no reason to question the date of the Erinton stone. See Forbes, *op. cit.*, p. 22.

41. See plates 18 and 19.

42. William Bradford, *History of Plymouth Plantation*, ed. Worthington C. Ford (Boston, Massachusetts, 1912), via *The Puritans: A Source Book of Their Writings*, ed. Perry Miller and Thomas H. Johnson (New York, 1963) Vol. 1, pp. 108–109.

43. Forbes, *op. cit.*, pp. 28–34.

44. *Ibid.*, p. 41.

45. *Ibid.*, p. 40.

46. *Ibid.*

47. *Ibid.*, p. 41.

48. *Ibid.*, p. 46.

49. *Ibid.*

50. *Ibid.*

51. *The Acts and Resolves, Public and Private of the Massachusetts Bay Colony*, Vol. X, 1720–1726, Appendix 5 (Boston, 1902) pp. 200 and 303.

52. Forbes, *op. cit.*, p. 59.

53. *Ibid.*, pp. 57–58.

54. *Ibid.*, p. 59.

55. *Ibid.*

56. *Ibid.*

57. *Ibid.*, *pp. 59–60.*

58. See the Forbes papers at the American Antiquarian Society, Worcester, Massachusetts.

59. *Ibid.*

60. Forbes, *op. cit.*, p. 67.

61. *Ibid.*

62. *Ibid.*, p. 99.

63. The Tingley stone bears the unmistakable mark of 19th century lettering forms suggesting that it was carved either in the closing years of the 19th or the early years of the 20th century. The groundskeeper, whose sense for dates is not all that it should be, told me that he remembered when the stone was put up by the last of the stonecarving Tingleys around the turn of the century or perhaps a bit later.

64. Benson, *op. cit.*

65. See Bibliographical Note 1A.

66. *Ibid.*

67. *John Stevens His Book 1705.* An undated facsimile copy of Stevens' daybook published by the Newport Historical Society. See page 33.

Aug. 9, 1727	John Cupitt	
	To one Tomb Stone	£ 6.0.0
	Too Two hundred bricks	0.12.0
	to 4 bushels lime @ . .	0.06.9
	to stone for foundation	0.07.0
	to carting Tombstone and stuff	0.05.0
	to Cutting Epitaph 215 letters @ 2D	1.15.10
	To Cutting *Two Cherubims heads*	0.12.0
	To Setting up Tombstone	0.18.0
		£10.16.7

68. Thus far only oral tradition supports the assumption that John Stevens III was born in 1760.

69. See Bibliographical Note 1A.

70. *John Stevens His Book 1705, op. cit.*, p. 18.

June 18, 1726. Brayton due to him	£0.3.0
by one Loade of gravestones	0.3.0
by one Tomb stone	0.6.0
March 5 by one Tomb stone and carting	0.18.0
by ½ bushel of apples	0.1.0
24 by one loade of stones	0.3.0
by ½ peck of beans	0.5.0
May 17 by one load of stones and carting	

71. Henry Bull, "The Bull Family of Newport," *Bulletin of the Newport Historical Society* (Newport, Rhode Island, 1931).

72. Erwin Panofsky, *Tomb Sculpture* (New York, 1964), see Lecture IV, pp. 67–96.

73. New England stonecarvers did not make a clear cut stylistic distinction between baroque and rococo forms. Some carvings enjoy both a sense of brittle lightness and fluttering motion while others retain the more ponderous slow moving forms of the baroque until the end of the 18th century. That there was some rococo influence cannot be questioned (see wasp-waisted figure on the Patience Watson stone), but it never became a significant carving style totally divorced from what had come before.

74. Forbes, *op. cit.*, p. 85.

75. See footnote 58.

76. Forbes, *op. cit.*, pp. 85–86.

77. *Ibid.*, p. 85.

78. *Ibid.*, p. 86.

79. Excluding the Erinton marker, the White stone of 1668 now seems to be the oldest surviving carving bearing a symbolic design in New England. It is highly unlikely that an earlier marker will be found soon.

80. The authenticity of the date of the White marker can only be established by the comparative method. As we know, colon separations and horizontal guide lines were characteristics of carving in Greater Boston in the 1650's. During the 1660's these stylistic archaisms were dropped by the more advanced but retained by the less gifted and more provincial carvers well into the 1670's. Indeed they surface again in the 18th century in the Connecticut Valley. If carvers in villages such as Watertown retained these marks well into the 1670's then it seems likely that they were retained until the late 1660's in Haverhill as well. Hence from the comparative epigraphical evidence alone it is more likely than not that the date may be taken as authentic. Similar symbols began to appear in Ipswich as early as 1674 suggesting that such motifs may have been in use some years earlier but have since vanished.

81. Forbes, *op. cit.*, p. 15.

82. Although it is possible that both the Hart stone of 1674 and the wood marker of 1714 were made by the same carver over a forty year period, it would seem more natural to assume that two carvers were at work until new evidence is forthcoming.

83. See footnote 58.

84. Forbes, *op. cit.*, pp. 77–78.

85. *Ibid.*, p. 78.

86. *Ibid.*, p. 10.

87. *Diary of Joshua Hempstead, The New London Historical Society Collections* (New London, Connecticut, 1901) Vol. I, p. 120.

88. *Ibid.*, p. 160.

89. *Ibid.*, p.VIII

90. *Ibid.*, p. IX.

91. Ernest Caulfield, "Connecticut Gravestones IX" *The Connecticut Historical Society Bulletin* (Hartford, Connecticut, 1963). Vol. 28, no. 1, p. 22.

92. *Ibid.*, p. 25.

93. Caulfield, *op. cit.*, Collins' earliest signed stones in Pachaug, Columbia, and Danielson are hardly legible today. Apparently Dr. Caulfield was able to read the following names some years ago: Hannah Tyler, Pachaug, 1726; James Danielson, Danielson, 1729; Elizabeth Gager, Columbia, 1730; Simeon Mearitt, Columbia, 1729; Joseph Coit, Pachaug, 1741. Since all these examples are purportedly signed it is a pity that they have eroded so badly.

94. Forbes, *op. cit.*, p. 111.

95. Caulfield, *op. cit.*, p. 28.

96. See plates 233A and 233B.

97. Caulfield, *op cit.*, Vol. 27, no. 3, p. 76.

98. Forbes, *op. cit.*, p. 108

Bibliographical Note

THE documentary evidence for the study of New England stonecarving must be described as inadequate. To date, only five stonecarvers' manuscripts have survived and they tell us almost nothing about the sources of their designs and what they may have meant to them. Many are merely lists of bills and payments.

The literature of Puritanism, although both abundant and prolix, remains curiously silent when it comes to mentioning the carved symbols which were so much a part of any proper New England burial. Conversely the literature bristles with numerous injunctions against idolatry and seethes with indignation whenever the subject of picturing the realms of heaven is mentioned.

As a contemplative act, the visiting of burial grounds was a much advised activity in the 17th and 18th centuries. Cotton Mather was an inveterate visitor throughout his active life but he did little to inform us of what he saw and what he thought (although his ideas on other subjects are more often than not discussed in tedious detail). Indeed, many notable Puritans such as Samuel Sewall seem to have spent many a pleasant afternoon conversing with the local stonecarver but we are never informed of what was discussed. Puritan literature is on the one hand lexiphanic and profuse and on the other hand intractable and granitic in its silences.

The Forbes papers at the American Antiquarian Society in Worcester, Massachusetts, contain accurate transcriptions of probated wills which list heretofore unknown stonecarvers. Dr. Caulfield has added to our knowledge of Connecticut carvers in his many publications. As yet there has been no attempt to photograph the actual documents. Such a project ought to be undertaken at once.

The stones themselves exist *in situ* (with several notable exceptions), but in the last twenty years there have been serious losses which will continue to mount. Little can be done at this time about the eroding effects of nature but surely sturdy fences can be built around the sites to dissuade vandals from destroying the old stones. Many of the most important monuments in Norwichtown, Connecticut, were recently toppled over and smashed, and Dr. Frank Sommer has informed me that an important Salem, Massachusetts, stone depicting Death and Time was recently pulverized by a madman. There is no end to such stories. The Colonial Arts Foundation has recently been established to save the stones and to provide a photographic record of all documents, major stones, and variants, but their work has been strapped by a lack of funds.

The Forbes Collection at the American Antiquarian Society contains some 1300 glass 5″ x 7″ negatives but only half have been printed up and there is no catalog. The Author's Index of New England Stonecarving, supported in part by funds from the Bollingen Foundation and later by the Colonial Arts Foundation, contains some 4000 photographs of stones indexed by site, carver, motif, and symbol. Nevertheless many important burial grounds remain to be documented and a photographic record of all the significant probate records has yet the be undertaken.

Important secondary publications on stonecarving can be exhausted after reading Mrs. Forbes' 1927 publication, the informative articles of Dr. Caulfield, my own publications, and Frederick Burgess' book on English carving. Other articles and numerous exhibitions of rubbings appear from time to time but the serious student will not find them particularly enlightening.

I. PRIMARY SOURCES

A. Manuscripts

1. Three manuscripts composed by the Stevens family survive in Newport, Rhode Island. The most important is entitled *John Stevens His Book 1705* in the Newport Historical Society. The second book, probably composed by John Stevens II, was begun in 1736, and the third dates from 1783 until 1794 and was probably composed by John Stevens, III. The latter two were originally in the collections of the John Stevens Shop in Newport but may now have passed to the Newport Historical Society. The first manuscript is composed of some ninety-four pages with consecutive dates running from 1724 until 1733. The earliest insertion is dated 1705 and probably reveals the hand of the first John Stevens. There is an additional insertion on page 40 citing a number of books read between February and July of 1767. On page 46 another insertion completes the book list and both were probably composed by John Stevens, III, who seems to have inherited the daybook after it had fallen into disuse. A notation on page 48 bears the date 1718 and later insertions continue until page 72. In the course of the document the carving of gravestones was mentioned no less than sixty-two times. For those concerned with the economic aspects of stonecarving this is an invaluable document.

2. In addition to the Stevens manuscripts, at one time the John Stevens Shop owned papers composed by John Bull. These too may have passed into the collections of the Newport Historical Society. According to Mrs. Benson they contain a great deal of material which does not directly relate to stonecarving and are of less significance than the Stevens papers.

3. The prominent stonecarver Joshua Hempstead composed a long diary which is now in the collections of the New London Historical Society. Composed of four bound volumes and some 750 closely written pages measuring 12″ x 17¼″, the first volume began on September 8, 1711, and the last notation is in 1758 in volume four. The only surviving diary of a New England stonecarver, the entries follow Hempstead through his daily activities which ranged from Judge of Probate to carpenter to carver of gravestones. In addition he seems to have been a land broker, a farmer, and a mariner. The first mention of stonecarving occurs on June 11, 1722, although prior to that time he seems to have busied himself making wooden coffins. In the course of this detailed account of the life and times of a New

England stonecarver we are never told where Hempstead got his designs nor what they may have meant to him, if anything.

4. Probate records exist in county seats and in state archives and in some cases reveal the names of heretofore unknown carvers. When lucky, the researcher will find that an executor kept a detailed list of accounts paid in the settling of an estate. In such cases the name of the stonecarver is likely to be revealed. In other cases the executor will submit only a totaled bill. In the majority of cases the executor's account was either not recorded or subsequently lost. Mrs. Forbes and Dr. Caulfield have combed the documents carefully.

B. Reprinted Documents

1. *The Diary of Joshua Hempstead, Collections of the New London Historical Society* (New London, Connecticut, 1901).
2. *John Sevens His Book 1705.* An undated facsimile edition published by the Newport Historical Society.

II. SOURCES

A. Some Major Publications Directly Relating to Burial Practices in New England and England in the 17th and 18th Centuries

1. John Weever, *Ancient Funerall Monuments* (London, 1631). A valuable account of English burial rituals on the eve of the colonization of New England.
2. *The Diary of Samuel Sewall, Collections of the Massachusetts Historical Society*, Fifth Series, Vols. V–VIII (Cambridge, Massachusetts, 1878). A chatty glimpse of New England burial practices in the early 18th century.
3. *The Acts and Resolves Public and Private of the Massachusetts Bay* (Boston, Massachusetts, 1902). Vol. X, Appendix V. Some prohibitions concerning New England burial rituals are mentioned.

B. Collected Papers and Photographic Archives

1. The Forbes Collection at the American Antiquarian Society contains transcriptions of important probated wills and in addition there is a collection of some 1300 5″ x 7″ glass negatives of New England gravestones taken between the wars. There is no index and only half the photographs have been printed. The collection is valuable because it documents many stones which have been destroyed in the last twenty-five years.
2. The author's Index of New England Stonecarving is a catalog of some 4000 gravestones indexed by site, symbol, stonecarver, and motif. The project was originally undertaken with the aid of a grant from the Bollingen Foundation and was later supported by funds from the Colonial Arts Foundation. Incomplete copies of the Index may be found in the Library of Congress, the Smithsonian Institution, and at the Winterthur Museum.

III. SELECTED SECONDARY SOURCES ON NEW ENGLAND AND ENGLISH STONECARVING

1. William Andrews, *Curious Epitaphs* (London, 1899). A collection of English epitaphs.
2. Esther Fisher Benson, "The History of the John Stevens Shop," *Bulletin of*

the Newport Historical Society (Newport, Rhode Island, 1963) Number 112.

3. Frederick Burgess, *English Churchyard Memorials* (London, 1963). The only recent book on the English vernacular tradition of stonecarving. There have been numerous publications on the cultivated art of tomb sculpture but these have little relationship to the more mundane craft practiced in New England in the 17th and 18th centuries and have been omitted from this list.

4. Ernest Caulfield, "Connecticut Gravestones," *Connecticut Historical Society Bulletin* (Hartford, Connecticut), Vol. 16, no. 1,4; Vol. 17, no. 1; Vol. 18, no. 4; Vol. 19, no. 4; Vol. 21, no. 1; Vol. 23, no. 2; Vol. 25, no. 1; Vol. 28, no. 1. Important probated wills are transcribed and other documentary information transmitted in these carefully composed articles. However, the author's attributions are far less secure than his documentary evidence and the reader should be warned against taking them for granted.

5. Harriette Merrifield Forbes, *Gravestones of Early New England* (Boston, 1927). The first serious publication on New England stonecarving and an invaluable guide to the field. There is no bibliography nor are the illustrations numbered. Mrs. Forbes omitted the transcriptions of the probated wills which can only be found in her papers at the American Antiquarian Society. The chapter on symbolism is weak but those on who the carvers were and what they did are strong.

6. Harriette Merrifield Forbes, "The Lamsons of Charlestown, Stone Cutters," "William Mumford Stone Cutter," "Early Portrait Sculpture in New England," "Symbolic Cemetary Gates in New England," *Old Time New England* (Boston, Massachusetts) Vol. XVII, no. 3; Vol. XVI, no. 3; Vol. XIX, no. 4; Vol. XXIV, no. 2. Mostly preparatory articles for Mrs. Forbes' 1927 publication. Some new information but not essential.

7. Allan I. Ludwig "Some Examples of Early New England Gravestones," *Graphis* (Zurich, Switzerland, 1963) Vol. 19, no. 108. "Stonecarving in New England," *New Haven Colony Historical Society Journal* (New Haven, Connecticut 1963) Vol. 12, no. 1. "Stone Carving in New England Graveyards," *Antiques* (New York, 1964) Vol. LXXXVI, no. 1.

8. Janine Lowell Ludwig, "The Forgotten Artists of Early America," *The New England Galaxy* (Sturbridge, Massachusetts, 1963) Vol. IV, no. 3.

9. Thomas C. Mann, *Over Their Dead Bodies: Yankee Epitaphs and History* (Brattleboro, Vermont, 1962). An amusing treatment of New England epitaphs with some crude line drawings of important Vermont stones.

10. Wilfred A. Norris, "The Old Burial Ground at Watertown, Massachusetts," "The Gravestones in the Old Burying Ground at Watertown, Massachusetts," *Old Time New England* (Boston, Massachusets) Vol. XVI, no. 1; Vol. XVI, no. 2.

11. Robert E. Pike, *Granite Laughter and Marble Tears* (New York, 1938). A collection of American epitaphs with some important photographs of New England stones.

12. Erich A. Taylor, "The Slate Gravestones of New England," *Old Time New England* (Boston, Massachusetts, 1924) Vol. XV, no. 2.

13. W. T. Vincent, *In Search of Gravestones Old and Curious* (London, 1896). A collection of epitaphs, rubbings, and line drawings of English stonecarving. A valuable adjunct to the more recent publication of Frederick Burgess.

14. G. A. Walker, *Gatherings from Graveyards* (London, 1837). A collection of English epitaphs and a dubious history of English tomb and churchyard sculpture.

15. Charles A. Wallace, *Stories on Stone* (New York, 1954). A good collection of American epitaphs.

IV. SELECTED SECONDARY SOURCES ON NEW ENGLAND HISTORY

1. Emery Battis, *Saints and Sectaries* (Chapel Hill, North Carolina, 1962).

2. Carl Bridenbaugh, *Mitre and Sceptre* (New York, 1962).

3. Richard S. Dunn, *Puritans and Yankees* (Princeton, N.J., 1962).

4. C. C. Goen, *Revivalism and Separatism* (New Haven, 1962).

5. Perry Miller, *Errand Into The Wilderness* (Cambridge, Massachusetts, 1956).

6. Perry Miller, *Jonathan Edwards* (New York, 1949).

7. Perry Miller, *The New England Mind: From Colony to Province* (Cambridge, Massachusetts, 1953). A work of major importance.

8. Perry Miller, *The New England Mind: The 17th Century* (Cambridge, Massachusetts, 1939). A work of major importance.

9. Perry Miller, *Orthodoxy in Massachusetts* (Cambridge, Massachusetts, 1933).

10. Edmund S. Morgan, *The Gentle Puritan: A Life of Ezra Stiles: 1727–1795* (New Haven, Connecticut, 1962). An important 18th century biography.

11. Edmund S. Morgan, *The Puritan Dilemma* (Boston, 1958). The best short introduction to Puritanism.

12. Edmund S. Morgan, *Visible Saints: The History of a Puritan Idea* (New York, 1963). A major work.

13. Samuel Eliot Morison, *Builders of the Bay Colony* (Boston, 1930).

14. Samuel Eliot Morison, *The Founding of Harvard College* (Cambridge, Massachusetts, 1930). 2 Vols. A major work.

16. Kenneth Murdock, *Increase Mather, the Foremost American Puritan* (Cambridge, Massachusetts, 1925).

17. Vernon Louis Parrington, *Main Currents in American Thought* (New York, 1927). Vol. I: *The Colonial Mind.*

18. Ralph Barton Perry, *Puritanism and Democracy* (New York, 1944).

19. Herbert Wallace Schneider, *The Puritan Mind* (New York, 1930).

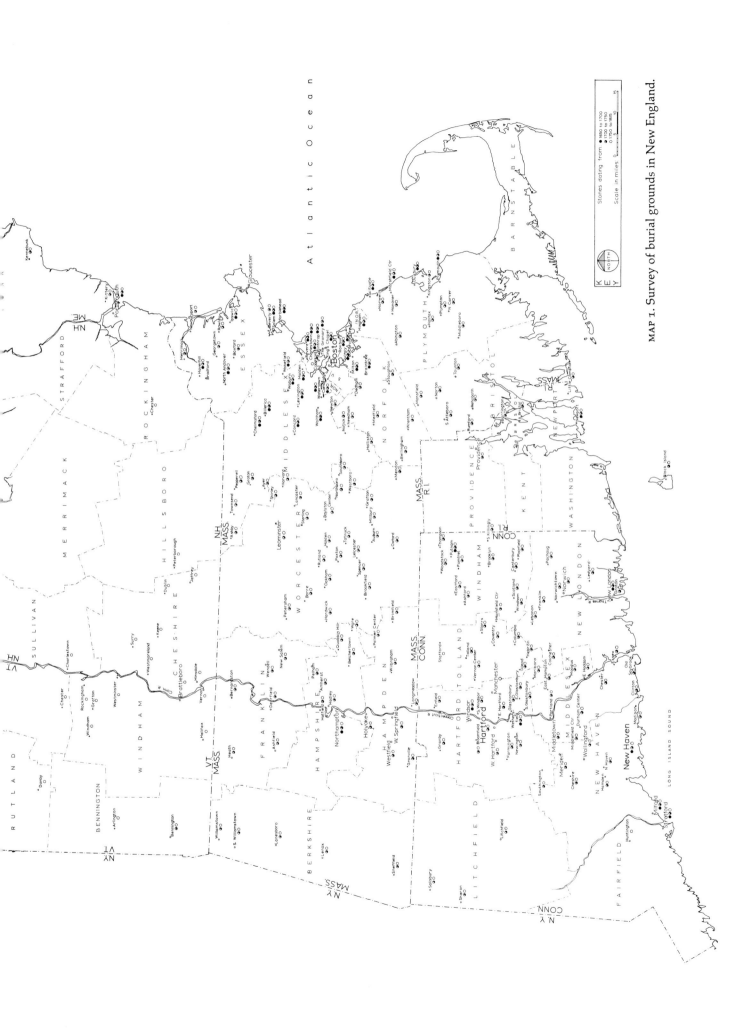

MAP 1. Survey of burial grounds in New England.

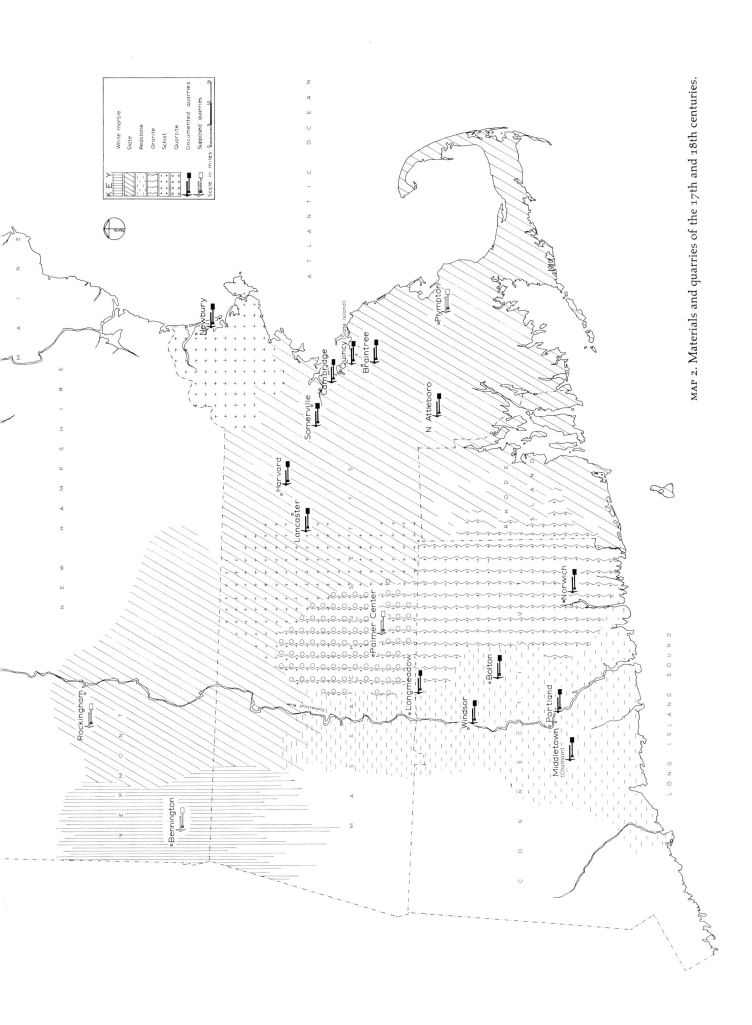

MAP 2. Materials and quarries of the 17th and 18th centuries.

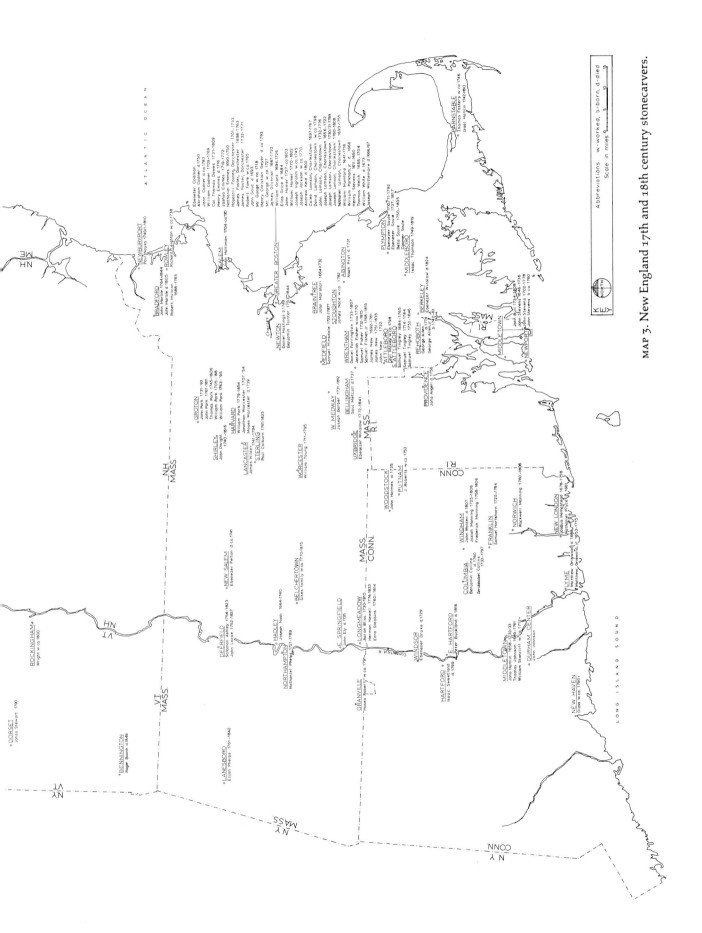

MAP 3. New England 17th and 18th century stonecarvers.

ATLANTIC OCEAN

KEY

NORTH

Abbreviations: w-worked, b-born, d-died

Scale in miles 0   5   10

NEWBURYPORT
Paul Noyes 1740/1-1810
ROWLEY
Richard Leighton w ca 1738
BRADFORD
John Hartshorne 1650-1738
John Marble d.1805
Robert Mulicen
1688-1765

SALEM
John Hancock

Ebenezer Codman
Abraham Codner d.1750
John Codner d. ca 1783
William Codner 1709-1769
Col. Thomas Dawes 1731-1809
Henry Emmes d.1796
Joshua Emmes 1719-1772
Nathaniel Emmes 1690-1750
Hopestill Foster, Dorchester 1701-1733
James Foster, Dorchester 1698-1763
James Foster, Dorchester 1732-1771
Robert Fowle w ca 1765
John Gaud d.1693
Mr Guage w ca 1718
Henry Christian Geyer d. ca 1793
Mr George w ca 1727
James Gillcrest 1687-1722
Elias Grice d.1684
John Homer 1727-ca 1803
William Homer 1770-1822
Joseph Ingraham w ca 1745
Joseph Jackson w ca 1770
Andrew Kent d. 1802
Caleb   Lamson, Charlestown 1697-1767
David   Lamson, Charlestown w ca 1798
John   Lamson, Charlestown 1656-1722
Joseph   Lamson, Charlestown 1732-1776
Joseph   Lamson, Charlestown 1760-1808
Nathaniel Lamson, Charlestown 1693-1755
William Mumford 1641-1718
William Parkman d. 1666
Henry Stevens 1811-1690
Thomas Welch 1655-1704
William White d. 1673
Joseph Whittemore d.1666/67

GREATER BOSTON

NEWTON
Daniel Hastings b.1729
Benjamin Tainter 1726-1844

MEDFIELD
Samuel Hinsdale

BRAINTREE
John Marshall 1664-1732

STOUGHTON
James Nace w ca 1782

WRENTHAM
Daniel Farrington 1733-1807
Jeremiah Fisher w ca 1770
Samuel Fisher 1732-1815
Samuel Fisher, Jr. 1768-1815
James New 1692-1781
John New   1722

ABINGTON
Noah Prat d.1731

PLYMPTON
Ebenezer Soule 1767-1792
Ebenezer Soule 1737-1817
Beza Soule w ca 1755-1835
Cooper Soule

MIDDLEBORO
Isaac Thomson 1749-1819

ATTLEBORO
James New 1692-1781
Samuel Tingley 1744-1765
Samuel Tingley 1714-1784
Samuel Tingley 1752-1846

REHOBOTH
Ebenezer Winslow d.1824

BERKELEY
George Allen 1774
George Allen, Jr.
d.1774-d.2-b.

PROVIDENCE
John Angell d.1756

BARNSTABLE
Thomas Fosters w ca 1746
Isaac Hamlin 1742-1860

NEWPORT

MASS.
R.I.

MASS.
CONN.

CONN.
R.I.

GROTON
John Park 1731-'93
John Park, 1761-1881
Thomas Park 1745-1806
William Park 1705-88
William Park 1763-'95

HARVARD
William Park 1779-1854
Jonathan Worcester 1707-'54
Moses Worcester d.1739

SHIRLEY
John Dwight 1740-1816

LANCASTER
James Wilder 1741-1794

STERLING
Paul Colburn 1761-1825

WORCESTER
William Young 1711-1795

W. MEDWAY
Joseph Barber 1731-1816

BELLINGHAM
Soul Metcalf d.1737

UXBRIDGE
Ebenezer Winslow 1772-1824

WOODSTOCK
John Holmes w 1725

PUTNAM
J. Roberts w ca 1753

WINDHAM
John Walden d.1807
Josiah Manning 1725-1806
Frederick Manning 1758-1806

FRANKLIN
Samuel Horsborn 1725-1784

NORWICH
Rockwell Manning 1760-1806

NEW LONDON
Joshua Hempstead 1678-1758
John Stevens 1646-1736
John Stevens 1702-1778
John Stevens b. ca 1760

MASS.
CONN.

NEW SALEM
Ebenezer Felton d.ca 1741

BELCHERTOWN
Sikes family w 1730-1815

DEERFIELD
Solomon Ashley 1704-1823
John Locke 1752-1857

HADLEY
Joseph Nash 1664-1740

NORTHAMPTON
Nathaniel Phelps 1721-1789

E. SPRINGFIELD
Joseph Ely d.1795

LONGMEADOW
Aaron Bliss 1733-1859
Herman Newell 1734-1833
Ezra Stebbins 1760-1814

GRANVILLE
Moses Roberts w ca 1791

WINDSOR
Ebenezer Drake d.1729

HARTFORD
Isaac Sweetland
1753-1799

E. HARTFORD
Peter Buckland d.1816

MIDDLETOWN
John Hamlin 1658-1723/33
Thomas Johnson 1669-1761
William Stancliff w 1722
John Johnson

DURHAM CENTER
John Johnson

LYME
Matthew Griswold d.1699
Matthew Griswold Jr. d.1755-1715

NEW HAVEN
Gigas w ca 1790

COLUMBIA
Benjamin Collins d.1760
Zerubbabel Collins 1733-1797

ROCKINGHAM
Wright w ca 1800

LANESBORO
Elijah Phelps 1761-1842

DORSET
Jonas Stewart 1790

BENNINGTON
Roger Booth d.1849

ATLANTIC OCEAN

ME
NH

NH
MASS.

VT
MASS.

VT
MASS.

NY
MASS.

NY
CONN.

Connecticut R.

LONG   ISLAND   SOUND

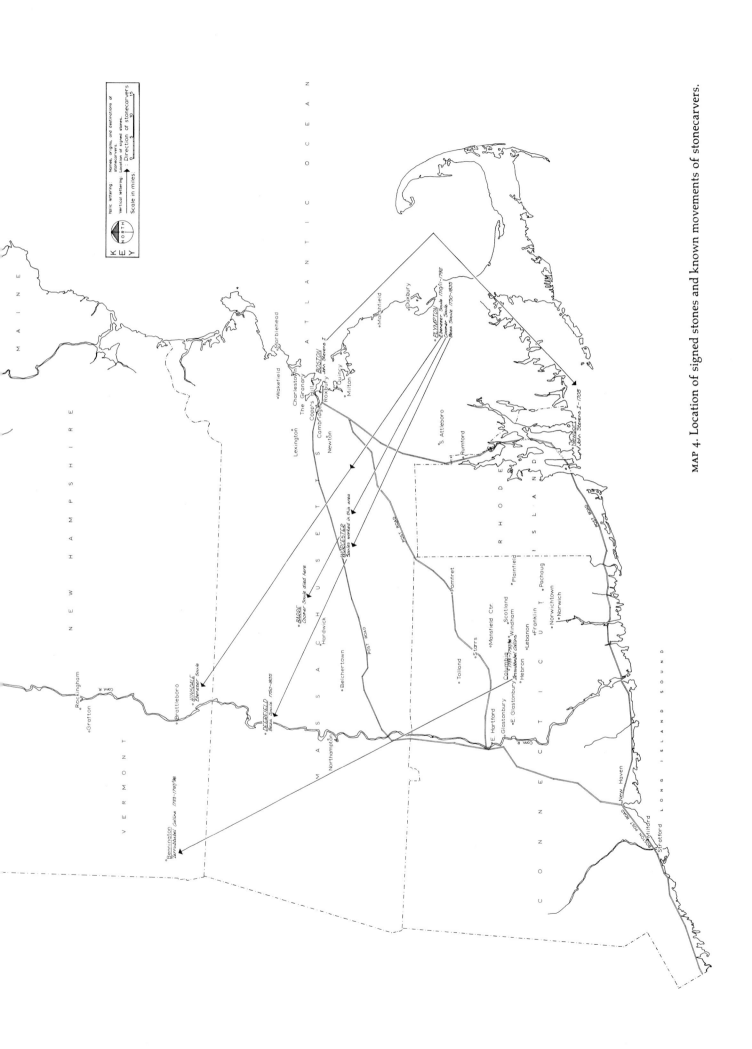

MAP 4. Location of signed stones and known movements of stonecarvers.

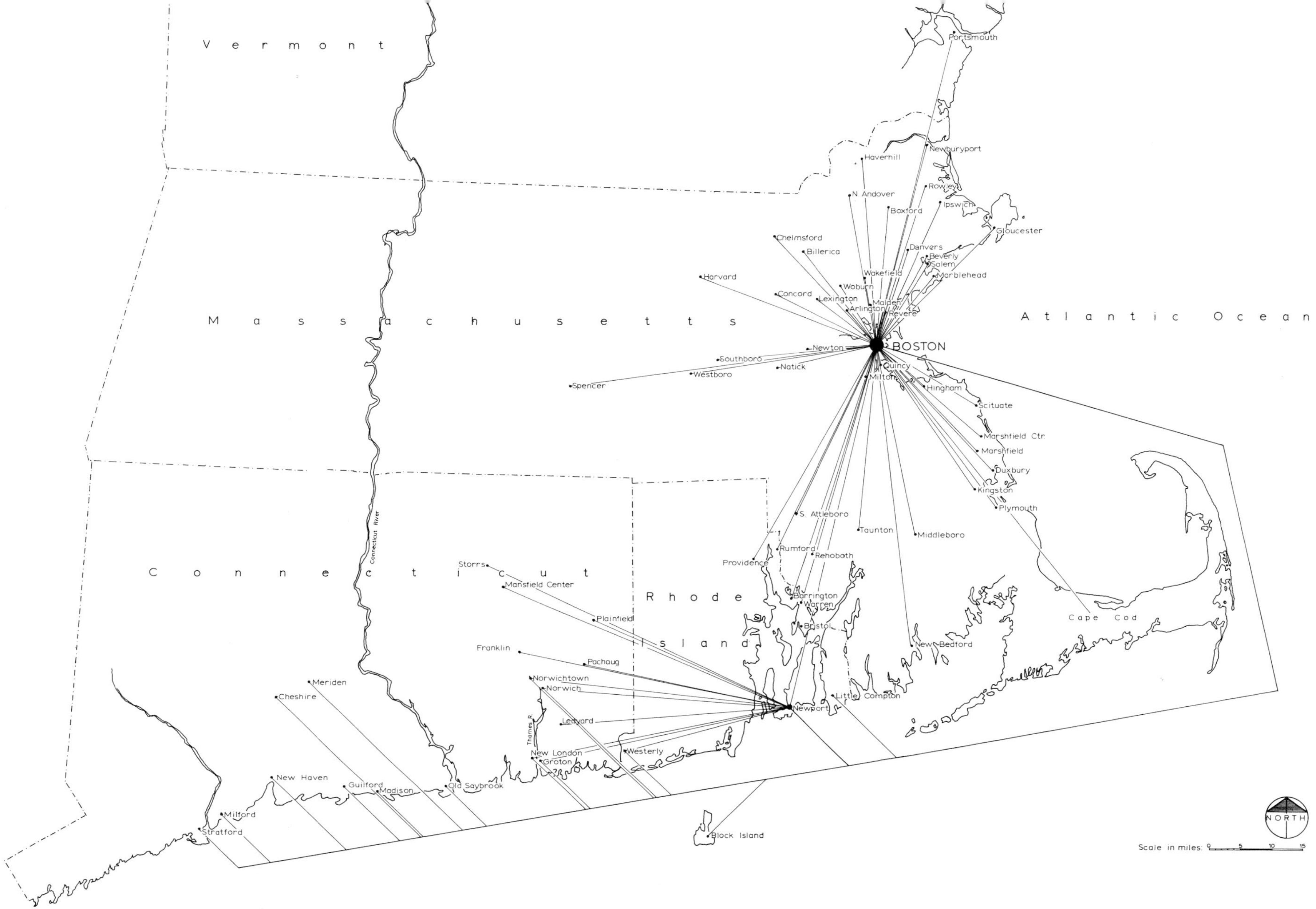

MAP 5. Diffusion of the provincial styles.

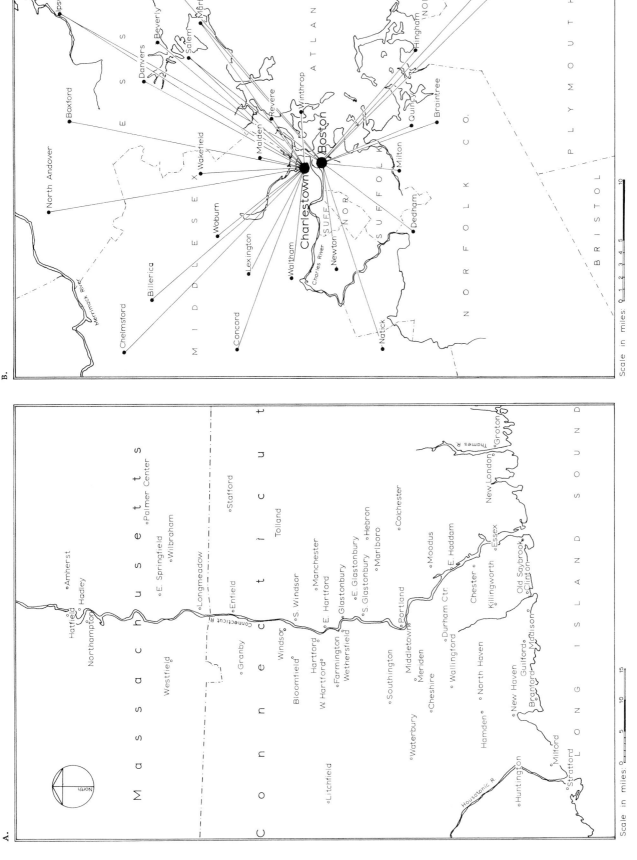

MAP 6. A. Connecticut Valley ornamental style, 1720–1800. B. Diffusion of the provincial baroque style in the 17th century in Greater Boston.

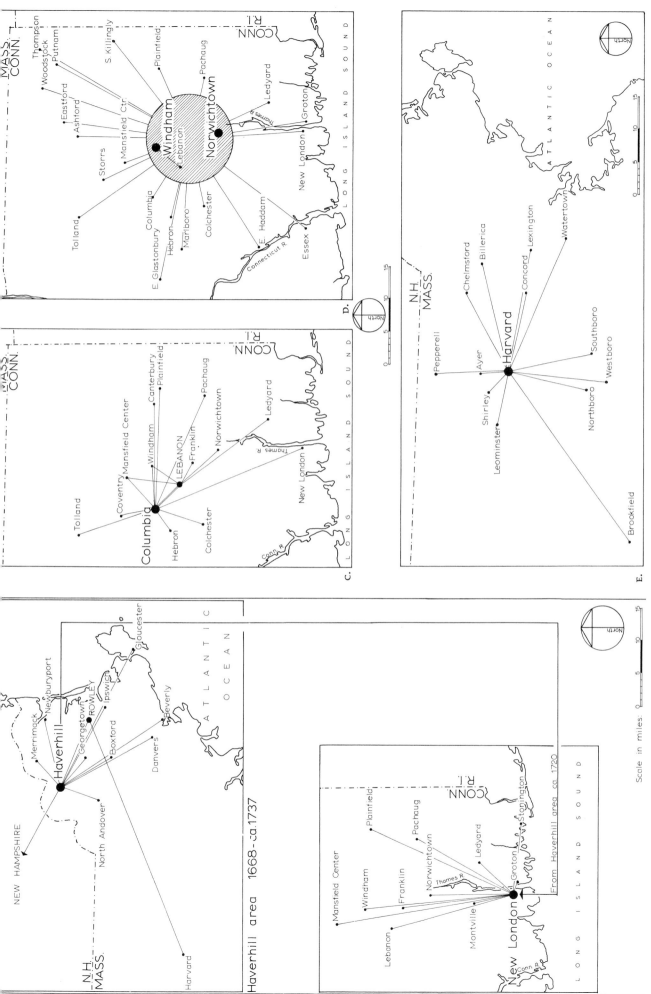

MAP 7. A. Haverill area, 1668–ca. 1737. B. Diffusion of the ornamental style: Phase 1, 1668–1730. C. Diffusion of the ornamental style: Phase 2, Eastern Connecticut, 1725–1750. D. Diffusion of the ornamental style; Phase 3, Eastern Connecticut, ca. 1750–1815. E. Diffusion of the ornamental style: Phase 3, Northern Massachusetts, ca. 1738–1760.

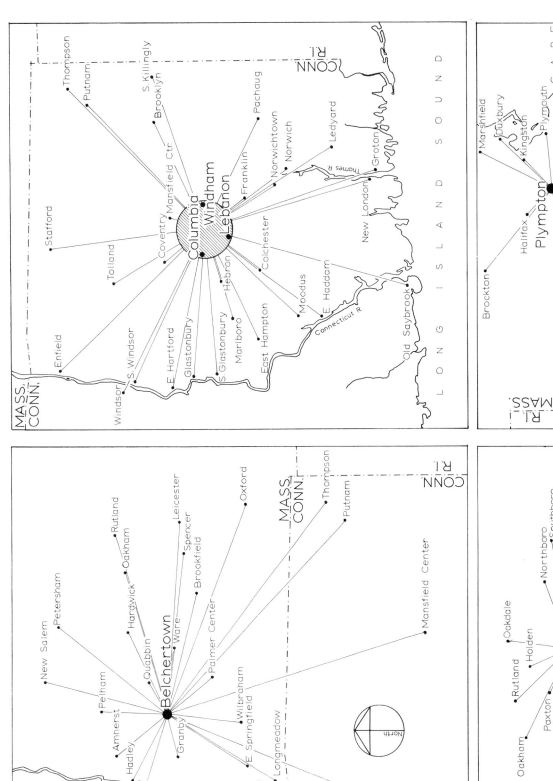

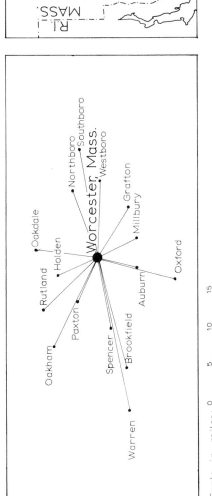

MASS.
CONN.

Thompson
Putnam
S. Killingly
Brooklyn
Pachaug
Franklin
Norwichtown
Norwich
Ledyard
Columbia
Windham
Lebanon
Coventry
Mansfield Ctr.
Stafford
Tolland
Colchester
Hebron
Moodus
Maribo
E. Haddam
East Hampton
S. Glastonbury
Glastonbury
E. Hartford
S. Windsor
Enfield
Windsor
Groton
New London
Old Saybrook
Connecticut R.
Thames R.

CONN.
R.I.

L O N G   I S L A N D   S O U N D

New Salem
Petersham
Rutland
Hardwick
Oakham
Pelham
Amherst
Hadley
Quabbin
Ware
Granby
Belchertown
Leicester
Spencer
Brookfield
Palmer Center
Wilbraham
E. Springfield
Longmeadow
Oxford
Northampton
Connecticut R.
Hartford
Mansfield Center
Putnam
Thompson

MASS.
CONN.

CONN.
R.I.

North

Oakham
Rutland
Oakdale
Holden
Paxton
Spencer
Brookfield
Warren
Auburn
Oxford
Millbury
Grafton
Westboro
Southboro
Northboro
Worcester, Mass.

Marshfield
Duxbury
Kingston
Plymouth
Brockton
Halifax
N. Carver
Plympton
Middleboro Ctr.
Taunton
Fall River
Buzzards Bay
C A P E
C O D
B A Y

R.I.
MASS.

Scale in miles: 0   5   10   15

MAP 8. Centers of geometric carving in the 18th century.

Index

Names in italics represent illustrated monuments and broadsides

Manning, Josiah, 401–409
Manning, Rockwell, 409
Mansfield Center, Connecticut, 67, 207, 334, 377, 380, 409, 412
Maples, Disire, 409, 412
Marblehead, Massachusetts, 82, 100, 237, 261, 277, 305, 322
Margate, Kent, 258
Marlboro, Connecticut, 124
Marshall, John, 59
Marshall, Joshua, 241
Marshall, Sarah, 148, 154
Marshfield, Massachusetts, 85, 148, 355, 394, 397
Martyn, Michael, 85, 299
Mason, Ann, 377
Mather, Cotton, 62, 196, 214
Mather, Increase, 223–225
Mattituck, Long Island, 326
May, John, 355
May, Sarah, 355
McCurdy, Ursula, 330, 331, 334, 353
McKeon, Sarah, 82, 316
Mediacy and immediacy, definition of, 44, 45
Memorials, wooden, in England, 241
Mendon, Massachusetts, 316
Menhir, 232, 233
Meriden, Connecticut, 274, 277, 341, 428
Merick, Abigail, 226, 232
Merrimack, Massachusetts, 365
Michel, Sary, 362
Middleboro Center, Massachusetts, 170, 350, 355, 358
Middlefield Center, Connecticut, 202
Middletown, Rhode Island, 202, 330
Migration of stonecarvers to New England, lack of evidence of, 263, 274
Milford, Connecticut, 160
Milk, divine, symbol of, 155
Miller, Alexander, 109
Miller, Perry, 4, 5
Milton, Massachusetts, 187
Mitchell, Elizabeth, 300
Modern art and rural stonecarving, connections between, 431
Montville, Connecticut, 380
Monuments, dating of, x
Moon, symbols of, 82; *see also* Cosmological symbols
Morgan, Edmund S., 4
Morgin, Isaac, 287, 358
Morison, Samuel Eliot, 4
Morse, Nathaniel, 59
Morton, Elizabeth, 168, 316
Morton, Thomas, 296, 299, 389
Mulican, Robert, 365
Mumford, Ann, 154

Mumford, William, 300, 314, 325
Munro, Pamela, 121, 216
Murdock, Kenneth, 4
Mutilated symbols, meaning of, in New England, 234ff
Muzzy family stone, 116
Mysterium Tremendum, 12, 13
Mystical vine, symbols of, 67, 77, 175, 180
Mysticism, 47–50; as realized eschatology, 48

"J. N.," 296–300
Neal children stone, 139, 236, 295, 296
Neoclassical: cinerary urns, 142; stonecarving in New England, 63, 121; first appearance of motifs in New England, 326; first use of classical temple façade in New England, 295; revival of, 295
Nereids, symbols of, 299
Newall, Nathaniel, 314
New England stonecarving, secular signs and religious symbols in, 8; secondary symbols, 14; repertory of symbols, 67–232
New Haven, Connecticut, 389
New Lights, 37, 38, 42
New London, Connecticut, 334, 377, 380, 382, 389
Newport, Rhode Island, 55, 100, 107, 148, 154, 202, 207, 216, 277, 325, 326, 330, 331
New Salem, Massachusetts, 412
Newton, Massachusetts, 296, 322
Newton, Isaac, 196
Nichols, Elizabeth, 109
Nisbitt, Sarah, 160
Noah, 187
Northampton, Massachusetts, 42, 109, 124, 180, 287, 412
North Andover, Massachusetts, 305, 362, 365
North Branford, Connecticut, 428
North Carver, Massachusetts, 355
North Haven, Connecticut, 394, 397
Norton, Elizabeth, 121, 261
Norwich, Connecticut, 124, 202, 330, 334, 409
Norwichtown, Connecticut, 121, 124, 128, 133, 189, 197, 202, 207, 225, 226, 334, 380, 382, 409
Nott, Reverend Abraham, 142

Old Lights, 37
Oldham family stone, 249, 254
Oliver, Mercy, 305
Ornamental style, xi, 237
Ornimorphic devices, 362, 365, 369, 371; first appearances in New England, 237; first appearance in eastern Connecticut, 377
Otto, Rudolph, 12–14
Oxford, Massachusetts, 148

Pachaug, Connecticut, 202, 216, 334, 380, 382

Paddy, William, 283, 287, 358
Pagan symbols on Puritan stones, 296–299; water deities, 300
Pain, William, 59
Paleo-Christian survivals of symbols, 66
Palmer Center, Massachusetts, 116, 142, 226, 334, 412
Palmer, Esther, 412
Palm of victory, symbol of, 124, 160; palms, 121, 180
Panofsky, Erwin, 8
Park family stone, 116
Parmele, Joel, 401
Parsons, Ithamar, 148
Peacocks, 121, 133; earliest use of symbol in New England, 296
Peaslee, Lydia, 202
Peaslee, Nathaniel, 365
Peaslee, Ruth, 362
Peck, Captain Samuel, 160
Pecker family stone, 226
Pember children stone, 85, 180, 277
Person, John, 82, 100
Pettefor, Anne, 258, 261, 263, 271
Phelps, Lydia, 389, 401
Philip, Robert, 57
Philo, 46, 187
Pickard, 369
Picks and shovels, symbols of, 77, 291; in Connecticut Valley, 394
Pierpont, Reverend Jonathan, 100, 197, 236, 305, 309, 313, 322
Pimble, Sarah, 263, 268, 426
Pin Hill quarries, 373
Pixlee family stone, 226
Plainfield, Connecticut, 109, 334, 380, 382
Plato, 46
Plats, Mary, 369
Plotinus, 51
Plymouth, Massachusetts, 67, 77, 85, 89, 148, 154, 168, 202, 214, 237, 274, 314, 337, 350, 355
Plymouth County, Massachusetts, 69, 350, 362
Plympton, Massachusetts, 355
Pogany, Madam, 350
Polychrome, use of in New England, 337
Pomeroy, Colonel Seth, 109, 124, 128
Poole, Jonathan, 82, 100
Portal symbols, 233; of Death, 142
Porter, Sarah, 124, 128, 148
Portland, Connecticut, 207, 397, 426
Post, John, 133
Portraiture, neoclassical, 338ff; first attempts at, 316; in Plymouth County, 316; first effigies in New England, 305
Portsmouth, New Hampshire, 365
Post, Samuel, 382

Poultney, Vermont, 387
Prentice, Thomas, 74
Preparation, doctrine of, 27, 37, 38
Priest, Hazadiah, 371
Primer, New England, 277
Proportion and proportionality, 23
Providence, Rhode Island, 88, 100, 121, 189, 202, 216, 234, 325
Provincial baroque style, xi, 237
Pseudo-Dionysius (Dionysius the Areopagite), 51
Pulborough, Sussex, 258
Puritan art, 3; background, 3–6; funerary art, 5; in New England, 65, 66, compared to Europe, Scotland, Ireland, and England, 65, 66; iconophobia, x, 18; imagery, logic of, 6; image making, ix; its freedom, 52; need for imagery, 4, 5; literature, 5; motives, 3; psychology, 5, rationalism, 27, 31, 32; religion, 21; dialectical unity of religion, 24; sacramental symbolism, 20; symbolism in religion until 1800, 33, 45; subjectivity, 5; enthusiasm, 33; use of symbols, 20, 34
Puritanism, definition of, 4; image of, modern, 3; orthodox, 21, 27, 37; neo-orthodox, 27, 37, 38; orthodoxy according to Edwards, 40–42; and Puritan art, 423, 424; relationship between religion, symbol, and imagery, 6, 42–44; relationship to the English Renaissance and Reformation, 3, 4; views of death, 77, 82, 107, 108
Putti, 322

Quakers, 4, 22, 27; and Puritans, 19; suppression of in New England, 19, 20
Quarles, Francis, 89, 216, 240, 274, 295
Quincy, Massachusetts, 133, 296

Rand, Silas, 371
Rawlins, Nathaniel, 241
Rawson, Reverend Grindall, 316, 322; first surviving true portrait, 316
Reed, Mary, 305
Reformation, 47
Reformed Remonstrant Church in Holland, 36
Rehbury, John, 249
Rehoboth, Massachusetts, 160, 322
Religious art and religious beliefs, connections between, 18
Religious symbolism, language of, 6–20; studies of in Europe and America, 6; words as religious symbols, 19
Remington, Jonathan, 154, 309
Rennals, Joseph, 380
Resurrection, symbols of, 108, 423
Revivalism, 20, 32

Thomists, 23

Thorney, Cambridgeshire, 249, 254, 258, 263, 389

Thurston David, 148

Tibbals, Reverend Joseph, 124, 401

Tillich, Paul, 15, 16

Time, attributes of, 82; scythe of, 148; felling a tree, 261; in primers, 277; Time and Death, allegories of, 88, 89, 100, 295

Tritons and Dagons, first appearance of in New England, 296ff

Tingley family, 325

Tingley, Rebekah, 160, 325

Titus, Emperor, 425; apotheosis of, 207; arch of, 139, 207

Toft, Cambridgeshire, 254

Tolland, Connecticut, 128, 133, 176, 380, 382

Tomb art, 8; tombs, coped and gabled, in New England, 232; tomb burials in New England, 232; tomb 85, the Granary, Boston, Massachusetts, 89; tomb as doorway, 233; tombs, Venetian and Florentine, 232

Tompson, Reverend Edward, 85, 148, 296, 300, 394

Tood [Todd?], Calup, 397

Tracy, Betsy, 124

Transubstantiation, 20

Treat, Dorothy, 338

Treat, Hannah, 338

Tree of life, symbols of, 14, 109–121, 142, 216, 362, with soul discs, 116; barren, 116, 121; budding, 116; cut branches, 109; trees qua palms, 121, 133; within disc sprouting vines, 121; tiara, 121; felled, 121, 261; birds in, 133

Trumbull children stone, 409

Trumpeting figures, symbols of, 109, 263

Tufts, Peter, 154, 309

Theory of types, 187

Turner, Captain, 300

Turner, Prudence, 305

Tyler, Jane, 409, 412

Types, theory of, 187

Typological symbols, 154, 187

Underhill, Evelyn, 50

Univoce predication, 23, 26, 28, 30

Urban, William Marshall, 11, 12

Urns, gadrooned, first appearance of in New England, 296

Usher, Bridget, funeral expenses of, 59

Vallar family stone, 258

Vanderlyn, John, 421

Vane, Governor, 35

Venetian and Florentine tombs, 232

Verbal symbols, passivity of in New England, 28

Vernacular and cultivated traditions in art, 424, 425; collapse of vernacular tradition, 421

Vine, mystical, symbols of, 67, 77, 175, 180; vine and grape symbolism, 168, 180

Virgin, Captain John, 316

Visual evidence, problems of, 6

Wakefield, Massachusetts, 82, 100, 109, 180, 197, 283, 291, 305, 313, 350

Walden, John, d. 1807, 409–412

Waldron, Captain Nathaniel, 326, 338

Walker, Dorothy, 128

Walker, Ephraim, 121, 180, 226

Walker, Samuel, 189

Wallingford, Connecticut, 277, 341

Wallis stone, 258

Walton, Miriam, 234

Warner, Calvin, 254

Washbun, Wilborah, 69, 160, 353

Watertown, Massachusetts, 100, 287, 291, 305, 371

Watson, Elizabeth, 350

Watson, John, 236, 237, 283, 291, 316, 355

Watson, Patience, 168, 316

Watts, Reverend Isaac, 274

Webb, Anna, 189, 409, 412

Webb, Bridget, 244, 263, 334, 341

Weever, Daniel, 142

Weever, John, 52–55, 57

Welch, Martha, 121, 128, 133, 216

Wellington, Sarah, 263, 389

West, Benjamin, 325

West, Joseph, 128

West, Deacon Joseph, 176

Westford, Massachusetts, 373

Wethersfield, Connecticut, 338, 389, 401

Wheate, Dr. Benjamin, 216

Wheeler, Moses, 287, 389

Wheelwright, John, 35

White, Buckland, 207

White, John, 226, 237, 358, 362, 365

Whitefield, George, 41

Whiting family stone, 121, 124, 202

Whitwell, Reverend William, 237, 322

Wightman, Reverend John, 341

Wilcom, Sarya, 216, 362

Willard, Samuel, 21–33, 82, 85, 107, 108, 139, 175, 202; his concept of symbolism, 21ff; on idolatry, 33

Williams, Anne, 401

Williams, Isaac, 133

Williams, James, 59

Williams, Timothy, 176

Windham, Connecticut, 377, 380, 382, 409

Windsor, Connecticut, 241, 263, 389

GRAVEN IMAGES *has been composed in Linotype Palatino by Finn Typographic Service, Inc., and printed in offset lithography by The Meriden Gravure Company. The binding is by Russell-Rutter Company, Inc. Designed by Raymond M. Grimaila.*

WESLEYAN UNIVERSITY PRESS, MIDDLETOWN, CONNECTICUT